FINISH
Carpentry

A Complete Interior & Exterior Guide

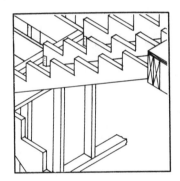
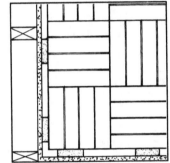
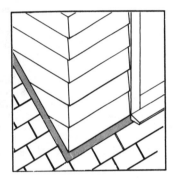

William P. Spence

Sterling Publishing Co., Inc. New York

Library of Congress Cataloging-in-Publication Data

Spence, William Perkins, 1925–
    Finish carpentry : a complete interior & exterior guide / William
P. Spence.
       p.   cm.
    Includes index.
    ISBN 0-8069-0700-2
    1. Finish carpentry.   I. Title.
TH5640.S64   1995
694—dc20
                                        95-20095
                                           CIP

Designed and edited by Rodman P. Neumann

11 12 13 14 15 16 17 18 19 20

Published by Sterling Publishing Company, Inc.
387 Park Avenue South, New York, N.Y. 10016
© 1995 by William P. Spence
Distributed in Canada by Sterling Publishing
c/o Canadian Manda Group, One Atlantic Avenue, Suite 105
Toronto, Ontario, Canada M6K 3E7
Distributed in Great Britain by Chrysalis Books 64 Brewery Road, London
N7 9NT England
Distributed in Australia by Capricorn Link (Australia) Pty. Ltd., P.O. Box
704, Windsor, NSW 2756 Australia
Manufactured in the United States of America
All rights reserved.

Sterling ISBN 0-8069-0700-2

Contents

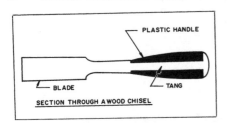
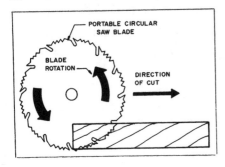
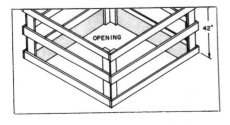
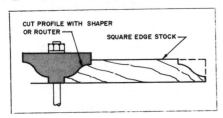

5 INSTALLING AND TRIMMING DOORS 66

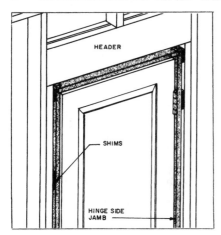

6 INSTALLING AND TRIMMING WINDOWS 86

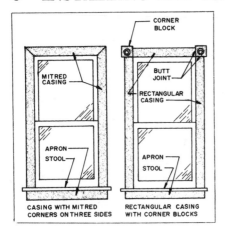

7 INSTALLING BASE, CROWN, AND OTHER MOULDINGS 103

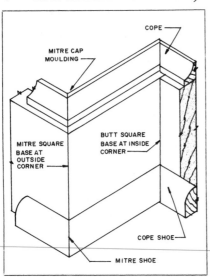

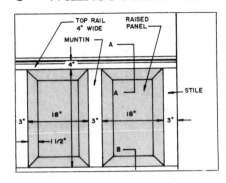
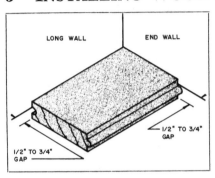
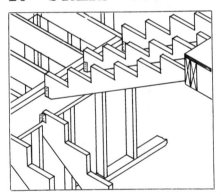
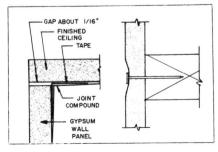

12 INSTALLING CABINETS 210

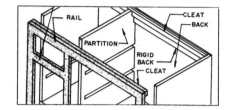

13 CORNICE CONSTRUCTION 227

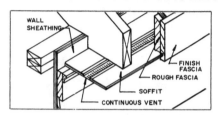

14 FINISHING THE ROOF 240

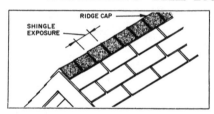

15 FINISHING THE EXTERIOR 259

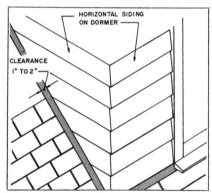

Preface

Finish Carpentry is designed as a guide for the beginning carpenter and should prove to be a valuable reference for the more experienced craftsman as well. It covers the various residential finishing operations on the interior and exterior of a building. While there are a number of ways to perform many of these jobs, those presented are typical of standard practice—what is being done.

A good job requires quality tools and the correct tools. The opening chapters show basic hand and power tools, how to use them, and the safety requirements that must be observed. Safety on the job is one of the responsibilities of the craftsman and Chapter 3, Safety, discusses mandatory safety requirements and behavior.

One of the important aspects of a fine interior finish is the selection of the mouldings. Chapter 4 gives information on the types of moulding, estimating the quantities needed, and proper storage. This is followed by chapters explaining how to install and trim doors and windows. Several ways to install the casing are presented. The interior trim is finished by installing base, crown, and other mouldings as shown in Chapter 7.

The interior wall finish information includes the installation of panelling, wainscoting, and gypsum wall board. These include various ways to install these materials, including cutting, proper nailing or gluing, and preparation of the joints between panels.

The finish floor information covers various types of wood flooring and gives detailed instructions on installation procedures. Finally the stairs can be finished, as explained in Chapter 10. This includes information on carpenter-built and factory-manufactured stairs. The procedures for figuring tread and riser sizes, laying out and cutting the stringer, and installing the landings are included.

In the kitchen and bath, cabinets must be installed. Recommended installation methods for standard and European cabinets are explained. Stock sizes are included along with information on using the architectural working drawings to select stock cabinets or to size and custom-build cabinets.

The finishing details for the exterior are covered in chapters on cornice construction and finishing the roof and exterior walls, event though the finish carpenter, per se, is only occasionally called on to do the exterior finish work. The various types of cornice construction are shown with detailed drawings that include providing for needed attic ventilation. The commonly used finished roofing materials—asphalt, wood, concrete, clay, slate, and metal—are described and typical installation details are shown. The exterior sidings applied by a carpenter include solid wood, wood shingles or shakes, plywood, hardboard, oriented strand board, vinyl, and aluminum. Installation details for each are shown.

This book will provide helpful information for finishing the interior and exterior of typical residential construction when wood products are used.

William P. Spence

Finish Carpentry Quality Standards

Finish carpentry involves production and installation of wood items that will be visible and become an important part of the interior and exterior appearance. The quality of the products and skill of the finish carpenter are essential to a satisfactory finished job. This requires that the manufactured wood products and the work of the finish carpenter be of high quality.

Quality standards for finish carpentry are published by The Architectural Woodwork Institute, 13924 Braddock Rd., Suite 100, Centerville, VA 22020. Its publication, *Architectural Woodwork Quality Standards*, provides detailed quality specification for trim, panelling, veneer work, cabinets, doors, staircases, and wood windows. It contains 17 sections, some directed at product manufacturers. It groups work into three quality categories: **Custom, Premium,** and **Economy.**

Custom Grade
The grade specified for most architectural woodwork. This grade provides a well-defined degree of control over the quality of workmanship, materials, and installation of a project. The vast majority of all work complies with **Custom Grade.**

Premium Grade
The grade specified when the highest degree of control over the quality of execution of the design intent, and the quality of all materials, workmanship, and installation is required. Usually reserved for special projects, or feature areas within a project.

Economy Grade
The grade which defines the minimum expectation of quality, workmanship, materials, and installation within the scope of AWI Standards.

Prevailing Grade
When the AWI Quality standards are referenced as a part of the contract documents and no grade is specified, AWI Custom Grade standards will prevail.

Exceptions to Grade
AWI recognizes the exceptional nature of some projects. These standards are a guide from which the design professional is free to deviate, often with the advice of an AWI manufacturer. The resulting products often exceed parts of this standard in design, engineering, workmanship, beauty, and function.

More than one grade of woodwork can be specified. For example, **Premium Grade** can be used in one or more locations and **Custom Grade** for the balance; or **Custom Grade** for designated public areas and **Economy Grade** for the service areas. In the selection of quality grades for service areas consideration should be given to cost and quality requirements of the job.

The sections in the standard follow.

   100 - Lumber

   200 - Panel Products

   300 - Standing and Running Trim

   400 - Architectural Cabinets

   500 - Panelling

   600 - Closet and Utility Shelving

   700 - Ornamental Work

   800 - Stairwork and Rails

   900 - Door Frames

  1000 - Exterior Windows

  1100 - Screens

  1200 - Blinds and Shutters

  1300 - Architectural Flush Doors

  1400 - Stile and Rail Doors

  1500 - Factory Finishing

  1600 - Modular Cabinets

  1700 - Installation of Woodwork

From the AWI Architectural Woodwork Quality Standards.
(Courtesy The Architectural Woodwork Institute)

1

The Carpenter's Toolbox

Finish carpenters are very skilled craftsmen. They must measure accurately, cut with great precision, make various joints, make strong assemblies with close-fitting joints, and smooth surfaces for finishing. They do such jobs as hanging doors, trimming door and window openings, installing base, crown, and other mouldings, installing panelling and wood flooring, building stairs, and installing hardware. To do these varied tasks requires a large set of high-quality tools. Many jobs require the skillful use of hand tools. Following are examples of hand tools commonly found in the carpenter's toolbox along with accessories to which the carpenter must give attention.

Clothing

Clothing should be comfortable and permit bending and other movement. Safety regulations require that items that could be caught in power tools such as long sleeves (roll them up) or scarfs (remove them) be secured. For safety's sake **steel-toed** leather shoes are recommended. However, plastic athletic shoes, as used for jogging, are available with steel toes; these are more comfortable than leather work shoes. Some form of **knee pads** are useful when installing baseboards and flooring.

Safety equipment such as **eye** and **ear protection** is required. Some jobs require a **mask** to prevent dust from entering your lungs. This is especially important when sanding, cutting, or shaping stock.

The **tool belt** is used by many finish carpenters (see **1-1**). It may be made from leather or a synthetic material. The belt has a variety of large pouches and small pockets in which small tools are carried. Larger tools are hung on the outside. Some of the tools placed in it are those used most frequently such as pencils, rules, and tapes. Some finish carpenters carry only the tools they need for the job at hand rather than

load themselves down with tools they likely will not need. There are work situations, as in close quarters or where the tools might scratch a wall or cabinet, in which case the belt is laid aside. Basically it is up to the craftsman to decide what to carry.

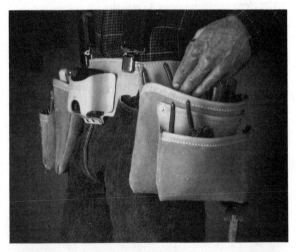

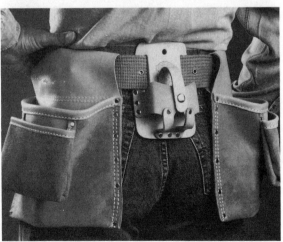

1-1 Two examples of a carpenter's tool belt with pockets and tool holders. (Courtesy McGuire-Nicholas Manufacturing Co.)

1-2 A shop pocket work vest designed to carry tools and fasteners. (Courtesy Fanteck, Inc.)

1-4 Accurate layouts can be made using a utility knife.

A shop pocket work vest is another garment designed to help the carpenter carry the tools and fasteners needed for a particular job. Some pockets are zippered to permit easy removal. The shoulders are padded, and it is made from a durable, cool, lightweight fabric (see 1-2).

Layout Tools

Finish carpenters do a lot of layout work. Commonly used layout tools are shown in 1-3. The **folding rule** and **tapes** are used to measure linear distances. **Squares** are used for layout and checking for squareness. The **T-bevel** is used for laying out and checking angles.

Various marking tools are used. Most common is the **pencil**; however, a line scribed with a **knife** is more accurate (see 1-4). Circles can be drawn with a **compass** or **trammel points,** and the exact location of holes to be bored or drilled is located with an **awl** (see 1-5). Also required is a **plumb bob** and sturdy **chalk line.** A metal **straightedge** 4 to 6ft (1.2 to 1.8m) long is also useful.

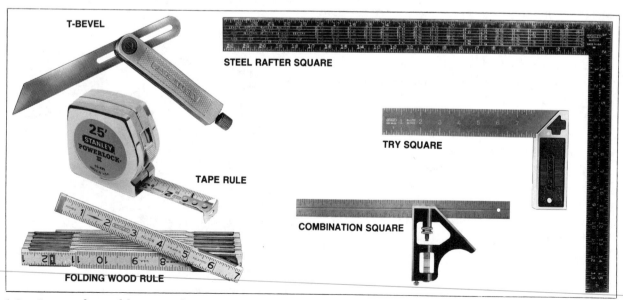

1-3 Commonly used layout tools. (© 1994 Stanley Tools)

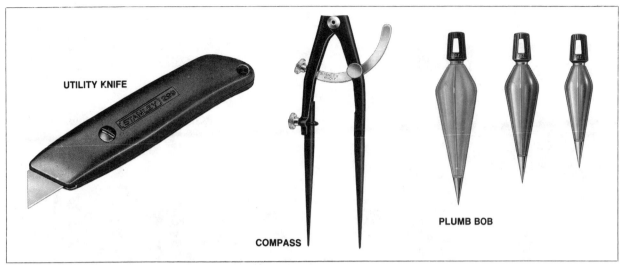

1-5 *Commonly used marking tools.* (© 1994 Stanley Tools)

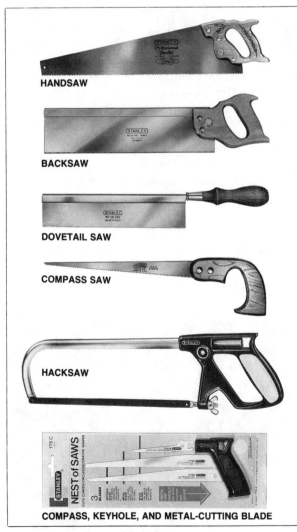

1-6 *Commonly used handsaws.*

Handsaws

While much sawing is performed with various power saws, there are situations where a good, sharp handsaw is needed. **Crosscut** and **rip saws** are used for rough cutting. They leave rough edges that, if exposed or used in a joint, must be smoothed. **Backsaws** and **dovetail saws** have fine teeth and produce a relatively smooth surface. They are used when an accurate cut is needed. The **compass** and **key hole saws** are used to cut internal openings such as an opening in a sheet of panelling for an electrical outlet. The **coping saw** is used to make curved cuts in thin stock and to cope the ends of moulding (see **1-6**). **Hand mitre boxes** are lightweight and convenient to use (see **1-7**).

1-7 *This hand-operated mitre box is lightweight and easy to move about the job.* (© 1994 Stanley Tools)

1-8   The two hand planes most frequently used on interior work. (© 1994 Stanley Tools)

Hand Planes

The most common type of hand plane used is the **bench plane.** It is available in several lengths. The longest, the **jointer plane** (24in or 610mm) is used to smooth long edges. Other types include the **fore plane** (18in or 457mm), **jack plane** (14in or 355mm), and the **smooth plane** (8in or 203mm) (see **1-8**). A **block plane** is a small plane (4 to 7in or 102 to 178mm) used to smooth end grain of stock (see **1-9**). The blade is set on a low angle enabling it to shear off the fibres in the end grain of a board.

1-9   A block plane is very small and is used to plane end grain.

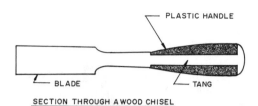

1-10   The best-quality wood chisels have the blade and tang forged as a single piece.

1-11   A typical set of wood chisels.

Chisels and Gouges

Chisels are used for a variety of jobs such as cutting rectangular openings or trimming joints. The best type of chisel has the blade and tang forged as a single piece. This permits it to be struck with a mallet (see **1-10**). A typical set will have chisels from ¼in (6mm) to 1½in (38mm) (see **1-11**).

A **gouge** is made like a wood chisel but the blade is formed into a V or U shape. It is used to make decorative cuts (see **1-12**).

1-12   Gouges are used to make concave cuts.

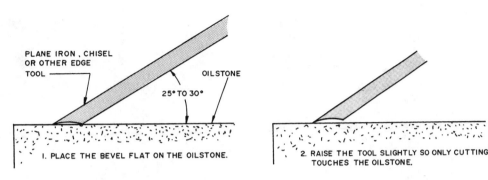

1-13   *The steps for setting the cutting edge to hone it to the correct angle.*

Sharpening Edge Tools

The most commonly used edge tools requiring sharpening are plane irons, chisels, gouges, and knives. If the cutting edge is a little dull but still has the proper shape and is not nicked, it can be sharpened (honed) on an **oilstone** or **waterstone**. Oilstones are lightly coated with a sharpening oil as the tool is moved over it, whereas waterstones use water. The oil or water prevents the surface of the stone from being clogged with metal particles. Stones are available in various degrees of coarseness.

The key to sharpening the edge tool is to hold it against the stone at the proper angle. Most plane irons, chisels, and gouges have a cutting edge of 25 degrees to 30 degrees.

To hone the cutting edge place the bevel flat on the stone. Raise the tool about five degrees so the cutting edge touches the stone (see **1-13**). Move the tool back and forth across the stone. Some prefer to move it in a figure-eight pattern (see **1-14**). Start with the coarsest stone, which is usually an 800 grit. After the bevelled side has been honed, move to a finer grit stone (1200 grit) and finally to the finest grit (6000), which puts a shiny finish to the cutting edge. Then turn the tool over and lay it flat on the finest stone. Move it back and forth several times to remove any burr left on the edge (see **1-15**).

1-14   *The cutting tool may be moved in a figure-eight pattern.*

1-15   *After dressing the cutting edge, lay the back side of the honed cutting tool flat on the oilstone and move it back and forth to remove any burr.*

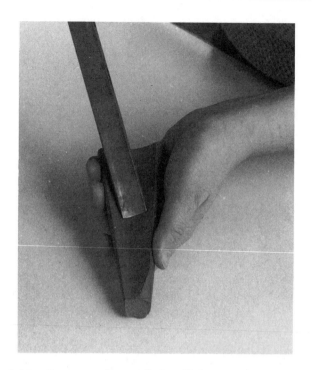

1-16 *Gouges with outside bevelled cutting edges are honed on the concave surface of the slipstone.*

1-17 *Gouges with inside bevelled cutting edges are honed on the convex surface of the slipstone.*

Gouges are honed using a **slip stone**. It has one surface concave and the other convex. Hone the outside bevel of a gouge on the concave surface (see **1-16**) and the inside bevel on the convex surface (see **1-17**). Knives are sharpened by placing the cutting bevel flat on the oilstone, raising the back edge slightly, and stroking it across the stone (see **1-18**).

If the cutting edge is nicked or the bevel is no longer concave, the edge must be ground before honing (see **1-19**). The tool is placed on the tool rest, which is adjusted so that the bevel on the tool is ground at the correct angle. Some grinders have tool-grinding attachments that hold the tool for grinding. A fine-abrasive cutting wheel must be used. After the grinder is started, the tool is moved up so that it just touches the wheel. It is immediately moved across the wheel in a parallel movement. Take very light cuts and keep the tool moving. Do not let the edge of the tool get too hot or it will turn blue, indicating it has lost its temper (hardness), and will not stay sharp very long. When the concave bevel is complete, hone to a fine cutting edge. Always wear safety glasses when using the power grinder (see **1-20**).

1-18 *Knives are sharpened in the same manner as other edge tools.*

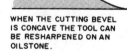

WHEN THE CUTTING BEVEL IS CONCAVE THE TOOL CAN BE RESHARPENED ON AN OILSTONE.

WHEN THE BEVEL IS WORN FLAT THE TOOL MUST BE REGROUND TO A CONCAVE CONDITION.

1-19 *When the concave surface on a cutting bevel is flat or nicked, the surface must be reground to restore it.*

1-20 *This plane iron is being ground using a tool holder set at the desired angle.* (Courtesy Delta International Machinery)

1-22 *Fine-toothed files tend to clog and need frequent cleaning.*

Finishing Tools

The most frequently used finishing tools are **files, cabinet scrapers, rasps,** and **surface forming tools.** There are a wide variety of files available. Those designed for use on wood include a **rasp, cabinet file,** and **wood file.** The rasp has very large teeth and removes wood rapidly, leaving a very rough surface. The cabinet file has finer teeth and can clean up a surface following the rasp. The wood file has the finest teeth but still leaves a fairly rough surface (see **1-21**). Metal-cutting files have very fine teeth and can be used on wood but they clog easily and need frequent cleaning. Files are available in flat, half-round, round, and triangular shapes (see **1-22**).

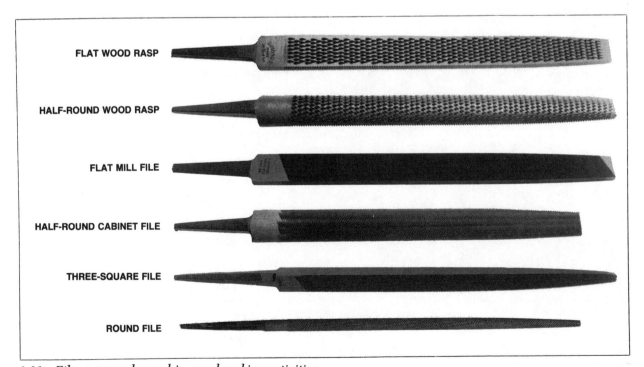

FLAT WOOD RASP

HALF-ROUND WOOD RASP

FLAT MILL FILE

HALF-ROUND CABINET FILE

THREE-SQUARE FILE

ROUND FILE

1-21 *Files commonly used in woodworking activities.*

REPLACEMENT BLADE

1-23 One of the many types of Surform forming tools. (© 1994 Stanley Tools)

Surface forming tools have a thin, perforated metal blade and serve the same purpose as files. The teeth on the blade are open so that the wood chips pass through the blade, reducing clogging (see **1-23**). When it gets dull a new blade is installed.

Flat files are used to smooth convex surfaces and half-round files are used for concave surfaces (see **1-24** and **1-25**).

1-24 Flat files are used to smooth convex surfaces.

1-25 Half-round files are used to smooth concave surfaces.

1-26 This rectangular handheld scraper provides a fine finish before sanding.

1-27 This scraper blade is held in a metal frame and is easy to use.

Cabinet scrapers are useful to give a final smoothness to a wood surface before sanding. They are available in handheld rectangular (see **1-26**) and curved types. Some have handles (see **1-27**). Hand scrapers are sharpened by filing the edge square and then burnishing each corner to form a cutting burr (see **1-28**).

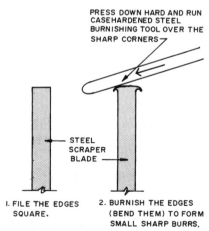

PRESS DOWN HARD AND RUN CASEHARDENED STEEL BURNISHING TOOL OVER THE SHARP CORNERS

STEEL SCRAPER BLADE

1. FILE THE EDGES SQUARE.

2. BURNISH THE EDGES (BEND THEM) TO FORM SMALL SHARP BURRS.

1-28 Scraper blades are sharpened with square corners which are then bent over to form a very small burr.

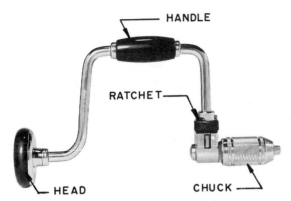

1-29 *The brace is used to hold bits that bore large-diameter holes.* (© 1994 Stanley Tools)

Drilling and Boring Tools

Larger-diameter holes are often bored with a **brace** and **auger bit** or one of the special large-diameter bits. Small holes are drilled with a push drill.

The brace, shown in **1-29,** hold the bits in its chuck. The bits have a tapered square tang that fits into the jaws in the chuck. An auger bit is shown in **1-30.** They are sold in sets beginning with a ¼in (6mm) diameter and going larger up to 1½in (38mm). The hole is bored more accurately if the center is punched with an awl, giving a recess for the screw to get started (see **1-31**). When boring with an auger bit or other special bits bore through from one side until the screw breaks through. Then remove the bit from the stock and finish the hole by boring through from the other side (see **1-32**).

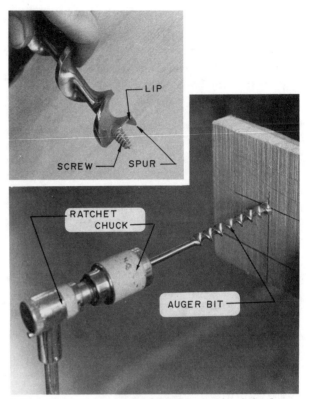

1-30 *Auger bits are held in the chuck of the brace and bore large-diameter holes.*

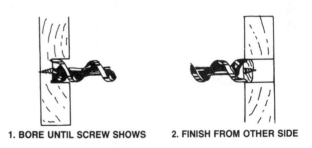

1. BORE UNTIL SCREW SHOWS 2. FINISH FROM OTHER SIDE

OR

BORE INTO SCRAP STOCK

1-31 *An awl is used to punch the center of a hole to permit the auger bit to be located accurately.*

1-32 *Two ways to bore through stock with an auger bit without spitting out the wood on the back side.*

When it is necessary, be certain the hole bored is perpendicular so the auger bit can be aligned with a square (see **1-33**). Holes to be on a specific angle can be lined up with a T-bevel (see **1-34**). Holes requiring a flat bottom are bored with a **Forstner bit.** They are sold in sets and are available in a range of diameters. Since a Forstner bit does not have a screw it will bore close to the back face without breaking through (see **1-35**). It has a tang on the end and is used in a brace.

The **expansive bit** in **1-36** has an adjustable cutter and can bore holes from ⅝ to 1¾in (16 to 44mm) diameter and a larger size will go from ⅞ to 3in (22 to 76mm) diameter (see **1-37**).

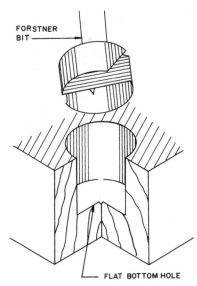

FORSTNER BIT

FLAT BOTTOM HOLE

1-35   *The Forstner bit will bore flat-bottomed holes.*

1-33   *A square may serve as a guide to keep the auger bit perpendicular to the stock.*

1-36   *An expansive bit has an adjustable cutter.* (© 1994 Stanley Tools)

1-34   *A T-bevel may be used to line up an auger boring on an angle.*

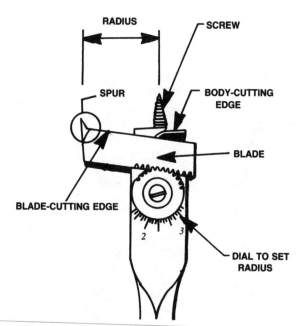

RADIUS   SCREW

SPUR   BODY-CUTTING EDGE

BLADE

BLADE-CUTTING EDGE

DIAL TO SET RADIUS

1-37   *The expansive bit has a dial for setting the radius of the adjustable cutter.*

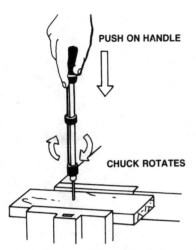

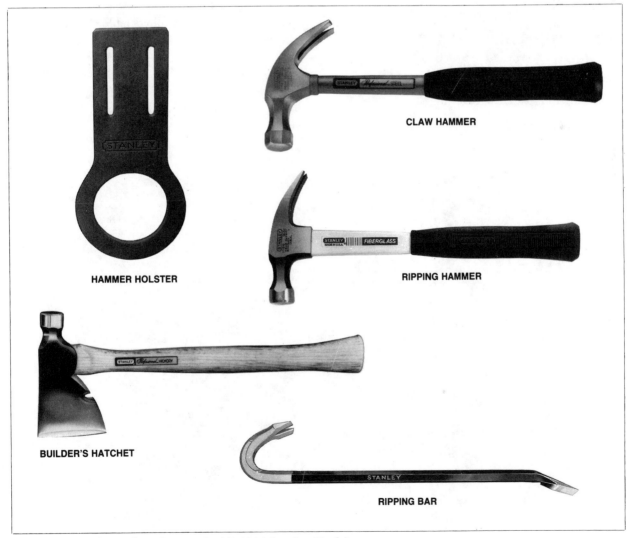

The **push drill** uses a fluted drill point. The drill sets have diameters from $\frac{1}{16}$ to $1\frac{1}{64}$in (1.5 to 4.4mm) (see **1-38**).

Other Tools

A variety of hammers are available. They should be high quality with a tempered face. Since most finish work requires careful nailing, lighter-weight hammers are often used. A 13oz (370gm) hammer is popular. Other weights available are 16oz (450gm), 20oz (570gm), and 22oz (625gm). Framing carpenters use the heavier sizes because they drive larger nails and hammer marks do not spoil the job because they are not seen. Some type of pry bar or ripping bar is useful especially when doing remodelling (see **1-39**).

1-38 A push drill uses a fluted bit that rotates as the handle is pushed down and released.

1-39 Commonly used striking tools. (© 1994 Stanley Tools)

1-40   *Hand screws have long parallel jaws.*

1-41   *C-clamps apply pressure by tightening the screw.*

Clamping tools commonly used are shown in **1-40, 1-41, 1-42,** and **1-43. Small portable vises** that clamp to a workbench or sawhorse provide excellent support. **A mitre clamp** to hold mitred corners for nailing is also valuable. There are a number of small tools required such as a **nail set, awl, levels, electric stud finder,** and several types of **pliers** and **adjustable wrenches.**

1-42   *Bar clamps are used to clamp long items.*

1-43 *A mitre vice holds mitred stock as it is being glued and nailed.*

Bonding Agents

Glues, adhesives, and **cements** are bonding agents used in wood construction. Glues are made from natural materials, adhesives from synthetic materials, and cements from rubber-based materials. Often bonding agents are used with mechanical fasteners such as nails or screws (see **1-44**).

The types of glues available are extensive and many are not of use to the finish carpenter. Following are some that are useful.

Glues

Two types of glues often used for cabinetwork are **liquid hyde glue** and **casein glue.** Liquid hyde glue is an animal product in liquid form. It will fill small gaps and chips in the joint and is used for interior work. It will set up in about two hours.

Casein glue is made from dry milk curds and is in powder form. It is mixed with water to form a thick cream. It is water-resistant and can be used on out-of-doors applications that are not directly exposed to the weather.

Adhesives

The most frequently used bonding agents are adhesives. They are classified under two types, **thermoplastics** and **thermosets.**

The major types of thermoplastics include **polyvinyl, aliphatic resin, alpha cyanoacrylate,** and **hot melts.** Polyvinyl is commonly called "white glue." It is sold in squeeze bottles and is ready to use. It sets up in about 30 minutes but the joint requires 24 hours

1-44 *A wide range of glues, adhesives, and cements are available.*

for a complete cure. Wood bonded with polyvinyl must have a moisture content of 6 to 10 percent.

Aliphatic resin is yellow and is stronger than the white polyvinyl adhesives.

Alpha cyanoacrylate is known as "Super Glue." It is not used on porous materials such as wood but bonds metal, plastics, and ceramic materials.

Hot melts glue wood and almost any other type of material. They are heated and applied with a special gum-like tool. They are not very strong and are used where strength is not important, such as bonding overlays to cabinet doors.

Thermoset adhesives are more resistant to heat and moisture than many bonding agents. The major types the finish carpenter may use are **urea-formaldehyde** and **resorcinol-formaldehydes.**

Urea-formaldehyde adhesives are sold as a powder. When mixed with water, a chemical reaction begins; therefore, do not mix more than will be used in a few hours. It is water-resistant and requires 16 hours' clamping time. In the store it is often called "plastic resin."

Resorcinal-formaldehydes produce a waterproof joint and are used on roof trusses and exposed surfaces where failure cannot be tolerated. They are sold in two containers; one contains the liquid resin and the other the catalyst. These are mixed and stirred. The joint must be kept clamped for at least 16 hours. One type is identified as Elmer's waterproof glue.

Cements

The two cements used in building construction are **contact cement** and **mastic.**

Contact cement is used to bond wood veneers, plastic laminates, and other decorative materials to a wood substrate. It is applied to both surfaces, allowed to dry, and then the surfaces are brought together (see **1-45**).

Mastic is a thick contact cement usually applied with a caulking gun to bond plywood subfloors to the joists and wall sheathing to the studs.

Tool Storage

Generally the finish carpenter will have a **tool-storage unit** built in the back of his/her truck or van. Many build their own storage boxes and shelves, while others buy metal units that fit in the back of the vehicle.

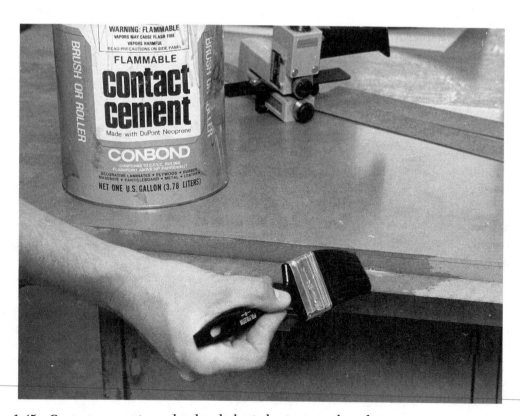

1-45   Contact cement is used to bond plastic laminate to the substrate.

Others use a metal tool chest of some kind that has large rollers. Many finish carpenters will not leave tool chests on the site overnight because of the danger of theft. Some form of small tool box with a handle can be used to move the tools needed that day from the truck to the building.

Electrical Power

The finish carpenter will need a variety of **electric extension cords.** Frequently the building will be without electricity, and power has to be brought in from an electric drop pole. It will have a meter and box into which a long, heavy-gauge electric wire can be run into the house. Some use 12- or 14-gauge thermoplastic-covered exterior wire for this long extension. In the building the wire connects to an electric box having one or more outlets. Smaller flexible wire cords run from the box to the area where lights or power tools are to be used. Extension cords must use wire with a large enough diameter to carry the load over the length of the wire (see **1-46**). Whenever there is any doubt about bringing power into the building, a qualified electrician should be consulted.

1-46 *Recommended extension cord sizes for use with portable electric tools.*
(**For Rubber Types S, SO, SR, SJ, SJO, SV, SP & Thermoplastic Types ST, SRT, SJT, SVP, SPT)**

Nameplate Amperes	Cord Length in Feet																			
	25	50	75	100	125	150	175	200	225	250	275	300	325	350	375	400	425	450	475	500
1	16	16	16	16	16	16	16	16	16	16	16	16	16	16	16	16	16	16	16	14
2	16	16	16	16	16	16	16	16	16	16	14	14	14	14	14	12	12	12	12	12
3	16	16	16	16	16	16	14	14	14	14	12	12	12	12	12	12	10	10	10	10
4	16	16	16	16	16	14	14	12	12	12	12	12	12	10	10	10	10	10	10	10
5	16	16	16	16	14	14	12	12	12	12	10	10	10	10	10	8	8	8	8	8
6	16	16	16	14	14	12	12	12	10	10	10	10	10	8	8	8	8	8	8	8
7	16	16	14	14	12	12	12	10	10	10	10	8	8	8	8	8	8	8	8	8
8	14	14	14	14	12	12	10	10	10	10	8	8	8	8	8	8	8	8		
9	14	14	14	12	12	10	10	10	8	8	8	8	8	8	8	8				
10	14	14	14	12	12	10	10	10	8	8	8	8	8	8	8					
11	12	12	12	12	10	10	10	8	8	8	8	8	8	8						
12	12	12	12	12	10	10	8	8	8	8	8	8	8							
13	12	12	12	12	10	10	8	8	8	8	8	8								
14	10	10	10	10	10	10	8	8	8	8	8									
15	10	10	10	10	10	8	8	8	8	8										
16	10	10	10	10	10	8	8	8	8	8										
17	10	10	10	10	10	8	8	8	8											
18	8	8	8	8	8	8	8	8	8											
19	8	8	8	8	8	8	8	8												
20	8	8	8	8	8	8	8	8												

Notes: Wire sizes are for 3-CDR Cords, one CDR of which is used to provide a continuous grounding circuit from tool housing to receptacle.

Wire sizes shown are A.W.G. (American Wire Gauge).

Based on 115V power supply; ambient temp. of 86°F (30°C).

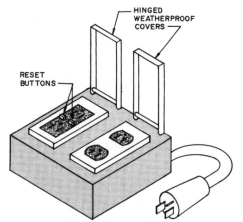

HINGED
WEATHERPROOF
COVERS

RESET
BUTTONS

1-47 A portable, ground-fault interrupter (GFI) used for protection against a fault, or short-circuit, where permanent GFI circuit protection has not been installed. Power tools are plugged into these outlets.

While portable power tools should always be double insulated to protect from electrical shock and the circuit being used should be grounded, further protection against a fault, or short-circuit, should be obtained by installing a **ground-fault interrupter** (GFI).

These units are plugged into the grounded circuit (see **1-47**). They sense an electrical fault current that would be too small to trip the normal circuit breaker but which could still flow through a person in contact with faulty equipment and a grounded surface. The GFI opens, or interrupts, the circuit, protecting the operator. It is especially needed when working on the ground or wet surfaces.

In addition the finish carpenter will need a couple **portable lights**, some **sawhorses**, and a lightweight **workbench**. **Step ladders** are essential and **scaffolding** is often required. Metal scaffolding can be rented and is more dependable than carpenter-built units.

Power Tools

Commonly used power tools include stationary and portable **circular saws, router, portable plane, electric drills** and **sanders, laminate trimmers, biscuit joiner, staplers, nailers,** and a **sabre saw.** All of these require accessories such as drills, bits, and blades. These are discussed in detail in the following chapter.

Note on Nominal Size

Boards and other lumber are typically designated by nominal size. Nominal means that the stated size approximately matches the size of the rough lumber before it is surfaced. The stated—nominal—size of the thickness and width of lumber differs from its actual size. Thus rough lumber 2 inches by 4 inches that is surfaced is actually closer to 1½ inches by 3½ inches, but it is still referred to as two-by-four lumber. In this book the nominal size "two-by-four" is written without units as 2 × 4. When a measurement is actual, the units are given. The same is true for one-by-six, four-by-four, etc. written as 1 × 6, 4 × 4, etc.

2

Power Tools

Finish carpenters use a variety of power tools to saw, drill, shape, nail, staple, and set screws. Some are **stationary** and others are **portable.** Stationary power tools are mounted on a base resting on the floor. Portable power tools are lightweight and are carried as the work progresses. Portable power tools are operated by electricity, batteries, and compressed air.

It is important to purchase only high-quality tools; anything less will not produce the work expected and could be dangerous. Select only tools that have their electrical system double insulated to ensure that electrical shocks are not possible. All tools should have guards on the cutting edges providing good protection. Be certain the manufacturer has a reliable service and repair system.

General Power-Tool Safety Rules

The construction industry is one of the more hazardous. Following are some general safety rules governing the use of power tools.

1. Wear some form of approved eye protection.

2. Use only tools with guards in place.

3. Be certain the electric cord and extension cord are not worn or damaged.

4. If the tool has a three-wire plug, be certain the source of electricity has a third-wire ground and use a ground fault interrupter (GFI).

5. Remove all rings, bracelets, necklaces, etc., that may become caught. Long hair can also be a problem and should be confined with a hair net.

6. Do not use a tool that is not in good condition.

7. Be certain the switch operates properly.

8. Use only sharp saws and cutters. Dull tools can cause accidents.

9. After changing a saw blade or other cutter, recheck before starting the tool to make certain it is properly seated and securely locked in place.

10. Work being cut must rest on a secure surface so it will not slip while being cut.

11. Avoid working when you are excessively fatigued.

12. Let the tool cut at its normal pace. Do not force or overcrowd to speed up the cut. This can cause kickbacks.

13. After finishing a cut let the saw or cutter stop rotating before laying the tool down.

The Occupational Safety and Health Administration (OSHA) requirements for power tools are detailed in the publication *Hand and Power Tools, OSHA 3080.* Order from OSHA Publication Office, 200 Constitution Ave., NW, Room N-3647, Washington, DC 20210.

Stationary Circular Saws

The stationary circular saw is used for a variety of cuts and produces more accurate results than the portable circular saw. The most common operations include ripping and crosscutting. When it has table extensions, it will accurately cut large panels such as plywood and particleboard. This tool can cause many accidents, so observing safety rules is very important. The saw in 2-1 has a 10in (25.4cm) blade and will cut stock 3¼in (82mm) thick at 90 degrees and 2⅛in (54mm) thick at a 45-degree mitre. It is light enough so that it can be easily moved around the construction job.

Circular Saw Safety

Following are safety recommendations for using a stationary circular saw.

1. Do not adjust saw while it is running.

2. Always wear safety goggles or safety glasses with side shields.

3. In some operations a dust mask should be used.

4. The saw table and the floor around the saw should be kept free from sawdust and debris.

5. When cutting wide stock, such as a plywood panel, use an auxiliary support to keep the panel level.

6. Keep all guards in place. Repair them if they do not function properly.

7. The blade should project no more than ⅛ to ¼in (3 to 6mm) above the work (see **2-2**).

8. Never reach over the blade or place your hands within several inches of it.

9. Never cut a piece of stock freehand. Always use a mitre gauge or the rip fence.

10. Do not stand directly behind the blade. Kickbacks do occur and can cause serious injury.

11. When ripping narrow stock use a push stick (see **2-3**).

12. Be certain the rip fence is parallel with the blade. This reduces binding and burning and possible kickbacks.

13. Do not use cracked or burned blades.

14. Blades that wobble or vibrate must be destroyed and discarded.

15. Be certain the blade is installed so that it rotates in the proper direction.

16. Place small, portable saws on a firm base at a convenient working height above the floor (see **2-4**).

17. Have someone help tail off the end when cutting long boards. A stand as shown in **2-5** can be used to support the end of long boards as they are ripped.

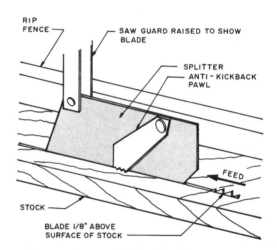

2-2   *The circular saw blade should not extend more than ⅛in (3mm) above the stock to be cut.*

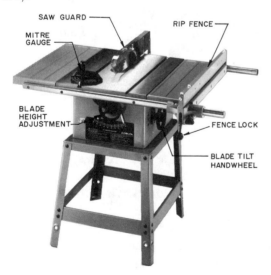

2-1   *This lightweight stationary circular saw can be moved around the building as required by the carpenter. (Courtesy Delta International Machinery Corp.)*

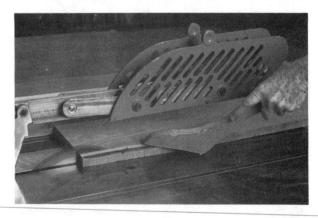

2-3   *Use a wood push stick to control wood when ripping narrow stock.*

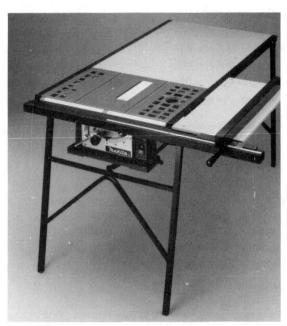

2-4 *This stand holds a small, portable circular saw, expands the size of the table, and raises the saw to a convenient working height.* (Courtesy Trojan Manufacturing, Inc.)

2-5 *A material support stand used to carry the end of long stock as it is being ripped on a table saw.* (Courtesy Trojan Manufacturing, Inc.)

18. Do not cut wet, cupped, or warped boards.

19. Do not use the rip fence as a stop when cutting short pieces to length. Use a stop block instead (see **2-6**).

20. Do not leave a running saw unattended. If you have to leave it, shut it off.

21. Use the proper blade for the job at hand.

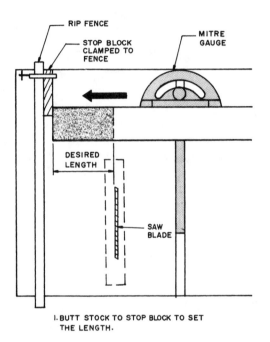

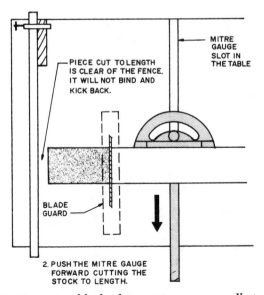

2-6 *Use a stop block when cutting many small pieces to length. Always keep a guard over the blade when crosscutting.*

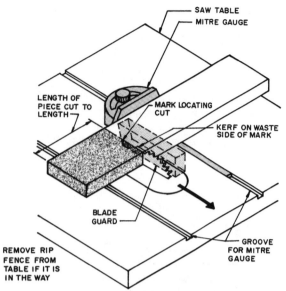

2-7 *To crosscut stock hold it against the mitre gauge, and move them together towards the blade. Be certain the rip fence is well clear of the stock. Always have the guard in place.*

Blade Selection

There are many varieties of circular saw blades available. The hole in the blade must match the diameter of the shaft on the saw. Following are the common types of blades.

A **crosscut blade** is used to cut stock across the grain. A **hollow-ground blade** is used for fine, smooth cuts. The teeth have no set, so it makes a very narrow kerf. A **ripsaw blade** has large set, chisel-like teeth and removes wood rapidly. It is used to cut with the grain. The **combination saw blade** has a combination of crosscut and rip teeth and is used for both ripping and crosscutting. The **plywood saw blade** is designed to cut plywood with a minimum of chipping and leaves a smooth surface.

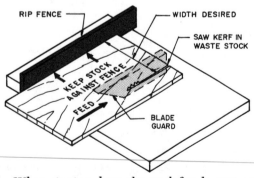

2-8 *When ripping, keep the stock firmly against the fence. Always have the guard in place.*

Circular Saw Parts

A typical saw is shown in **2-1**. Before operating a saw, be certain you are familiar with the operating parts and adjustments. Usually the switch is located on the front within quick and easy reach. Two handles below the table are used to raise and lower the blade and tilt it for cutting on angles.

Crosscutting

Following are steps for crosscutting stock (see **2-7**).

1. Set the mitre gauge on the desired angle. Slide it in the groove in the table.

2. Crank the blade up so it protrudes ⅛in (3mm) above the stock to be cut.

3. Place the saw guard over the blade.

4. Be certain the trip fence is moved over, out of the way. Remove it from the saw if necessary.

5. Place the stock to be cut on the table and firmly against the mitre gauge.

6. Start the saw. Do not begin to cut until it reaches its full speed.

7. Holding the board firmly against the mitre gauge, slide it into the saw. Sight through the guard to see that the mark on the board lines up with the saw blade and that the blade will cut on the waste side of the line.

8. Push the board and mitre gauge on past the saw. Then remove the board from the mitre gauge.

9. If the scrap end cut off is small, use a stick to push it off the table or wait until the blade stops turning to remove it.

Ripping

Following are steps for ripping stock.

1. Measure the required distance between the saw blade and rip fence. Measure from the edge of the teeth bent towards the fence.

2. Raise the blade so that it is ⅛in (3mm) above the thickness of the stock to be cut.

3. Place the guard over the blade.

4. Start the saw. Do not begin to cut until the spinning blade has reached full speed.

5. Place the straight, smooth edge of the board against the fence. Do not try to rip stock with curved or warped edges.

6. Hold the stock against the fence and feed it into the saw. Keep an even pressure (see **2-8**).

7. Have someone on the other side of the saw to receive long boards. They must only support the stock and should not pull on it.

8. When the end of the stock nears the saw, use a push stick to move the stock past the saw. If the boards is 12in (30.5cm) or wider, you can safely move the stock with your hand if you keep your hand against the rip fence.

Radial-Arm Saws

A radial-arm saw is a type of circular saw that has the blade above the table, and it moves on an arm that extends over the table. A typical radial-arm saw is shown in **2-9**. This will rip and crosscut as well as cut mitres.

The blade is mounted directly onto the motor. The motor and blade are raised and lowered by a crank on the top of the column. They also move horizontally by gliding along the arm. The blade can be tilted to cut on an angle. The blade must be installed with the teeth pointing down towards the table and rotating towards the fence. This action helps hold the stock being cut against the fence (see **2-10**).

2-9 *A lightweight radial-arm saw that can be easily moved about as the carpenter works. (Courtesy Delta International Machinery Corp.)*

Radial-Arm Saw Safety
Following are safety recommendations for using a radial-arm saw.

1. Never operate unless all guards are in place.

2. Be certain the blade is installed so that it rotates in the proper direction. If it is not, the saw will tend to run out towards the operator.

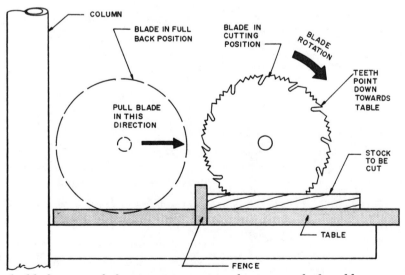

2-10 *The teeth on the blade on a radial-arm saw must point down towards the table at the outside, opposite the fence.*

3. When ripping be certain to feed the stock into the blade from the proper direction (see **2-11**).

4. When crosscutting hold the stock firmly until the blade is clear of the stock.

5. Keep both hands clear of the blade at all times. Never reach across the front of the saw.

6. Always return the blade/motor assembly to the full rear position after crosscutting a board.

7. Set the anti-kickback device so that it is slightly below the surface of the stock.

8. When ripping, be certain the blade is parallel with the fence. If not, binding will occur which will produce a damaging kickback.

9. Be certain to use the spreader device when ripping to keep the stock from binding behind the blade after it has been cut.

10. When ripping stock, use a push stick to feed stock past the saw.

11. Never cut anything freehand. Always keep the stock tight to the fence.

12. Do not cut wet, cupped, or warped wood.

13. When ripping make certain the blade is rotating towards you.

Ripping

1. Move the yoke out on the arm. Release the clamp and rotate it 90 degrees. Lock it to the arm so that the distance between the blade and the fence is the size desired. Set it so that the blade is rotating towards the board as it it is fed into the saw (refer to **2-11**).

2. Be certain all adjustments are locked tight.

3. Lower the blade so that it just touches the wood table. It should cut a shallow kerf in the table when turned on.

4. Adjust the anti-kickback device so that it is slightly below the surface of the stock.

5. Adjust the blade guards so that the blade is covered.

6. Turn on the power. Recheck to be certain that the blade is rotating upwards towards you.

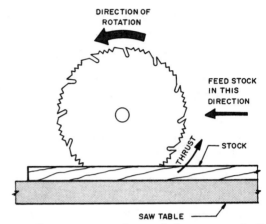

2-11 *When ripping with a radial-arm saw, feed the stock into the blade from the side where the teeth are rotating upwards.*

7. Place the smooth edge of the stock against the fence and feed into the blade. Do not rip curved, warped, or wet stock.

8. When the end of the stock approaches the blade, use a push stick to feed it past the blade.

Crosscutting

1. Adjust the arm to the desired angle of the cut. Lock it tightly in place.

2. Lower the blade so that it cuts a slight kerf in the wood table.

3. Adjust the anti-kickback device so that the fingers are just above the surface of the stock.

4. Place the blade-motor yoke back against the column so that the blade is clear of the front of the fence.

5. Place the stock firmly against the fence. Do not cut warped stock.

6. Turn on the saw.

7. Hold the stock to the fence with one hand. Be certain your hand is clear of the path of the saw. With the other hand move the saw forward into the stock. Hold it firmly so that you control the rate of cut (see **2-12**).

8. When the cut is complete, return the yoke to the rear position with the blade behind the fence. Then you can move the cut pieces of stock from the table.

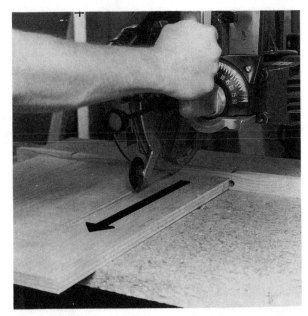

2-12 *When crosscutting, hold the stock firmly against the fence, keep the guard in place, and keep your hands clear of the path of the saw.*

Mitring

To cut a **flat mitre,** rotate the arm right or left to the required number of degrees, which is usually 45 degrees. There is an automatic stop, setting the arm on this angle. Place the stock against the fence and cut in the same manner as crosscutting (see **2-13**).

A **compound mitre** is cut with the radial-arm saw by adjusting the arm to the correct angle and tilting the motor unit to the correct number of degrees (see

2-13 *Mitres are cut by pivoting the radial arm to the desired angle, and cutting in the same manner as crosscutting stock.*

2-14). The stock is placed against the fence and cut the same as for a flat mitre. To cut a compound mitre on a 45-degree angle forming a 90-degree corner, tilt the blade to 30 degrees and place the arm at 35.25 degrees.

2-14 *A compound mitre requires that the saw be set on an angle (as for a regular mitre) and tilted to the required angle to produce the desired cut.*

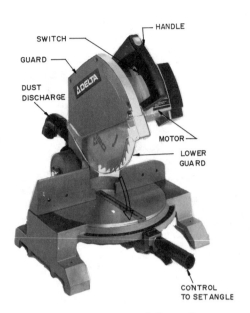

2-15 *A power mitre saw is used for making square and angled cuts.* (Courtesy Delta International Machinery Corp.)

Mitre Saws

The mitre saw is used to cut mitres and crosscut narrow stock. It resembles the radial-arm saw except that the blade-motor unit swings up and down on a pivot and may be adjusted to swing right and left on various angles (see **2-15**).

Mitre saws are specified by the diameter of the blade. A 12in (30.5mm) saw will crosscut 2 × 8 stock at 90 degrees and 2 × 6 and 4 × 4 stock at a 45-degree mitre. It will also mitre 5¼in (133mm) crown moulding and 5½in (140mm) base moulding. A 10in (25.4mm) saw will crosscut 2 × 6 stock at 90 degrees and 2 × 4 stock at 45 degrees.

Mitre Saw Safety

1. Always leave all guards in place.

2. Be certain the blade revolves down towards the table.

3. Since the saw swings down, it is necessary to be especially alert and keep your hands well clear of the cutting area.

4. Hold the stock firmly against the fence.

5. As soon as a cut is complete, release the switch.

6. Always hold stock against the fence. Never try to cut freehand.

2-16 *This portable lightweight stand holds the mitre saw at a convenient height and provides portability.* (Courtesy Trojan Manufacturing, Inc.)

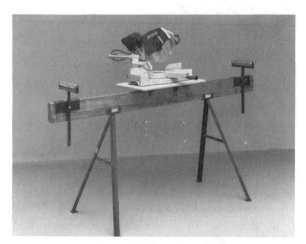

2-17 *Steel sawhorse legs and a wood base can provide a simple work stand for a mitre saw.* (Courtesy Trojan Manufacturing, Inc.)

7. Be certain the spring that lifts the saw to an upright position is properly adjusted. Do not use the saw if it will not automatically raise to the up position when released.

8. Secure the mitre saw to a firm base that holds it at a comfortable working height (see **2-16**). Another mitre saw stand is shown in **2-17**).

Cutting Mitres

1. Set the saw on the desired angle. Lock it tightly in place.

2. Place the stock firmly against the fence.

3. Turn on the saw.

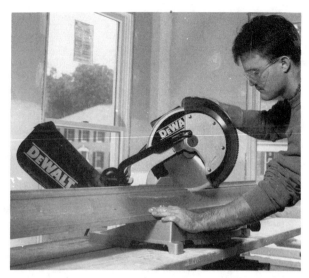

2-18 *This moulding is being cut on a mitre using a power mitre saw.* (Courtesy DeWalt Industrial Tool Company)

4. Once you are certain your hands are clear, and the stock is firm against the fence, lower the blade and complete the cut (see **2-18**).

5. Release the switch and raise the saw. Be careful of the blade because on most saws it is still rotating. Some models have a brake to slow down the spin in a very short period of time.

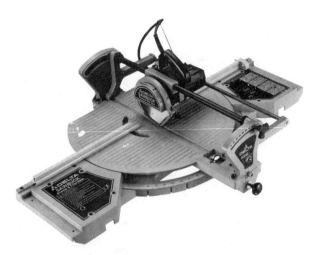

2-19 *A framing and trim saw.* (Courtesy Delta International Machinery Corp.)

Frame and Trim Saws

A versatile saw that can crosscut and mitre wide stock is the frame and trim saw shown in **2-19**. It will crosscut stock up to 2¾in (70mm) thick and 16in (40.6cm) wide and mitre 1¾in (44mm) stock 12in (30.5cm) wide at 45 degrees (see **2-20** and **2-21**).

2-20 *The framing and trimming saw can mitre wide stock.* (Courtesy Delta International Machinery Corp.)

2-21 *The framing and trimming saw produces accurate crosscuts.* (Courtesy Delta International Machinery Corp.)

2-22 *The framing and trim saw can use a dado head to cut dadoes.* (Courtesy Delta International Machinery Corp.)

It can also be used to cut dadoes commonly used for stair and cabinet construction (see **2-22**). The saw head can be tilted to cut compound mitres.

When using the frame and trim saw, observe the safety rules for the use of mitre and radial-arm saws.

2-24 *This sabre saw is making an internal cut in a thin piece of plywood.* (Courtesy Black & Decker, Inc.)

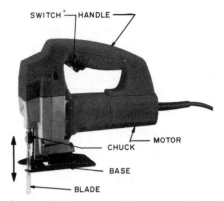

2-23 *A sabre or bayonet saw.* (Courtesy Milwaukee Electric Tool Corporation)

Sabre or Bayonet Saws

The sabre or bayonet saw is primarily used to cut curves and internal cuts. However, it can be used for crosscutting, ripping, and mitring but is not as accurate as other types of saws. A typical sabre saw is shown in **2-23**. Light-duty sabre saws are used to cut thin materials such as plywood sheets (see **2-24**). Heavy-duty sabre saws can be used to cut 2in (51mm) stock. Several brands will cut stock up to 5in (127mm) thick (see **2-25**).

Manufacturers provide a variety of blades for various purposes (see **2-26**). Thin wood is best cut with a fine-tooth blade such as one with 12 teeth per inch. A blade with 10 teeth per inch is used on thicker panels. If cutting 2in (51mm) stock, a blade with six teeth per inch will produce the fastest cut. Some blades will cut

2-25 *Sabre saws can cut stock up to 1½in (38mm) thick.* (Courtesy Black & Decker, Inc.)

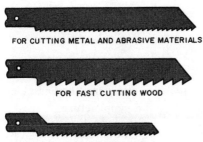

FOR CUTTING METAL AND ABRASIVE MATERIALS

FOR FAST CUTTING WOOD

FOR SCROLL CUTTING WITH SMALL RADIUSES IN WOOD UNDER 1/2" THICK

2-26   Several of the many types of blade available for use with a sabre saw.

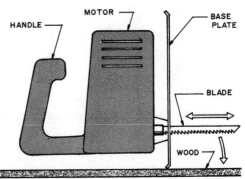

1. REST BASE PLATE ON THE WOOD. START THE MOTOR. SWING THE BLADE TO THE SURFACE OF THE WOOD.

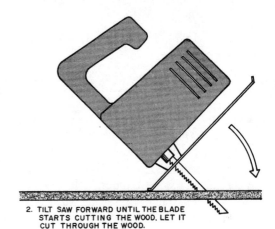

2. TILT SAW FORWARD UNTIL THE BLADE STARTS CUTTING THE WOOD. LET IT CUT THROUGH THE WOOD.

3. ROTATE THE SAW UNTIL THE BASE PLATE IS FLAT ON THE WOOD AND CUT IN THE NORMAL MANNER.

metal and plastics and can be used to cut through nails. Thin, hard metals and very thin woods are cut with a blade having 24 teeth per inch. A blade should always have two teeth in contact with the material. Thicker, softer metals require a blade with 14 teeth per inch.

Internal cuts can be made by drilling holes at the corners of the area to be removed. The blade is lowered into the hole and the cut proceeds in a normal manner. Internal cuts in thin stock can also be made by plunge-cutting. The back edge of the base is placed on the panel surface. The saw is started and the blade slowly lowered to the wood surface. It cuts its way through the panel until the saw base is flat on the surface. The cut proceeds in the normal manner (see **2-27**).

Sabre Saw Safety

1. Unplug the saw before changing blades.

2. Check to be certain the blade is securely held in the chuck.

3. As you cut, keep the cord out of the way.

4. When beginning a cut, place the base firmly on the wood surface before touching the blade to the wood.

5. If the blade gets stuck, turn off the power and slide the blade clear.

6. When plunge-cutting, use blades designed for that purpose.

7. After cutting, the blade is very hot, so do not touch it.

8. Do not force the saw to cut faster than normal.

9. Do not use dull blades.

2-27   Sabre saws are used to make plunge cuts through thin panels.

10. Be sure the wood to be cut is held so that it will not slip.

11. Let the saw get to full speed before starting to cut.

12. Keep all fingers on top of the board.

2-28 *A reciprocating saw.* (Courtesy Milwaukee Electric Tool Corporation)

Reciprocating Saws

A reciprocating saw operates much like the sabre saw. A blade is held in a chuck and moves back and forth to produce a cutting action (see **2-28**). It will saw wood, metal, and plastic. A variety of blades are available for cutting various materials. It does not produce accurate cuts but is used for rough cutting operations such as cutting notches for pipes, holes for electric outlet boxes, metal duct work, sawing wood, and cutting pipe. It is a versatile saw and useful for many operations (see **2-29**).

2-29 *A reciprocating saw can be used to cut openings in materials such as this subfloor for a heat register.* (Courtesy Milwaukee Electric Tool Corporation)

Reciprocating Saw Safety

1. Observe the safety rules listed for the sabre saw.

2. Use the shortest blade that will do the job.

3. When plunge-cutting use the foot piece and blade specified by the manufacturer.

4. Before making a blind cut, as into a wall, be certain no electric wires or plumbing are behind the surface.

5. Hold the tool by the insulated gripping surfaces.

Portable Circular Saws

The portable circular saw is probably the most frequently used power tool on a framing job. It is also the *most dangerous*. Carelessness and improper use cause serious accidents.

A typical saw is shown in **2-30**. Popular saw sizes are 7¼in (184mm) and 8¼in (209mm) diameters. However, they are available from 5in (127mm) to 10in (254mm) in diameter. They are used for crosscutting and ripping solid lumber, plywood, and other panel products. There are many types available, and the purchaser needs to consider possible uses in his/her selection. Factors to consider are the blade size, power available to the blade, guards, provision for grounding, whether it has a brake on the blade, weight, and type of drive.

The saw cuts from the bottom of the material, so that it produces a smoother cut at the bottom. This means the best surface of the stock should be placed down, and the cut made from the other side (see **2-31**).

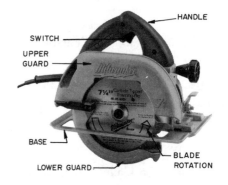

2-30 *This portable circular saw has an electronic brake to rapidly slow down the blade after a cut is finished.* (Courtesy Milwaukee Electric Tool Corporation)

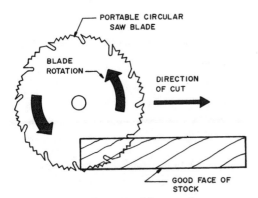

2-31   The blade of a portable circular saw cuts up from the bottom of the stock.

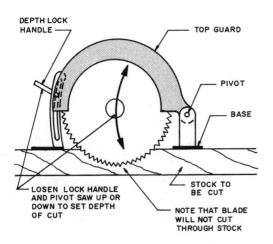

I. THE SAW SWINGS ON THE PIVOT TO SET THE DEPTH OF CUT.

NOTE: BOTTOM GUARD IS NOT SHOWN BUT MUST ALWAYS BE IN PLACE.

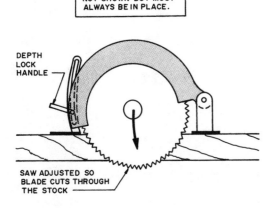

2. LOOSEN THE LOCK HANDLE AND LOWER THE SAW UNTIL THE BLADE EXTENDS 1/8" BELOW THE BOTTOM SURFACE OF THE STOCK.

2-33   The depth of cut on a portable circular saw is set by raising or lowering the saw in relation to the base plate.

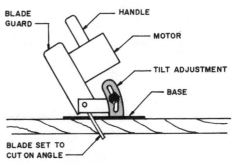

2-32   The portable circular saw can be tilted on its base to cut bevels.

The angle the blade makes with the surface can be adjusted from 90 degrees to 45 degrees. This permits producing bevel cuts on ends and edges. To do this the base it unlocked and pivoted to the angle desired (see 2-32). The depth of cut can be adjusted by loosening a lock on the base and pivoting it up or down to expose more or less of the blade below the base (see 2-33).

When installing a blade, be certain it is on the arbor, so that the teeth cut up from the bottom, as shown in 2-31. Usually the blade is marked with an arrow on the outside face indicating the direction of rotation.

Crosscutting can be done freehand, if accuracy is not important (see 2-34). A straightedge clamped to the stock will provide a fence against which the saw can slide. This provides a more accurate cut.

2-34   The portable circular saw can be used to cross-cut stock. (Courtesy DeWalt Industrial Tool Company)

2-35 This portable panel saw system provides a guide so that large panels may be cut accurately. (Courtesy Penn State Industries)

Ripping can also be done freehand, keeping the blade cutting along a line drawn on the surface. Long straightedges or straight stock can be clamped to the surface to produce a more accurate cut. One such device is shown in **2-35**. The aluminum track is clamped to the stock, and the saw is attached to a carriage that rolls along the track. A precision circular saw table is shown in **2-36.** The saw mounts on a carriage that slides on two round rails. It can be set up to make precision straight cuts, mitre cuts, or cuts on a variety of angles. An adaptation of this uses round tracks and a mounted portable circular saw to function as a panel saw (see **2-37**).

The same types of blade described for stationary circular saws are available for use on portable saws.

2-36 This unit makes precision straight cuts and may be set to cut a range of angles. (Courtesy Tinkerdell, Inc.)

Portable Circular Saw Safety

1. Do not use blades that are dull, cracked, or that wobble.

2. Keep the extension cord clear of the work. Be certain the cord is long enough to let you finish the cut. A short cord may jerk the saw back, causing a kickback.

3. The piece being cut must be clamped or otherwise held firmly in place.

4. Never hold a piece of wood in your hand while trying to cut it. It must be firmly held on some stationary object.

5. Do not try to cut small pieces of wood.

6. Set the depth of cut so that the blade protrudes no more than ⅛in (3mm) below the wood being cut.

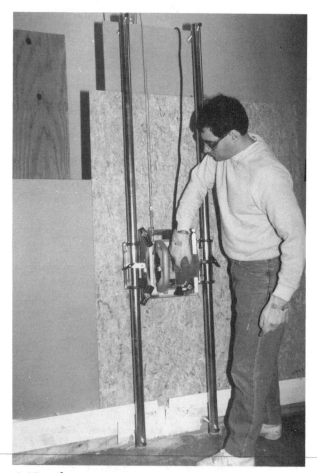

2-37 This unit turns a portable circular saw into a panel saw. (Courtesy Tinkerdell, Inc.)

7. Never *ever* place your hands below the wood being cut.

8. Allow the blade to reach full speed before starting to cut.

9. A bind between the saw and wood could cause a kickback. If the saw binds, release the switch immediately. Put a wood wedge in the kerf to hold it open before trying to continue the cut.

10. Do not use the saw if the guards are not working.

11. After finishing a cut, let the guard close and the blade stop, before moving it to another position.

12. Never use a dull blade. A dull blade will cause kickbacks and burning of the blade.

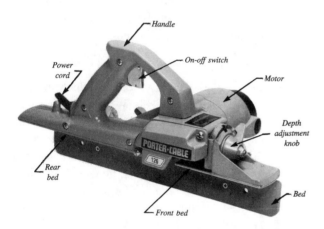

2-38 *A portable electric plane.* (Courtesy Porter-Cable Corporation)

13. Do not force the saw to cut faster than its normal pace.

14. Remove pitch and resin buildup from the blade.

15. Do not cut wet wood. This increases friction and loads the blade with wet sawdust.

16. When cutting large pieces, have provision to keep the pieces from falling when the cut is completed. A helper is often a good solution.

Portable Electric Planes

Portable electric planes are used to smooth edges of stock and faces of narrow boards. They will cut chamfers, rabbets, butt joints, and tenons. The width of the cutter is generally about 3in (76mm) and a typical depth of cut in a single pass is $1\frac{1}{64}$in (4.4mm). The depth of cut is regulated by raising or lowering the front shoe (see **2-38**).

To use the electric plane, set the desired depth of cut as specified by the manufacturer. Do not set it too deep. It is better to take two light cuts than one overly deep cut. The fence slides along the face of the board and keeps the plane moving in a straight line. Start the motor, and let it reach full speed. Place the front shoe on the board, and slide the plane along the surface. Hold the plane as specified by the manufacturer. At the start of the cut keep most of the downward pressure on the front shoe. As the end of the surface is reached, keep most of the pressure on the rear shoe (see **2-39**).

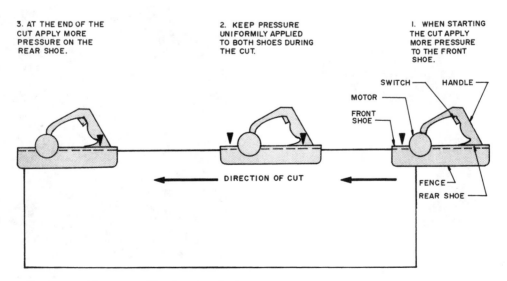

2-39 *How to take a cut with a portable electric plane.*

Portable Electric Plane Safety

1. Be certain the cutters are sharp and installed as recommended by the manufacturer.

2. Allow the cutter head to reach full speed before starting a cut.

3. Use thinner cuts on harder woods.

4. Hold the tool as recommended by the manufacturer. Large planes require two hands. Small block planes can be held with one hand.

5. Be certain the stock is held securely. Otherwise the plane will throw it back.

6. Keep both hands above the plane.

7. Do not feed faster than it seems to cut easily.

8. When possible, avoid cutting knots, especially with deep cuts.

2-40 A reversing, portable electric drill with a keyless chuck. (Courtesy Milwaukee Electric Tool Corporation)

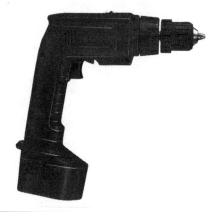

2-41 This is a 12-volt keyless, cordless portable electric drill. (Courtesy Milwaukee Electric Tool Corporation)

Portable Electric Drills

Portable electric drills are available in a wide range of sizes and features. Some have electric motors connected to 120V outlets by a cord, and others are battery operated and are called cordless drills. Typical electric drills are shown in **2-40** and **2-41**. Most small drills have a pistol-grip handle and can be operated with one hand. Larger, more powerful drills have a pistol grip and a second handle to control the torque produced by large-diameter drills.

Electric drills operating on 120V current are specified by the chuck size and the amperage of the electric motor. The chuck size indicates the maximum diameter drill shank it will hold. Most frequently used sizes are ⅜ and ½in (10 and 13mm). Typical amperage ratings run from 3 to 10 amps. Battery-operated cordless drills are specified by chuck size and the available voltage. Common chuck sizes are ⅜ and ½in, and voltages of 7 to 13 are typical. The one shown in **2-40** has a keyless chuck.

Bits are installed in key-type chucks which are then tightened with a key (see **2-42**). When using straight-shank twist drills, insert the round shank into the chuck but do not let any of the twisted flutes enter. Drills with no flutes, such as a spade bit, are inserted into the chuck as far as they will go (see **2-43**). It is recommended that the chuck be tightened by inserting the key and tightening at all three holes in the chuck. The bit can be released by inserting the key in any one of the holes.

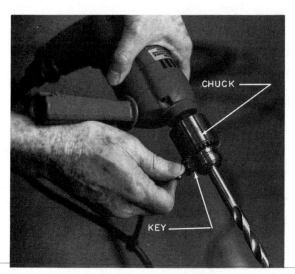

2-42 This chuck is tightened with a chuck key. (Courtesy Black & Decker, Inc.)

When drilling holes, be certain to keep the drill perpendicular to the work. If it drifts off to an angle, the bit may break or may bind in the work. When bits in large, powerful drills bind, the tool could twist out of your hands, causing injury.

Some drills can have the speed of rotation varied and the direction of rotation can be reversed. These can be equipped with a screwdriver bit and used to drive screws. A very low speed of rotation is used.

Portable Electric Drill Safety

1. Do not use a drill if the switch does not operate properly.

2. Remove the chuck key before starting the drill.

3. Always hold the tool securely.

4. Do not force the drill bit into the work.

5. Use sharp drill bits.

6. If the drill bit binds in the work, immediately release the switch. Free the bit from the work before proceeding.

7. When the drill is about to break through the back of the stock, reduce the pressure.

8. Drill bits get very hot, so do not touch them immediately after finishing a hole.

9. Keep drill bits clean and free of wood chips or resin deposits.

10. Be certain the work being drilled is firmly supported.

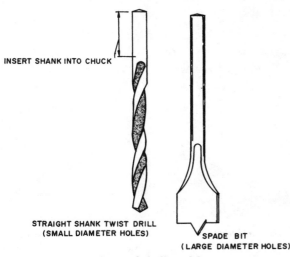

INSERT SHANK INTO CHUCK

STRAIGHT SHANK TWIST DRILL
(SMALL DIAMETER HOLES)

SPADE BIT
(LARGE DIAMETER HOLES)

2-43 *A commonly used drill and bit.*

Electric Drywall Screwdrivers

Gypsum drywall is commonly secured to wood and metal studs with special screws. These are driven with an electric screwdriver. When the screw is tight the clutch releases the drive (see **2-44**). Cordless electric screwdrivers are also available (see **2-45**).

2-44 *Gypsum wallboard can be installed with special screws driven with an electric screwdriver.* (Courtesy DeWalt International Tool Company)

2-45 *Cordless electric screwdrivers are convenient to use.* (Courtesy Milwaukee Electric Tool Corporation)

2-46 A portable electric router.

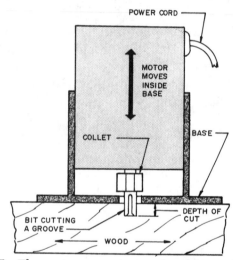

2-47 The router motor is raised and lowered to set the depth of cut.

2-48 The router can be mounted below a router table and serve as a light-duty shaper. (Courtesy Porter-Cable Corporation)

Portable Routers

The portable router is used to make decorative cuts and joinery. It consists of two major parts, the motor and the base (see 2-46). On the end of the motor shaft is a collet that holds the router bits. The motor moves up and down inside the base. This adjustment sets the depth of cut (see 2-47). A lock binds the motor and base together when the proper depth has been set. For general uses a one-horsepower router will be adequate. A finish carpenter will most likely want a two- or three-horsepower router so that deeper cuts may be made. In 2-48 is a router table. The router is mounted below the table with the cutter extending above it. This is operated like a shaper.

A **laminate trimmer** is used to trim high-pressure plastic laminates, as used on countertops, so it is flush with the edge of the substrate. It is a small, lightweight unit that operates similar to a router (see 2-49).

Router Safety

1. Do not make deep cuts and overload the router. Limit cuts to ⅛ to 3/16in (3 to 5mm).

2. Before changing the cutter, unplug the power cord.

3. Stock to be routed should be clamped to sawhorses or a workbench.

4. Hold portable routers with two hands using the handles provided on the machine.

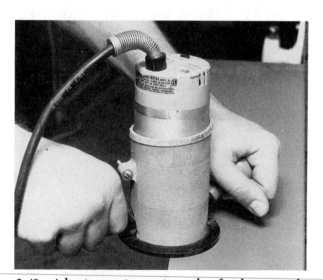

2-49 A laminate trimmer is used to finish cutting the edge of countertop plastic laminate after it has been bonded to the substrate.

5. Laminate trimmers are designed to be held with one hand.

6. Never place your hands near the rotating cutter.

7. When routing an outside edge of the stock, move the router in a *counterclockwise* direction.

8. Be certain the bit is correctly installed.

9. Do not let the rotating bit become tangled in your clothing. Remove rings, jewelry, long hanging clothing, and put long hair in a hair net.

10. Wear eye protection and a face shield.

11. Do not use dull router bits.

Router Bits

There are dozens of router bits available. Some produce various shapes on the edges of stock; others produce decorative cuts on the surface; and others still are used to cut grooves (see **2-50**). The cutting edges are made from carbon steel and are available carbide tipped. The carbon-steel bits are less expensive but the carbide-tipped will last much longer. Those who do a lot of routing will most likely use carbide-tipped cutters. Carbide cutters can also be used to trim plastic laminates, particleboard, and plywood. Some have a pilot tip which is a small roller on the end of the bit.

It rolls along the edge of the board and controls the width of the cut.

Routing on Edge

Begin by clamping the stock firmly to a workbench or sawhorses. Then set the depth of cut. If it appears to have a heavy cut, set it to take a lighter partial cut first, and then set the bit to take a full cut for the second pass. Light-duty routers may require more than two passes for a deep cut. Overloading may also damage the cutter.

Once the stock is secure and the depth set, plug in the router.

Most bits used to shape edges have a pilot tip riding along the edge of the stock. This controls the horizontal depth to which the bit will enter the wood (see **2-51**).

To begin the cut, start the motor and let it get to full speed. Place the base flat on the workpiece and slowly move the cutter into the wood until the pilot tip touches the edge. Move the router from left to right in a steady motion. Experience will show you how fast to move. If you go too slow the cutter will burn the wood. If you go too fast the cut may be bumpy rather than smooth. At the end of the cut lift the router (see **2-52**).

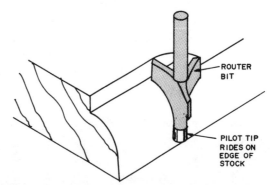

2-51 *Many shaper cutters are made with a pilot tip to help control the horizontal depth.*

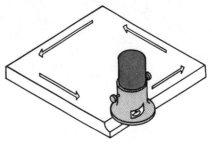

2-52 *Move the router from left to right.*

2-50 *A few of the router bits available for routing edges and decorating surfaces.*

2-53 *This router control system permits many edge mouldings and decorative surface cuts to be accurately completed.* (Courtesy Tinkerdell, Inc.)

In **2-53** is a router control system that mounts the router on a moving carriage that slides on side bars. The stock is placed on the table below the router and clamped in place. The router can be moved to cut rabbets, dadoes, edge mouldings, or decorative surface cuts.

Decorative Routing

The decorative router cutters do not have a pilot, so the router must be guided by a template or the router guide that is usually supplied with the router. The router guide is used to make straight cuts as shown in **2-54**. A circular decorative cut may be made by placing a circular guide on the rods from the straight guide (see **2-55**). Rotate the router counterclockwise.

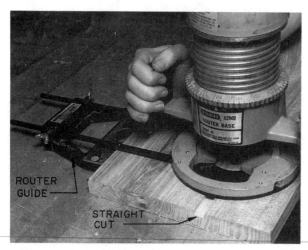

2-54 *This router guide is used to make accurate, straight cuts.*

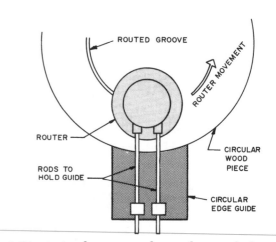

2-55 *A circular router edge guide is used when routing circular edges.*

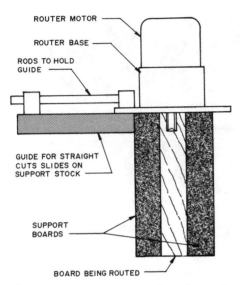

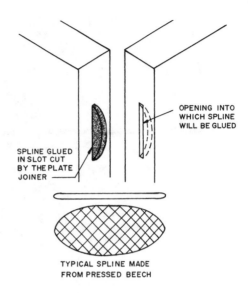

ROUTER MOTOR

ROUTER BASE

RODS TO HOLD
GUIDE

GUIDE FOR STRAIGHT
CUTS SLIDES ON
SUPPORT STOCK

SUPPORT
BOARDS

BOARD BEING ROUTED

SPLINE GLUED
IN SLOT CUT
BY THE PLATE
JOINER

OPENING INTO
WHICH SPLINE
WILL BE GLUED

TYPICAL SPLINE MADE
FROM PRESSED BEECH

2-56 *When routing grooves in the edges of stock, clamp support boards on each side to provide a broader surface.*

Cutting Grooves

Grooves can be cut on the edges of the stock by following the setup shown in **2-56.** The commercial straight guide is used to keep the bit in the desired location on the stock. It helps if the stock is supported by wood support strips on the side. This makes it easier to adjust the guide.

Biscuit Joiners

A biscuit, or plate, joiner (see **2-57**) uses a small cutter to cut short, circular kerfs in the edges of wood to be joined. Pressed-wood splines, often called biscuits or plates, are glued into these kerfs holding the wood parts together. They are commonly used on edge-to-edge, butt, and mitre joints (see **2-58**).

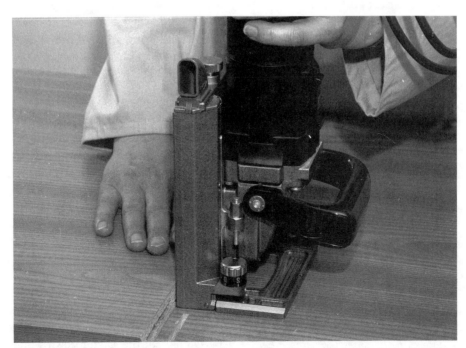

2-57 *The biscuit, or plate, joiner cuts small circular kerfs in the edges of stock to be joined.* (Courtesy Colonial Saw Company)

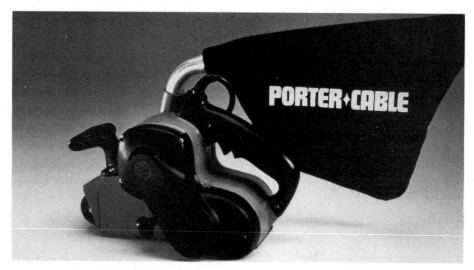

2-59 *This heavy-duty belt sander will remove wood rapidly.*
(Courtesy Porter-Cable Corporation)

Portable Sanders

The two commonly used portable sanders are for belt- and pad-type finishing. The belt sander is primarily used for removing large amounts of wood on flat surfaces (see **2-59**). They are available in a variety of sizes. The size is indicated by the length and width of the belt with 3×21in and 4×24in (76×533mm and 102×610mm) being widely used. Some have a dust bag attached to reduce the dust in the air.

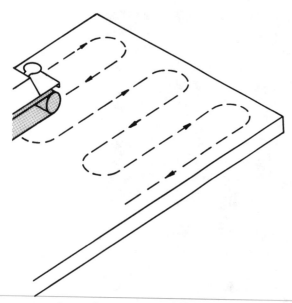

2-60 *This is the pattern to follow when using a belt sander.*

Using the Belt Sander

Before starting the belt sander be certain the belt is properly installed. The sander has tracking knobs on each side which need frequent adjustment to keep the belt running straight on the pulleys.

Clamp the stock to be sanded or it will be thrown across the room when the moving belt is placed on it. Place the sander flat on the piece, grip the handles firmly, and turn on the power. Immediately move the sander following the pattern in **2-60.** The strokes should overlap and be short. Always sand with the grain.

Belt Sander Safety

1. Unplug the power cord before changing the abrasive belt.

2. Be certain the switch is OFF before plugging in the power cord.

3. Clamp pieces to be sanded to a workbench or sawhorses.

4. Keep both hands on the handles provided on the sander.

5. Keep the power cord out of the way. Some run it over their shoulder.

6. Do not set the sander down while the belt is still turning.

2-61 A *finishing sander*. (Courtesy Porter-Cable Corporation)

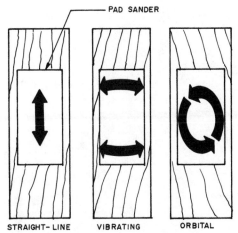

2-62 *Finishing sanders are available that produce different sanding patterns.*

Finishing Sanders

Finishing sanders are used to produce a smooth finished surface, after the heavier belt sander has already been applied. One type has a rectangular pad (see **2-61**) that may be moving in an orbital, straight-line, or vibrating direction (see **2-62**). The pad is covered with abrasive paper held to the pad with clamps on each end. Since it is a finish sander, generally fine-grit abrasive papers are used.

When using the pad sander work with the grain. Do not bear down on the sander to try to speed up removing a defect; use a coarser paper or go back to the belt sander instead. A vibrating sander and an orbital sander may be moved in any direction across the board. Straight-line sanders must be moved with the grain.

A very fine finish can be obtained using a random-orbit finishing sander (see **2-63**). Sanding pads are bonded to the pad with pressure-sensitive adhesive-backed paper. It can be moved in any direction without leaving any scratch marks. It is used for the final sanding operation.

2-63 *A random-orbit finishing sander.* (Courtesy Porter-Cable Corporation)

2-64 *Power nailers can be used for many of the jobs performed by the finish carpenter.* (Courtesy Senco Products, Inc.)

Power Nailers and Staplers

Power nailers speed up the work of the finish carpenter. They can be used for almost any work that needs to be accomplished. Jobs such as installing doors, casing, baseboard, and cabinetwork are examples where power nailers and staplers are helpful (see **2-64**). Power nailers operate off of an air compressor. However, a cordless type is available. Some nailers drive small brads as required when installing small trim and

2-65 *Portable air compressors are required to operate many of the tools used by finish carpenters.* (Courtesy Hilti, Inc.)

mouldings. Brad sizes range from ⅝in to 1⅝in (15 to 42mm). A finish nailer is used for installing light and heavy trim, panelling, and stair parts. Finish nails range from 1 to 2in (25.4 to 50.8mm) in length. Heavy-duty nailers are used by framing carpenters and drive nails up to 16d (3½in or 89mm).

Power staplers also find use on interior work but are used in places where the staples will not be seen.

Air Compressors

It is important to have an air compressor supplying a constant air stream at the required **pressure**. Air pressures from 80 to 100 psi (551 to 689 kPa) are common. The air supply must also provide the required **lubrication** to the power tool as specified by the manufacturer. Water condenses in the air tank and must be regularly drained. Filters are used to keep the air clean and remove abrasive sludge created by rust and dust in the air supply system. The air intake filter must be frequently cleaned (see **2-65**).

Power Nailer and Stapler Safety

1. Before operating, study the owner's manual and observe all operating recommendations.

2. Treat the tool as you would a gun. *Never* point it at anyone even as a joke. The projected fastener can cause serious physical damage.

3. Keep both hands behind the nail-ejecting tube.

4. Keep your feet and legs behind and clear of the tool.

5. Wear safety glasses.

6. Use only the fasteners designed for the tool and recommended by the manufacturer.

7. Keep the tool tight against the surface being fastened. Do not let it bounce.

8. Maintain the recommended air pressure.

9. When making repairs or adjustments, disconnect the tool from the air line.

10. Do not use a nailer that will discharge a nail when the end of the tool is not against a surface.

3

Safety

Working in the construction industry exposes individuals to a vast array of dangerous situations. The contractor is responsible for overseeing that the construction site meets recommended safety regulations. On large jobs a full-time safety supervisor is present. Regardless of the actions of others, the prevention of accidents falls largely upon the knowledge and skills of each individual worker. Regulations alone will not protect the individual unless everyone on the job observes them. Many accidents occur due to the *improper use* of **tools, ladders,** and **scaffolding.**

In 1970 the United States government acted to assure safe and healthful working conditions by passing the Occupational Safety and Health Administration Act which established the Occupational Safety and Health Administration (OSHA).

U.S. Occupational Safety and Health Administration

OSHA regulations applicable to the construction industry are available in a single volume. It is titled *Construction Industry, OSHA Safety and Health Standards (29 CFR 1926/1910)* and can be purchased from the Superintendent of Documents, Congressional Sales Office, U.S. Government Printing Office, Washington, D.C. 20402. Other specialized publications are available such as *Personal Protection Equipment, OSHA 3077,* and *Hand and Power Tool Safety, OSHA 3080.*

On-Site Housekeeping

Many accidents can be averted by proper on-site housekeeping. Following are some recommendations.

1. Keep the area around the building clear of debris.

2. Keep the interior of the building, including stairs, halls, aisles, walkways, and open floor areas, free of debris.

3. Remove all nails from scrap lumber.

4. Avoid fires by removing flammable materials or storing them in fire-safe containers.

5. Keep all electrical cords free of entanglement with loose materials and in good repair.

6. Wipe up spilled liquids on areas that may cause workers to slip.

7. Build protective barriers around openings on the site or in the building that may cause falls (see **3-1**).

8. When dropping materials to the ground, barricade the drop area. Drops over 20ft (6.1m) high should be made using a chute.

Worker Safety

The employer is responsible for requiring the wearing of appropriate **personal protective equipment** in all operations where there is an exposure to hazardous conditions. Each individual should have the proper

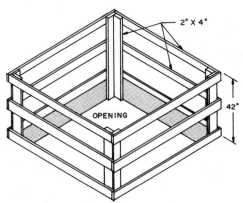

3-1 Temporary openings must be protected by a guard rail.

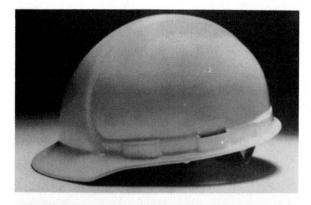

3-2 *This Type 2 hard hat has a head rest mounted inside the shell of the hat.* (Courtesy Cabot Safety Corporation)

personal safety equipment. In some cases the contractor provides some equipment, but basic safety items are usually provided by each worker. Following are some things to observe:

1. Always wear a **hard hat** in areas designated as "Hard Hat Areas." The hard hat lining must be adjusted so that it sits firmly on the band inside (see **3-2**). Protective hats are available in two types. Type 1 has a full brim not less than 1¼in (32mm) wide and Type 2 is brimless with a peak extending forward.

2. Purchase hard hats certified to meet the specifications in *American National Standards Institute, Z89.1-1969, Safety Requirements for Industrial Head Protection.*

3. Never wear a hard hat over another hat.

4. Wherever it is not feasible to reduce the noise levels or duration of exposures to those levels specified by OSHA regulations, **ear protection devices** must be provided and used. Plain cotton is not an acceptable protective device (see **3-3**).

5. **Eye and face protection equipment** is required when machines or operations present potential eye or face damage. Eye and face protective equipment must meet the requirements speci-

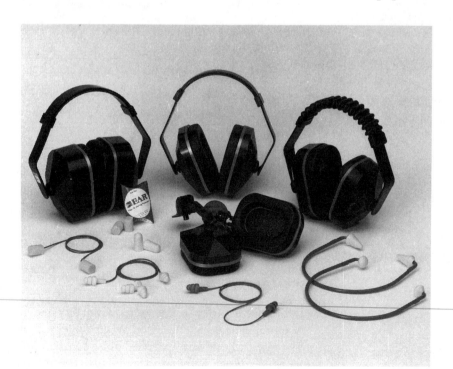

3-3 *Ear-protection devices such as these are required for noise levels above those considered safe by U.S. OSHA regulations.* (Courtesy Cabot Safety Corporation)

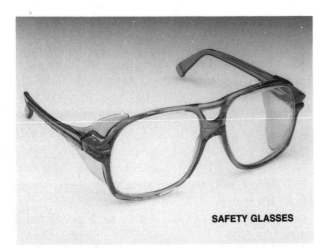

SAFETY GLASSES

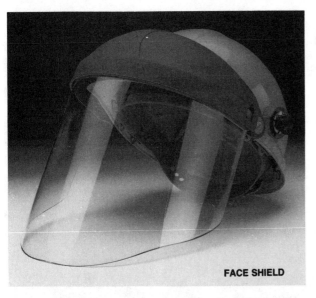

FACE SHIELD

PROTECTION GLASSES

3-4 *Eye protection can be accomplished with several types of approved eye-shielding equipment.* (Courtesy Cabot Safety Corporation)

fied in *American National Standards Institute, Z87.1-1989, Practice for Occupational and Educational Eye and Face Protection* (see **3-4**).

6. Face and eye protection equipment must be kept clean and in good repair.

7. When employees are exposed to harmful respiratory substances **respiratory protective devices** must be used. Selection of a respirator should be made according to the guidelines in *American National Standards Practices for Respiratory Protection Z88.2-1980* (see **3-5**).

8. When working aboveground where falls are likely, **lifelines, safety belts,** or **lanyards** should be used for employee safeguarding. These should be sized and secured as specified in OSHA requirements.

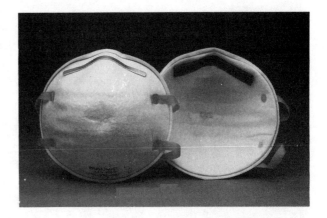

3-5 *Two types of respiratory-protection devices.* (Courtesy Cabot Safety Corporation)

9. Many situations require that the worker wear **safety shoes** having a steel toe covering.

10. Clothes should be loose enough to permit easy bending but not loose enough to get caught in moving tools.

11. Long hair should be enclosed in a hair net.

Power Tool Safety

The use of power woodworking tools is covered in Chapter 2. General safety recommendations as well as specific requirements for each tool are discussed there.

Ladders

Finish carpenters use **step** and **straight ladders**, and occasionally **extension ladders** (see **3-6**). It is important to purchase high-quality ladders that meet OSHA requirements. Detailed OSHA information on ladders and stairways is available in the publication *Stairways and Ladders, OSHA 3124*. Order from OSHA Publication Office, 200 Constitution Ave., NW, Room N-3647, Washington, DC 20210.

National safety codes for portable ladders available from the American National Standards Institute include *ANSI-14.1-14.2-56, Safety Code for Portable Metal Ladders*.

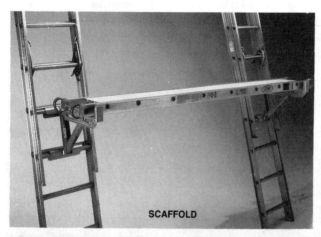

SCAFFOLD

STEPLADDER

STEPLADDER

EXTENSION LADDER

STRAIGHT LADDER

3-6 Commonly used types of ladder. (Courtesy Keller Industries)

Using Straight and Extension Ladders Safely
Following are recommendations to be observed when using ladders.

1. Never use a ladder that is defective. Examine regularly for cracked, broken, or missing parts.

2. Place ladders where they are out of the normal traffic pattern followed by workers on the job. This prevents them from accidentally being bumped or knocked down.

3. The ladder must have an approved type of non-skid feet.

4. When necessary, nail blocking to keep the feet from sliding.

5. Clear the area of debris where the ladder is to be used.

6. When raising a straight extension ladder, prop the feet against a fixed support to keep them from sliding (see **3-7**).

7. The top of the ladder should extend three feet above the top of a wall. This provides support for activities such as going up on a roof (see **3-8**).

8. Use a ladder that is the correct length for the job. Extension ladders are adjustable and make it easy to vary the length (see **3-9**).

9. The feet of the ladder should be away from a wall a distance equal to one-fourth of the working distance as shown in **3-8**.

10. When ascending or descending a ladder, keep your hands on both rails and face the ladder.

11. Observe the load limitations specified for the ladder. They must support at least four times the maximum intended load.

12. Ladders are not designed to carry loads when they are in a horizontal position, so do not use them as scaffolding.

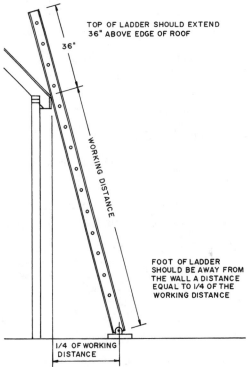

3-8 *Proper way to position a straight or extension ladder.*

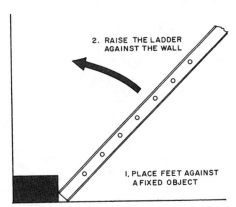

3-7 *When raising a ladder, place the feet against a solid object.*

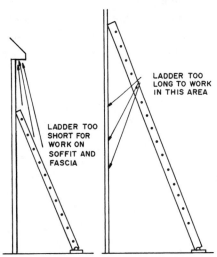

3-9 *A ladder must be the proper length for the work to be accomplished safely.*

13. Do not lean out away from the ladder. If you cannot reach something, move the ladder closer to it.

14. Keep your shoes clean and dry.

15. Do not stand on the top three rungs of a straight or extension ladder.

16. Allow a three-foot overlap between sections of a 36ft extension ladder. A four-foot overlap is required when using 48ft extension ladders.

17. Metal ladders that could conduct electricity should not be used near energized lines or equipment. Conductive ladders must be prominently marked as conductive.

Using Stepladders Safely

1. Observe the maximum load-carrying capacity specified.

2. Be certain that the ladder is fully open and that the braces are fully extended, locking the legs in place.

3. All four legs must be firmly set on a level surface.

4. Do not stand on the top two steps. These are usually marked "no step."

5. Discard any stepladder that is defective. Check it regularly for splits and loose parts.

Scaffolding

The most commonly used scaffolding is commercially made from metal pipe welded into units that are assembled on the job. These are freestanding and do not rely on attachment to the building for vertical support. It is important that the feet be placed on a solid material such as 4in (10.2cm) concrete blocks or heavy wood members set level on the ground. The scaffolding is usually tied to the building to stabilize it and help resist tilting (see **3-10**).

Sometimes site-built scaffolding is used. It may be freestanding (independent) or built to fasten to the wall of the building (single pole) and rely on the wall for part of the structural frame.

Detailed OSHA regulations for scaffolding are also in the publication *Construction Industry, OSHA Safety and Health Standards (29 CFR 1926/1910)*. For full details secure a copy of the report.

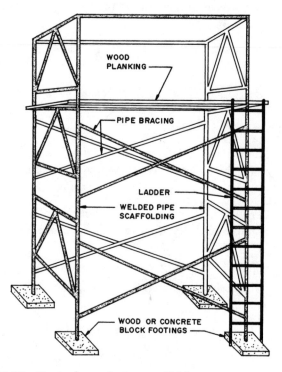

3-10 Typical metal pipe scaffolding.

4

Moulding

A wide variety of moulding profiles are available for interior and exterior use. Satisfaction with the finished job depends on the selection of the moulding profile, the use of mouldings made from quality materials, and the installation by a skilled finish carpenter. Mouldings are available from three sources: stock mouldings, special mouldings made to order by a moulding manufacturer, and carpenter-made mouldings.

Stock mouldings are those manufactured in large quantities and sold by local building materials suppliers. The actual designs and sizes available vary from region to region. It is less costly to use stock mouldings than have specially designed mouldings made. However, the choice of profiles is limited.

The choice of the mouldings to be used in new construction is made by the architectural designer in consultation with the owner of the building under construction. With old construction being remodelled or renovated, an interior designer may be involved in such specification. The carpenter must be certain the specified mouldings are used and should not make a substitution without written approval from the designer or owner.

In addition to local building materials suppliers, mouldings can be bought from a number of mail-order supply houses. They have catalogs of mouldings they cut, and orders are placed by phone or mail. The material is shipped to the construction site. Some of these companies will also manufacture **specially designed mouldings.** Mouldings are available in a variety of wood species as well as moulded high-density polymer plastics.

The quality of wood mouldings varies depending on the species of wood used and the method of cutting them. While the production of stock mouldings is a mass-production process, the cutting tools must be kept sharp and the profile of the cutters consistent so that smooth, accurately cut profiles are produced. Some companies supply wood mouldings that are fireproofed and prefinished. Prefinished mouldings must be handled carefully so that they are not damaged during shipping, storage, cutting, and installation.

Examples of some of the commonly available wood mouldings are shown in **4-1** on the following page. **Baseboards** cover the lower edge of the wall where it meets the floor. **Base caps** are attached to the top of some types of baseboard to give an attractive profile. **Base shoes** are placed on the floor where the baseboard meets the floor. **Crown mouldings** are used where the wall and ceiling meet and are also used on exterior cornice construction. **Casing** is used to trim the interior edge of door and window frames; it covers the space between the frame and the interior wall finish material. **Chair rails** are applied to the wall in rooms, such as a dining room, where chairs may rub against the wall. **Picture rails** are applied on the wall near the ceiling and are shaped to hold a metal hook used to hang pictures. **Door stops** are nailed inside the door frame such that the door closes against them when it is closed. **Panel moulding** is used to provide a profile on the top of wood panelling and to the outer edge of casing. A variety of **corner** and **cove mouldings** are available. Corner mouldings are used to protect wall corners from damage. Cove mouldings find a wide range of applications, including use on inside wall corners.

A wide variety of mouldings that are cast or extruded from **plastics** are available. They can have a smooth or simulated wood-grain finish. Examples of polyurethane architectural moulding profiles are shown in **4-2.** They are available in the same basic types as wood but, since they are moulded or extruded, the surface design features can be more de-

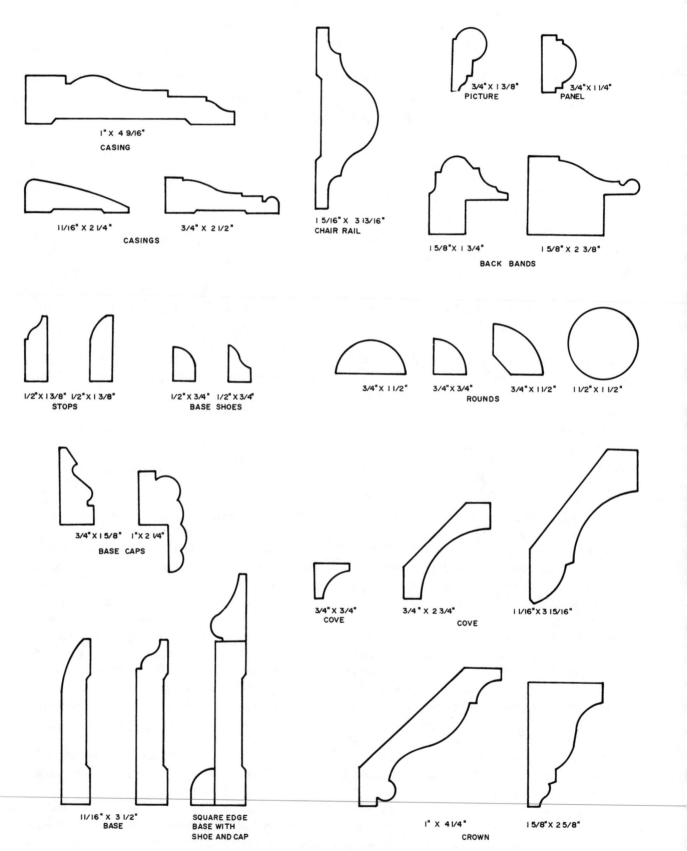

1" X 4 9/16"
CASING

11/16" X 2 1/4"

3/4" X 2 1/2"

CASINGS

1 5/16" X 3 13/16"
CHAIR RAIL

3/4" X 1 3/8"
PICTURE

3/4" X 1 1/4"
PANEL

1 5/8" X 1 3/4"

1 5/8" X 2 3/8"

BACK BANDS

1/2" X 1 3/8" 1/2" X 1 3/8"
STOPS

1/2" X 3/4" 1/2" X 3/4"
BASE SHOES

3/4" X 1 1/2"

3/4" X 3/4"

3/4" X 1 1/2"

1 1/2" X 1 1/2"

ROUNDS

3/4" X 1 5/8" 1" X 2 1/4"
BASE CAPS

3/4" X 3/4"
COVE

3/4" X 2 3/4"
COVE

1 1/16" X 3 15/16"

11/16" X 3 1/2"
BASE

SQUARE EDGE
BASE WITH
SHOE AND CAP

1" X 4 1/4"

1 5/8" X 2 5/8"

CROWN

4-1   A few examples of the many stock wood mouldings manufactured.

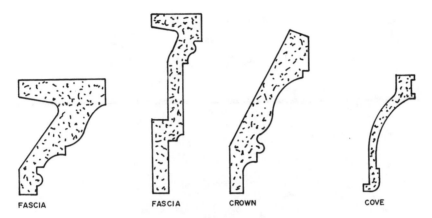

FASCIA   FASCIA   CROWN   COVE

4-2   Profiles of some of the polyurethane architectural mouldings available.

tailed and elaborate than commonly found on wood mouldings. They are made in heights as much as 15in (38.1cm) and more. Plastic mouldings can be used inside or outside the building. They are impervious to rot, will not warp, and will stand up to the elements. Manufacturers will also produce custom-design mouldings. Strip mouldings, such as crown mouldings, are available in 16ft (4.9m) lengths. Plastic mouldings can be painted or stained. Some types are very flexible

and may be bent to desired contours (see **4-3**). They can be cut with a saw or knife and installed with adhesive.

Another form of moulding is made using a metal-wrapped wood core. The metals used are brass, copper, and chrome. The metal surface is polished and sealed with a transparent lacquer coating. They are available in the same types as described for wood moulding.

4-3   Plastic architectural mouldings are moulded in very detailed profiles. (Courtesy Flex Trim, Inc.)

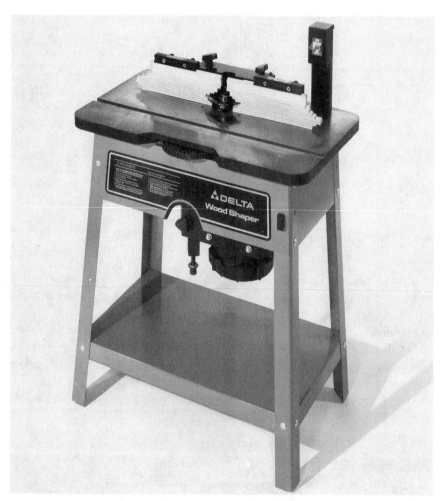

4-4   *A wood shaper used to cut profiles on wood parts.* (Courtesy Delta International Machinery Corp.)

Wood Moulding Grades and Species

The selection of the grade and species of wood moulding influences the cost and the quality of the finished job. Basically the products can be divided into two major types, **paint grades** and **stain or natural finish grades**. Paint-grade mouldings permit the painter to fill any joints and nail holes, sand the surface smooth, and cover these with an opaque coating. Stain grade requires more careful cutting of joints and avoiding too many joints by using long lengths when possible. This requires the highest level of skilled joinery and installation.

Paint grades are usually softwoods because these have a smooth, tight grain and are less expensive. Commonly used species include various types of pine, such as White, Idaho, Northern, Ponderosa, as well as Sugar and Yellow hemlock, poplar, fir, and red-wood, and occasionally a hardwood such as maple, beech, or birch. Stain-grade mouldings are commonly some type of hardwood such as oak, walnut, birch mahogany, or cherry. The choice of grade and specie is made by the designer and owner. Stain-grade mouldings are not usually stocked by local building materials suppliers, so an order for these mouldings must be placed well in advance of when they are to be needed so that they can be manufactured.

Hardwood mouldings are more difficult to nail and frequently the holes have to be drilled for the nails. Obviously, hardwood mouldings will withstand bumps and abrasions better than softwoods. If for some reason moisture is a possible problem, moulding made from rot-resistant wood, such as redwood, cedar, or cypress, can be used.

Detailed information on wood mouldings of various designs and species is available from the Architectural Woodwork Institute, 2310 S. Walter Reed Drive, Arlington, VA 22206-1199.

Custom-Made Mouldings

While most **custom-made mouldings** will be manufactured to the designer's specification by a moulding manufacturer, a finish carpenter can produce some types using common power woodworking tools. A typical production moulding machine feeds the wood au-

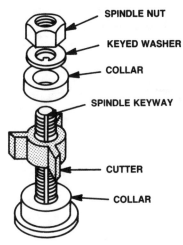

4-5 *The three-lip shaper cutter is mounted on the shaper spindle.*

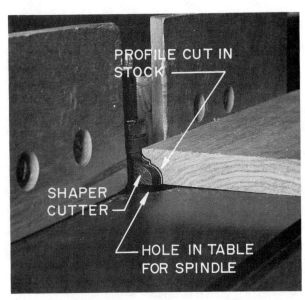

4-7 *The shaper cutter extends above the table and out beyond the fence, letting it cut a profile in the stock passing by it.*

tomatically through the machine past a set of knives ground to the shape desired. The designer will produce a full-size drawing of the shape of the moulding desired. The manufacturer will then grind a set of knives to this profile. In addition to the desired profile, the grade and specie of wood must be specified.

Carpenter-Made Mouldings

The finish carpenter can produce special mouldings using a woodworking shaper, circular saw, and a portable router. Specific details for operating each of these machines is available in woodworking books.

A shaper is shown in **4-4.** It uses a three-lip cutter having the profile ground in the edges of each lip (see **4-5**). A wide variety of cutters with various profiles are available; some are shown in **4-6.** The shaper cutter extends through a round opening in the shaper table. The cutter is raised and lowered until the desired profile is exposed. The wood is placed against a fence and moved into the rapidly rotating cutter (see **4-7**). Always feed the stock against the direction of rotation of the cutter (see **4-8**). Remember that the direction of rotation of the cutter on a shaper can be reversed by a simple switch; so it is important to feed the stock from the proper direction.

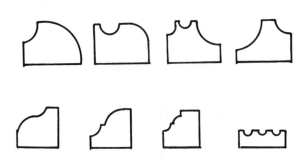

4-6 *Some of the profiles available on standard shaper cutters.*

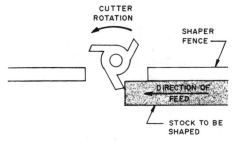

4-8 *Feed the stock to be shaped into the rotation of the cutter.*

Small mouldings can be cut with a portable router. (The router is discussed in Chapter 3.) It is advisable to use a sufficiently powerful router such as one that has one or more horsepower. A variety of bits are available in various profiles. The stock to be shaped will have a square edge against which the router-bit guide rides. The cutter removes the wood forming the profile (see 4-9). The depth of cut used influences the profile cut. This is adjusted by raising and lowering the motor (see 4-10). Notice in 4-11 how this adjustment changes the profile of the moulding.

Mouldings produced with a router can be made more easily and more accurately if the router is mounted on a router shaper table (see 4-12). The router is mounted upside down below the table. A fence is used to guide the stock past the cutter. This is much the same operation as using a shaper.

The stationary circular saw (discussed in Chapter 3) can be used to cut a limited variety of mouldings using the circular saw blade. It can cut bevels and rabbets using the rip fence as a guide. To cut a bevel, the blade is tilted to the desired angle, and the stock is placed against the rip fence and moved past the blade (see 4-13). To cut a rabbet, the saw is set to the desired depth of cut, and the width of the rabbet is set between the blade and the fence and this is cut. Then the stock is turned over, the fence reset, and the second cut is made as shown in 4-14.

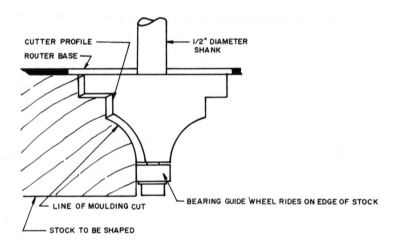

4-9   The router bit has a bearing guide wheel to help control the depth of cut.

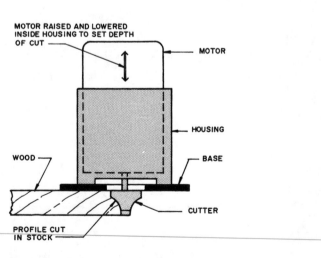

4-10   The base of the router rests on the surface of the wood, and the motor is raised and lowered to adjust the cut.

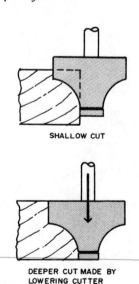

4-11   The shape of the moulding is changed when the motor is raised or lowered.

4-12 *This router is mounted on a router table making it operate much like a shaper.*
(Courtesy Porter-Cable Corporation)

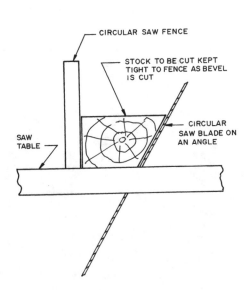

4-13 *Bevels are cut on a circular saw by tilting the blade.*

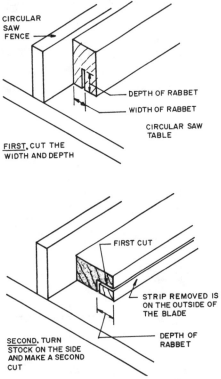

4-14 *How to cut a rabbet on a circular saw.*

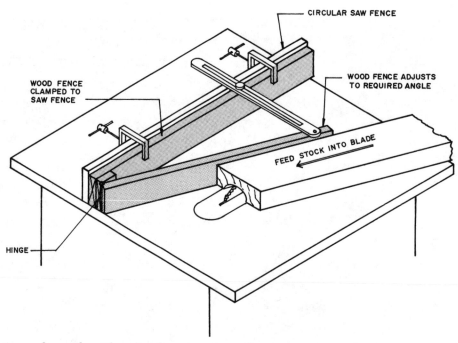

4-15   Cove cuts can be made with a circular saw using a fence set on an angle.

Cove cuts can be made by feeding the stock across the saw on an angle. An adjustable fence can be made as shown in **4-15**. It is clamped to the rip fence and adjusted to the desired angle. The size and shape of the cove is varied by adjusting the angle. Make some trial cuts in waste stock until the desired cove shape is produced. Tightly lock the adjustable fence at this angle. Raise the blade so that it protrudes ¼in (6mm) or less above the surface of the table. Place the stock against the temporary fence, and push the wood across the saw. Then raise the saw blade ⅛ to ³⁄₁₆in (3

to 4.5mm) higher and repeat the cut. Continue until the depth of the cove required is reached. Cove mouldings of various profiles can be made by combining the cove cut with other cuts on a shaper, moulding head, or with a router as shown in **4-16**.

There are a number of moulding heads available for use on the circular saw. They replace the saw blade and have cutter blades much like those used on shapers and routers (see **4-17**). The stock to be cut is placed against the rip fence and moved over the rotating moulder head. Manufacturers' instructions should be carefully studied and observed when using moulding heads on circular saws.

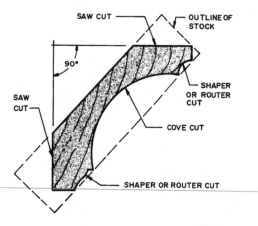

4-16   Cove mouldings can combine cove cuts and other profiles.

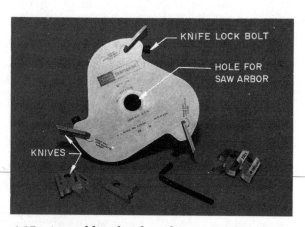

4-17   A moulding head used on a circular saw.

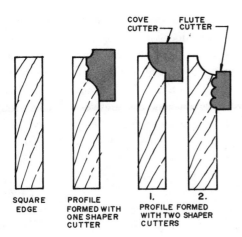

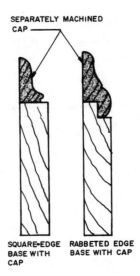

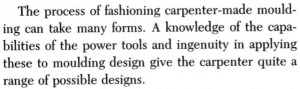

4-18 *Carpenters can make base and casing using shaper cutters.*

4-19 *The base can have a separate profiled cap moulding.*

The process of fashioning carpenter-made moulding can take many forms. A knowledge of the capabilities of the power tools and ingenuity in applying these to moulding design give the carpenter quite a range of possible designs.

Start with good-quality, kiln-dried, straight stock free of knots, warps, and other defects. In some cases, square-edge stock becomes the baseboard or door and window casing. It can have various profiles cut, if a more decorative design is desired. Selected examples are shown in **4-18**. If a baseboard with a finished cap is desired, the cap could be purchased ready-made or made by the carpenter as shown in **4-19**. The square-edge base may require a rabbet in the top edge. The base cap can be machined on the edge of a wider board and cut to width (see **4-20**).

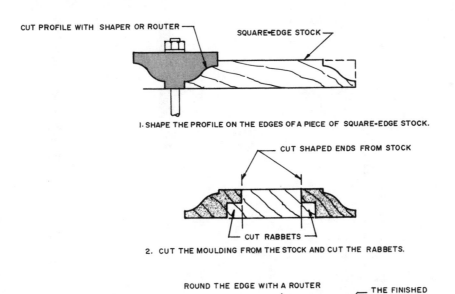

4-20 *Typical carpenter-made base cap moulding.*

When the carpenter proceeds to make the moulding, it is best to make trial cuts on scrap stock before cutting into the more expensive material. Mouldings to be painted can be cut from white pine or other softwoods. These can be purchased cut to standard widths and planed to standard thicknesses. If hardwoods are to be used, they are usually sold in random widths and lengths and are not surfaced. It will be necessary to have hardwoods planed to thickness and cut and squared to the desired widths. It is more difficult to get long pieces of hardwoods, so more joints will occur as the moulding is installed than with soft woods.

Estimating Quantities of Moulding

Trim and moulding may be ordered by **specifying lengths** for certain installations or by giving the **total number of lineal feet** required. Often lengths are specified for casing doors and windows. Quantities of this type are ordered by giving descriptive information such as the width, profile, and length of each piece.

For example, to case an interior door, each side would take two pieces long enough to run the 6'-8" length plus the width of the moulding required for a mitre. In most cases, a 7'-0" piece would be long enough. However, without detailed specifications, casing is sold in two-foot lengths starting with 6ft; so four 8ft pieces would be required for the trim on both sides.

The head casing will vary by door width, but if it is a 2'-8"-wide door, it will have to be that long plus twice the moulding thickness for mitre on each end plus up to about ½in for the setback from the door frame. Therefore, a 2'-8" door plus ½in plus 5½in for twice the 2¾in-wide casing gives a finished length of 3'-2" for the head casing. Two pieces could be cut from one 8ft length with 1'-8" waste. Three pieces could be cut from a 10ft piece with 6in waste. Some door and window manufacturers supply casing in required lengths for the units (see **4-21** and **4-22**).

Most mouldings are sold by the lineal foot and are installed using the lengths received. This is frequently referred to as running moulding. These mouldings can be joined with scarf joints to form the required long pieces. In most cases, therefore, the exact lengths received are not critical. Base, shoe, crown, cove, panel, and other mouldings are usually ordered by giving the total number of lineal feet needed. This figure includes the number of feet actually required plus a percentage for waste. A waste factor of 10 to 15 percent is typically used.

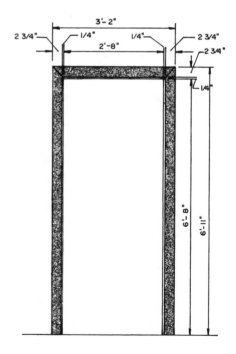

SIDE CASING — 4 PIECES 6'-11" (BOTH SIDES OF OPENING)
HEAD CASING — 2 PIECES 3'-2"

SIDE CASING — CAN GET ONE PIECE FROM 8'-0" STOCK OR TWO FROM 14'-0" STOCK.
HEAD CASING — CAN GET TWO FROM 8'-0" STOCK OR THREE FROM 10'-0" STOCK.

4-22 *Estimating the casing needed for an interior door.*

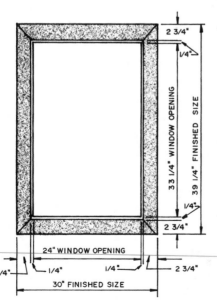

4-21 *Estimating the casing needed for a window.*

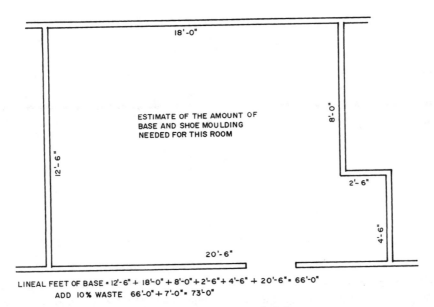

LINEAL FEET OF BASE = 12'-6" + 18'-0" + 8'-0" + 2'-6" + 4'-6" + 20'-6" = 66'-0"
ADD 10% WASTE   66'-0" + 7'-0" = 73'-0"

4-23   Estimating the quantity of base and shoe moulding needed for a room.

An example is shown in **4-23**. To figure the amount of base, the length of the perimeter was found, ignoring openings, to be 66ft. A 10 percent waste factor was added to give a total of 73 lineal feet of base and shoe to be ordered. The quantity received may be slightly more than this, because the supplier will send the lengths on hand that add up close to the amount ordered.

Securing and Storing Wood Materials

The general contractor with the consultation of the owner and designer purchases the finish materials in most job arrangements. The species of wood, quality of all materials, and so on may be stated in the specifications and be part of the general contract. When the finish carpenter arrives on the job the materials should be there.

However, many small jobs require the finish carpenter to choose and purchase these materials. As always, the obligations of the contract between the carpenter and contractor must be observed. As discussed, mouldings are available in various grades and species, and these choices influence the cost of the materials.

When the moulding is delivered to the job, it must be **stored flat on a dry surface**. Storage inside the building on the dry wood subfloor is best. If the subfloor is wet or if the material is stored on a concrete garage floor, plastic sheeting must be placed below it. The material must also be covered with plastic to protect it from moisture. All drywall plaster work must be finished and completely dry before storing the stock in the building. The building must be ventilated to reduce the moisture in the air. The wood moulding is kiln dried for interior use and will absorb moisture from the air. It is recommended that the wood products be allowed to be in the building a few days before they are used so that they can equalize their moisture content with that in the air.

5

Installing and Trimming Doors

Interior doors are hung and trimmed only when the building is near completion. The windows already should be in place, and the drywall installed, taped, and sanded. The finished flooring may or may not be in place; if it is not, the carpenter may have to make allowances for it as the door frame is installed. Door framing and hanging can require some sawing and planing which might soil a carpet.

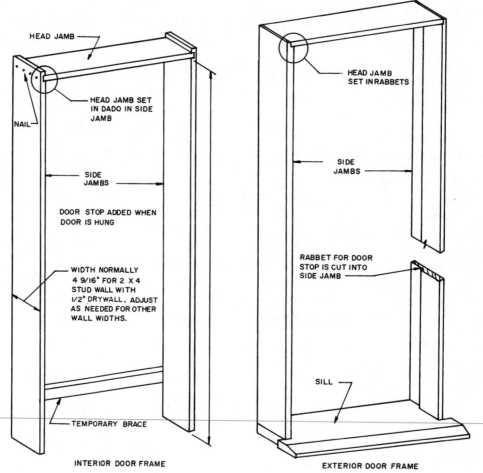

HEAD JAMB

HEAD JAMB SET IN DADO IN SIDE JAMB

NAIL

SIDE JAMBS

DOOR STOP ADDED WHEN DOOR IS HUNG

WIDTH NORMALLY 4 9/16" FOR 2 X 4 STUD WALL WITH 1/2" DRYWALL. ADJUST AS NEEDED FOR OTHER WALL WIDTHS.

TEMPORARY BRACE

INTERIOR DOOR FRAME

HEAD JAMB SET IN RABBETS

SIDE JAMBS

RABBET FOR DOOR STOP IS CUT INTO SIDE JAMB

SILL

EXTERIOR DOOR FRAME

5-1 *Typical interior and exterior door frames.*

Installing doors requires the finish carpenter to work very carefully. The frame must be absolutely square and plumb. A poorly installed frame can cause a door to bind, or always swing open, or refuse to stay open. In any case, it is an annoying situation and a sure sign that the finish carpenter did not do a good job.

First the rough opening must be checked and corrected, if necessary. Once this has been accomplished the door frame may be installed.

Typical **interior** and **exterior door frames** are shown in **5-1**. A typical interior door frame is ¾in (19mm) thick softwood. The height and width made for standard door sizes for interior doors are typically 6'-8" (2033mm) high and range from 2'-0" (610mm) to 3'-0" (915mm) in width in 2in (51mm) increments. Exterior doors are typically 6'-8" (2033mm) high through 7'-0" (2135mm). Widths range from 3'-0" to 3'-6" (915 to 1067mm), though wider sizes are available. Interior doors are 1⅜in (35mm) thick, and exterior doors are 1¾in (44mm) or 2¼in (57mm) thick.

The depth of the door frame depends on the width of the finished wall. A typical situation is shown in **5-2**. In this example the actual wall width is 4½in (114mm), while the stock frame is 4⁹⁄₁₆in (116mm). This extra width is essential to provide allowances for any variation in wall thickness. If the frame happens to be too wide, it can be planed narrower. If, for some reason, the wall is a little too wide, the gypsum drywall can be shaved a little so that it is behind the casing.

There are several **framing situations** to be considered. These include (**1**) high-quality factory-made door frames, (**2**) assembled door frames with prehung doors, (**3**) assembled door frames with prehung doors and casing on one side, (**4**) split-jamb, and (**5**) carpenter-made frames. The basic installation techniques are the same for all types of frames.

Types of Door

The style of door and the material from which it is made are specified by the designer or owner. This information is shown on the working drawings or in the specifications. The sizes of the doors are given in a door **schedule** (a keyed, reference list with specifications) that is on the working drawings.

There are many styles and types of interior door manufactured. Examples of those most commonly used are shown in **5-3**. The solid-wood door with wood **panels** is a popular choice. Various panel configurations are available that can be used for interior or exterior doors. They are made in softwoods for painting and in hardwoods for stained or natural finishes. The wood panels can be replaced with glass or louvres. A door with a similar appearance is moulded from wood fibres, commonly referred to as hardboard. The surface is embossed to create the appearance of a wood grain. These moulded doors have the advantage of being dimensionally stable, thus reducing the possibility of warping. The panel design door comes factory-primed and -ready for the finish coat of paint.

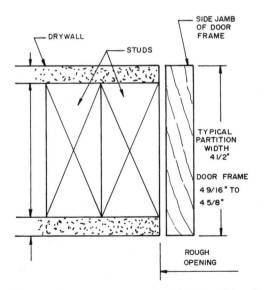

5-2 *This is the most commonly found width of an interior partition.*

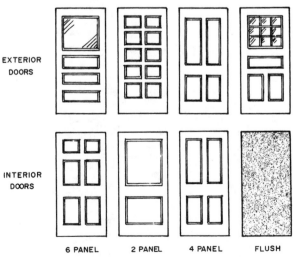

5-3 *A few of the many interior and exterior door styles.*

Another popular style of the door is the **flush door**. The hollow-core flush door is built with a wood frame and internal bracing of cardboard or wood strips that form a honeycomb interior. Over this internal structure plywood veneers or plastic laminate are glued, providing a smooth, flush door face. They are available in a wide variety of hardwood veneers. The flush door is also available with a solid core. The solid-core flush door is heavier and stronger; it is generally used as a exterior door, because it provides great resistance to damage from fire or potential intruders. The same style is made from moulded hardboard. The exterior surface has embossed wood grain and is available in a variety of natural color finishes, such as oak and walnut.

Many exterior doors in use today have a **steel** or **fibreglass** outer surface over a wood-framed interior structure. The voids inside the door are filled with polyurethane foam, providing better insulating qualities than a wood door. Steel-sheathed doors are primed, ready for paint. Fibreglass doors are embossed with a wood-grain pattern, and can be stained to the color of various wood and finished with a clear urethane top protective coating. They can also be painted. Steel doors have the disadvantage of denting if struck. Fibreglass doors resist such denting. Both are highly weather resistant and do not absorb moisture or warp or twist.

Handling Doors on the Job

Doors are very expensive, and the property owner expects each one to be installed free of damage. When handling and storing doors on the job observe the following:

1. Store flat in a clean, dry place. Place cardboard between the stacked doors to protect them from damage.

2. Protect doors from exposure to excessive heat, moisture, dryness, or direct sunlight.

3. When handling doors, wear gloves or be certain your hands are clean.

4. When moving doors, lift them clear of the floor, and carry them. Do not drag them across one another or across the floor.

5. Store doors in the area in which they are to be installed for a few days, so that they can adjust to the relative humidity of the area before they are hung.

6. If wood doors are to be stored for any length of time on the job site, seal all edges and ends with an effective wood sealer to prevent absorption of moisture.

Door Hands

Before the door frames can be hung, the finish carpenter must ascertain the **swing**, or **hand, of the door**. The hand of a door refers to which side of the jamb will have the hinges and which the lockset. This relates to the way the door will swing. An examination of the floor plan shows which way the designer wants the door to swing. The carpenter must install the frame to produce this result.

While there is not universal agreement on determining the hand of a door, the following is a typical procedure.

The hand of a door is determined by looking at it from the "outside." For example, you view a bedroom door from the hall to determine the hand. You view an exterior door from outside the building. The various possible hand designations are shown in **5-4**.

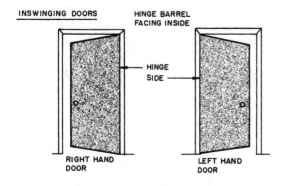
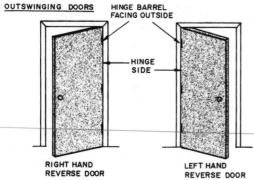

5-4   *How to specify the handedness of a door.*

When you view the door from the **outside**, in the standard designation of handedness—right hand, left hand—the door will **swing away** from you. If the hinges are on the right side, then, in this case the door is a **right-hand door**. If, however, you view the door from the outside, but the door swings **towards** you, e.g., into the hall, then this is designated as a **reverse door**. Thus, in this instance, if the hinges are on the right side, the door is then a **right-hand reverse door**. Likewise, when the door is viewed, as always, from the outside, and the door swings towards you, but the hinges are on the left, then that door is a **left-hand reverse door**. Note that the lockset opening is on the side opposite the hinges.

When ordering sets, it is necessary to specify the hand of the door. Some locksets are designed so that they can be changed to fit either hand.

Checking the Rough Opening

The framing carpenters who built the exterior walls and framed the interior partitions are responsible for framing door openings to hold the door, its frame, and to leave room for making adjustments to set the frame plumb. It is advisable to check the size of the rough openings to see that they are correct. If they are too large, additional material may be added to the trimmer stud to reduce the size. If the opening is too small, the studs will have to be removed, repositioned, and a longer header built. Commonly used rough opening data are given in **5-5**. Also check to see that the gypsum drywall was installed properly so that it can be covered by the door jamb.

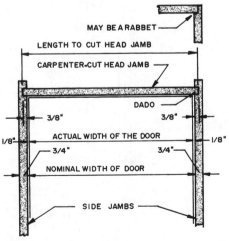

5-6 The door frame is sized to allow for space between the door and frame.

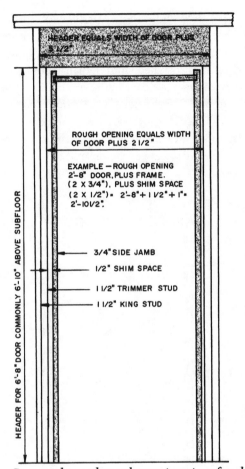

5-5 Commonly used rough opening sizes for doors.

Installing Prefabricated Door Frames

Prefabricated door frames are available cut to size, ready to install. The jamb stock can also be bought in lengths and cut to size on the job. Carpenter-made jambs must have the head jamb cut longer than the distance between side jambs to allow for it to be inserted in the dado in each side jamb. Actual door widths are usually ¼in (6mm) narrower than the stated size. For example, a 2'-8" (513mm) is actually 2'-7¾" (506mm) wide. This provides the space required between the door and frame. The space allowed varies, but ⅛ to ⁵⁄₃₂in (3 to 4mm) on each edge is common (see **5-6**).

If the building is to have a hardwood floor, it is easier to install the floor first, and then set the door frame on top of it. However, many carpenters prefer to set the frame first, placing it on the subfloor. The hardwood flooring has to be fitted around the base of the side jambs or the jambs may be cut off to allow the flooring to slide under them. Another technique is to raise the bottom of the jamb above the subfloor a distance equal to the thickness of the hardwood flooring when it is installed, rather than trimming later.

An example of the door frame set on the subfloor is shown in **5-7**. The frame is 1in (25mm) longer than the door. This leaves a space below the door for carpet. In some cases it is necessary to trim a little off the bottom of the door to get the desired clearance above the floor.

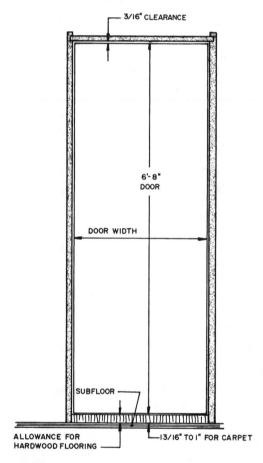

5-7 The height of the door frame head may vary depending on the type of finished flooring.

Another consideration is locating the head of the frame above the floor. In most cases the head of the door frame and the heads of the windows are kept the same distance above the floor. When this is the case, the desired height can be marked on the studs that form the rough opening, and the door frame head lined up with this. This may require the bottom of the frame to be raised slightly above the subfloor, but this space will be hidden by the carpet.

Once the height and floor decisions have been made the door frame can be installed as follows:

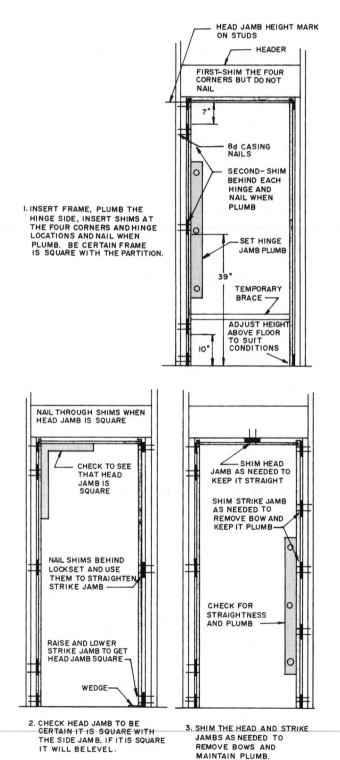

5-8 The basic steps for installing an interior door frame.

1. Set the frame in the rough opening. Position it so that the head is in line with the height mark. Nail the side jamb with the hinges to the trimmer stud first (see **5-8**). Use a 6ft level to be certain the jamb is plumb and in the same plane as the wall. Insert wedge-shaped shims between the stud and jamb to adjust the jamb to a plumb position (see **5-9**). It is best to use shims made for this purpose. While wood shingle scraps can be used, they tend to split and fall out when nailed or cut to length.

2. Insert shims from each side of the wall, and tap lightly until they bind. Adjust until the jamb is plumb. Place the first shims near the top and bottom of the jamb. Nail through the jamb and shims with 8d casing nails to secure the frame to the stud. Place the nails in the center of the jamb so that they are covered by the door stop. Do not set the nails until the frame installation is complete. Additional shims are placed where each hinge is to be located. Other shims can be added, wherever needed, to produce a plumb jamb. (Interior doors should have three hinges.) Cut off the shims so that they are flush with the edge of the jamb.

3. Check to be certain that the jamb is square with the partition. Use a framing square as shown in **5-10**.

4. Move the strike jamb (the side to have the lock) up and down until the head jamb is horizontal and at right angles with the hinge side jamb. The head jamb is held in place by the strike side jamb, which is now nailed in place.

5. Place shims near the top and bottom of the strike jamb. Check to see that it is at right angles with the head jamb and is plumb. Nail through the shims into the stud with 8d casing nails. Place shims behind the jamb in the areas where the lock will be located. Place other shims, as needed, to get the jamb straight.

6. Finally shim the head jamb to prevent it from eventually bowing.

7. The frame can be checked for squareness by measuring the diagonals of the opening. They must be exactly the same length. The real test comes when the door is placed on the hinges. Check the opening around the edges to be certain it is uniform and that the door opens and closes properly.

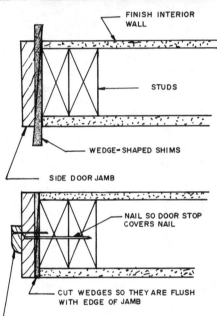

5-9 *Use wood wedges between the frame and studs to set the frame plumb. (Courtesy Senco Products, Inc.)*

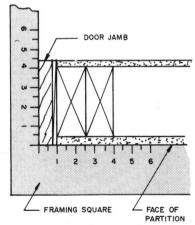

5-10 *Be certain the jamb is at right angles to the face of the partition.*

Installing Factory-Assembled Jambs with Prehung Doors

Prehung doors come with the frame assembled and the door hung on the frame with hinges. Usually the door is prebored for the installation of a lockset. The door frame is made from a good-quality wood, usually a softwood, and it fits inside the studs forming the rough opening as shown in **5-11**.

To install the jamb, remove the door from the frame. Place the frame into the rough opening, plumb and nail the hinge side to the trimmer stud in the rough opening. Wedge, as necessary, to get the side jamb plumb, and be certain it is square with the surface of the wall. Then put the door back on the hinges. Since the frame is held only on one side, care must be taken not to damage the frame. Close the door inside the frame, and adjust the top and latch-side frames so that the gap between the door and the frame is uni-

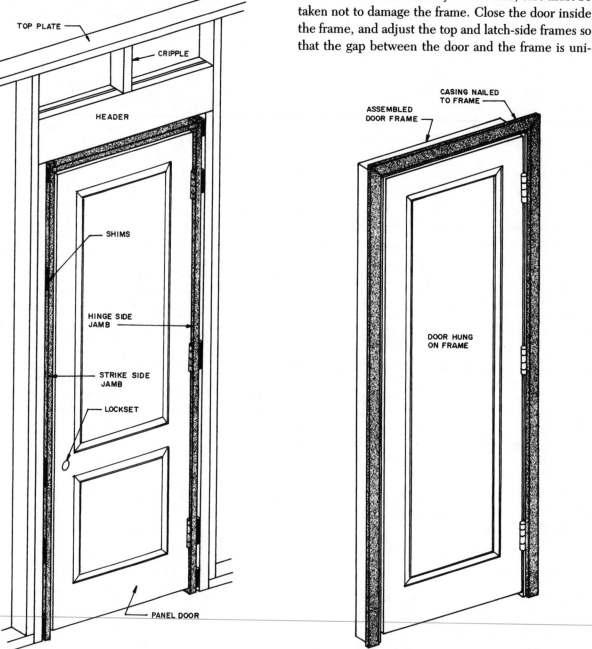

TOP PLATE

CRIPPLE

HEADER

SHIMS

HINGE SIDE JAMB

STRIKE SIDE JAMB

LOCKSET

PANEL DOOR

CASING NAILED TO FRAME

ASSEMBLED DOOR FRAME

DOOR HUNG ON FRAME

5-11 *A preassembled interior door frame with the door also hung at the factory.*

5-12 *A preassembled interior door frame with both the door hung and casing applied at the factory.*

form. The size of the gap depends on the decision of the manufacturer, but is usually about ⅛ to ³⁄₁₆in (3 to 4.5mm). Place shims along the latch-side jamb, adjusting until the gap is uniform. Nail through the jamb and wedges into the trimmer stud. When the jamb is plumb, and the door operates properly, set the nails. Be certain to place shims behind hinges and the lockset as described for factory-made door frames.

Installing Prehung Doors with Casing in Place

A typical prehung unit with casing applied on one side of the jamb is shown in **5-12**. While some carpenters simply set the unit in the rough opening, check it for plumb, and nail the casing to the studs, this does not produce the strongest installation. It is far better to shim it from the side without the casing and nail through the shim and casing into the stud as described earlier for factory-made frames. The casing can then be nailed to the wall stud to hold the unit plumb while the shims are installed and nailed.

Installing Split Jambs

Some manufacturers make door frames in two pieces so that they join with some type of tongue-and-groove joint. They often have the casing already nailed to each side. The two halves are slid into the rough opening from opposite sides, and the casing is then nailed to the studs. They can be shimmed from one side and nailed through the joint, but this is difficult (see **5-13**).

Carpenter-Built Door Frames

Door frames to be painted can be cut from good-quality, kiln-dried softwoods such as white pine. If hardwoods are required, these are usually sold unsurfaced and in random widths and lengths. They must be planed to thickness, one edge cut straight and smoothed, and then cut to the required width. Allow extra width so that the edges of the stock can be jointed smooth. Some carpenters make the finished width ¹⁄₁₆in (1.5mm) more than the wall thickness.

After the stock is the required width, cut three or four ⅛in (3mm) deep saw cuts, evenly spaced in the back side. This helps control warping. Stock for interior door frames should be at least ¾in (19mm) thick (see **5-14**).

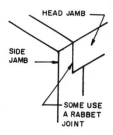

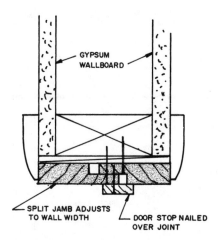

5-13 A split jamb can be adjusted to accommodate varying wall thicknesses.

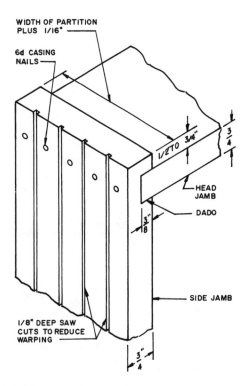

5-14 A typical layout for carpenter-built interior door frames.

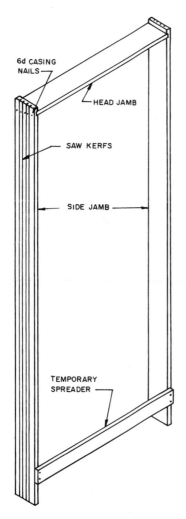

6d CASING NAILS

HEAD JAMB

SAW KERFS

SIDE JAMB

TEMPORARY SPREADER

5-15 *The assembled interior door frame.*

Rabbet or dado the top of the side jambs to hold the head jamb. Nail through the side jamb into the head jamb with three 6d casing nails. Nail a spreader strip between the side jambs near the floor; this stiffens the unit so that it does not come apart during installation and holds the side jambs parallel (see **5-15**).

The length of the side jambs can be determined by the size of the door and the type of finished floor. Remember to allow space below the door to the subfloor for carpeting or other finish flooring.

Installing Exterior Doors

Exterior door frames are shipped to the job site completely assembled. They have the exterior moulding nailed to the frame. The frame is thicker than interior door frames and usually has a rabbet around the edge to receive the door as shown in **5-16**. Many exterior doors, such as those with metal and fibreglass skins, are shipped with door frames already fitted to them, and the doors are prehung. If this is the case, remove the door before installing the frame.

The exterior door frame is installed as described for interior door frames. It must be level and plumb. It is nailed to the studs through the side jamb, and shims are used to position it properly. The brick moulding can be nailed to the studs to stiffen the installation. Notice that the jamb is rabbeted to receive the door; this replaces the door stop used on interior doors. If

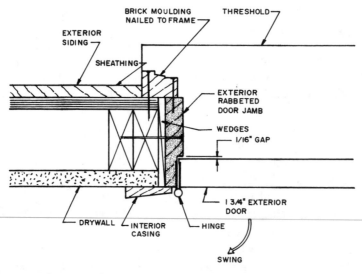

BRICK MOULDING NAILED TO FRAME
THRESHOLD
EXTERIOR SIDING
SHEATHING
EXTERIOR RABBETED DOOR JAMB
WEDGES
1/16" GAP
1 3/4" EXTERIOR DOOR
DRYWALL
INTERIOR CASING
HINGE
SWING

5-16 *The exterior door frame has a rabbet cut to serve as a door stop.*

the door is not prehung, it may be necessary to trim it to fit the door frame opening.

If solid-wood panel or flush doors are used that are not prehung, the width of the door may have to be changed to allow it to fit into the door frame rabbet. The best way to do this is with a power jointer or portable power plane (refer to Chapter 2). These tools will remove a uniform thickness of wood the entire length of the door. It is essential that the edges of the door remain parallel.

Often the door must be trimmed to length. Wood doors are made with a wide bottom rail providing plenty of material to allow shortening without weakening the door. They should be cut with a very sharp, fine-toothed circular saw. Use a guide clamped to the door to get a straight cut (see **5-17**). Care must be taken to prevent chipping along the edge of the cut. It is advisable to cut the bottom edge of exterior doors on a slight angle (bevel) so that when the door closes it will fit snugly against the weatherstripping on the threshold (see **5-18**). Some carpenters sometimes put a slight bevel on the hinge and lockset sides on exterior doors as well (see **5-19**). This provides a little extra clearance as the door swings open.

There are a number of ways that the threshold is designed on preassembled exterior door frames. The carpenter does not need to make any adjustments in the door. One example of a threshold is shown in **5-20**.

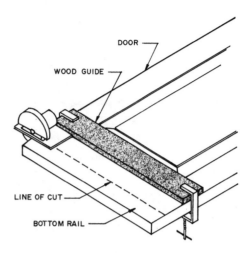

5-17 Use a guide when trimming doors to length with a portable circular saw.

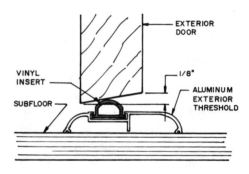

5-18 The bottom edge of exterior doors is sloped so they fit snugly against the vinyl insert on the threshold.

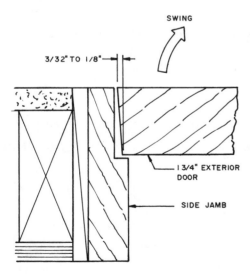

5-19 The slight bevelling of the edges of the door allows a little extra clearance when the door swings open.

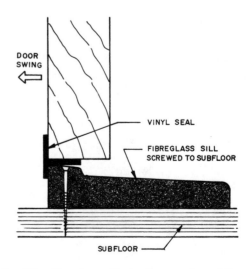

5-20 The fibreglass sill sits flat on the subfloor.

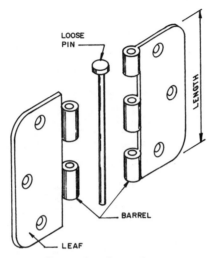

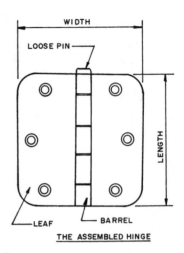

5-21 *A butt hinge typically used to hang doors.*

Installing Hinges

When prehung doors and frames are used, the hinges are already in place. When frame kits are used or the carpenter builds the frames, the hinges must be located and mounted on the jamb and the door.

The hinges commonly used are **lose-pin butt hinges**. For most doors in residential construction, the residential-grade butt hinge is adequate. For heavy doors commercial-grade or ball-bearing hinges are recommended. The parts of a hinge are shown in **5-21**. Butt hinges used to hang doors are swaged; this means that the leaves are bent to provide a small space between them when the door is closed (see **5-22**).

Recommendations for selecting the height of a hinge are shown in **5-23**. While these are not mandatory sizes, they do provide a guide. Doors that are heavier than usual or doors on openings that will have considerable use should use larger hinges of commercial quality or have additional hinges.

Hinge dimensions are specified by giving the height of the leaf (parallel with the barrel) and the width, which is measured when the hinge is open in a flat position. The width chosen relates to the thickness of the door and to the clearance between the open door and the wall that is required to clear the casing or other wall mouldings. The clearances provided by various width hinges for the most commonly used door thicknesses are shown in **5-24**. These are based on the assumption that the mortise stops ¼in (6mm) from the edge of the door. Examples of how the information in **5-24** applies to 1⅜in (35mm) and 1¾in (44mm) thick doors is shown in **5-25**. While the exact locations of hinges can vary, the placement in **5-25** is typical. Interior and exterior doors should have three hinges.

5-23 *Recommendations for selecting hinge sizes.*

Door Thickness	Door Width	Hinge Height
1⅜″	up to 32″	3½″ or 4″
	33″ or larger	4″ or 4½″
1¾″	up to 36″	4½″*
	36″ to 48″	5″*
	over 48″	6″*
2¼″	up to 42″	5″ heavy**
	over 42″	6″ heavy**

* Use heavy-weight hinges for heavy doors.
** Use heavy-weight ball for bearing hinges.

5-22 *Door hinges are swaged.*

Selecting the proper width hinge.

Door thickness (inches)	Hinge Width When Open (inches)	Clearance of Door from Wall Provided with Mortise Stopping ¼″ from Edge of the Door (inches)
1⅜″	3½″	1¼″
	4″	1¾″
1¾″	4″	1″
	4½″	1½″
	5″	2″
2¼″	5″	1″
	6″	2″

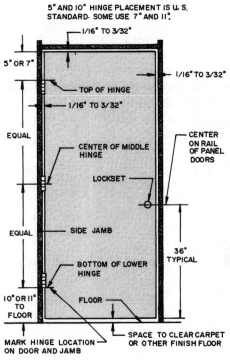

5-25 *Vertical location of hinges on doors.*

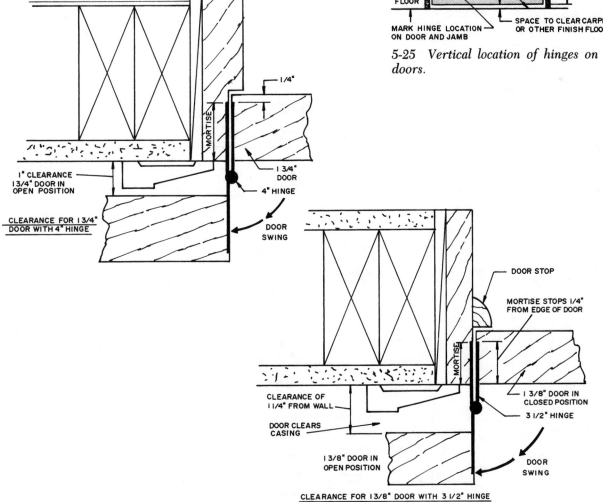

5-24 *When selecting the proper width hinge, the required clearances must be considered.*

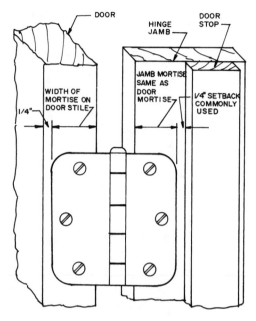

5-26 *Laying out the hinge on the door and side jamb.*

The layout of the hinge on the jamb and door is shown in **5-26**. Hinges are available with round or square corner leaves.

The steps to manually cut the **hinge mortise** (also called a **gain**) are shown in **5-27**. This is used to produce square corner mortises. Begin by laying out the edges of the hinge, and then mark the thickness of the leaf to establish the depth. Use a wood chisel to outline the edges of the mortise, and then cut a series of crosscuts along it. Use the chisel to remove the surface to the required depth.

Round corner mortises are cut with a portable router and a template. The metal template is clamped to the door or jamb (see **5-28**). The straight router bit will cut a flat bottom and must be set to cut to the required depth. The router is moved around the template, cutting the exterior profile, and then used to remove the material in the mortise. The finished hinge mortises are shown in **5-29**.

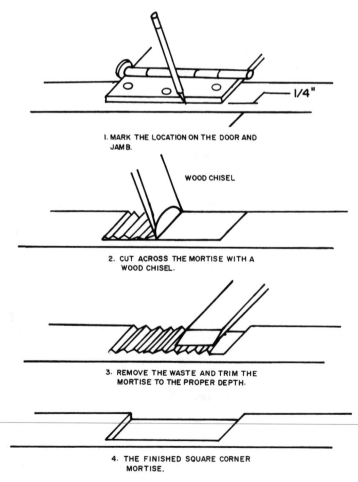

1. MARK THE LOCATION ON THE DOOR AND JAMB.

2. CUT ACROSS THE MORTISE WITH A WOOD CHISEL.

3. REMOVE THE WASTE AND TRIM THE MORTISE TO THE PROPER DEPTH.

4. THE FINISHED SQUARE CORNER MORTISE.

5-27 *The steps to hand-cut a mortise for a square corner hinge leaf.*

Now the hinges can be installed. Install the hinges on the door, being certain the loose pin is located so it is removed by *pulling up*. Otherwise it will eventually fall out. Remove the pin from the hinge, and install each leaf in the mortises on the door and jamb.

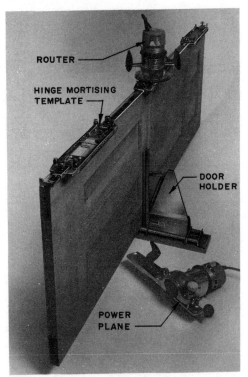

5-28 *Mortises for hinges are cut using a hinge-mortising template and a portable router. Notice the door holder used to steady the door.* (© 1994 Stanley Tools)

Bore small-diameter holes for each screw. This provides a better seat for the screw and reduces the chance of splitting the wood. Be certain the hinge is firmly touching the back side of the mortise. Some carpenters set the screws slightly *off center* towards the back of the mortise to be certain that the hinge firmly presses against the back of the mortise (see **5-30**). Once the hinges are installed, set the door in place, and see if the hinge barrel can slide together. Often minor adjustments are needed at this point. Also check the clearances around the edges of the door. The space should be $\frac{1}{16}$ to $\frac{3}{32}$in (1.5 to 2.4mm) wide and uniform in width. If the space on the lockset side is too small, remove the hinges from the door, and cut the mortise a little deeper. If the space at the lockset side is too large, remove the hinges, and place pieces of hard, incompressible cardboard or wood veneer in the mortise under the hinge.

5-30 *The hinges are mounted on the door and frame.*

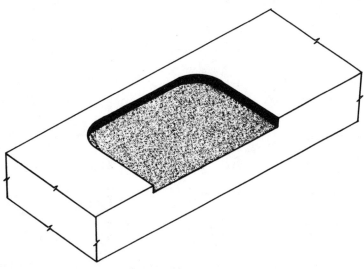

5-29 *This is a mortise cut for a round-cornered hinge leaf.*

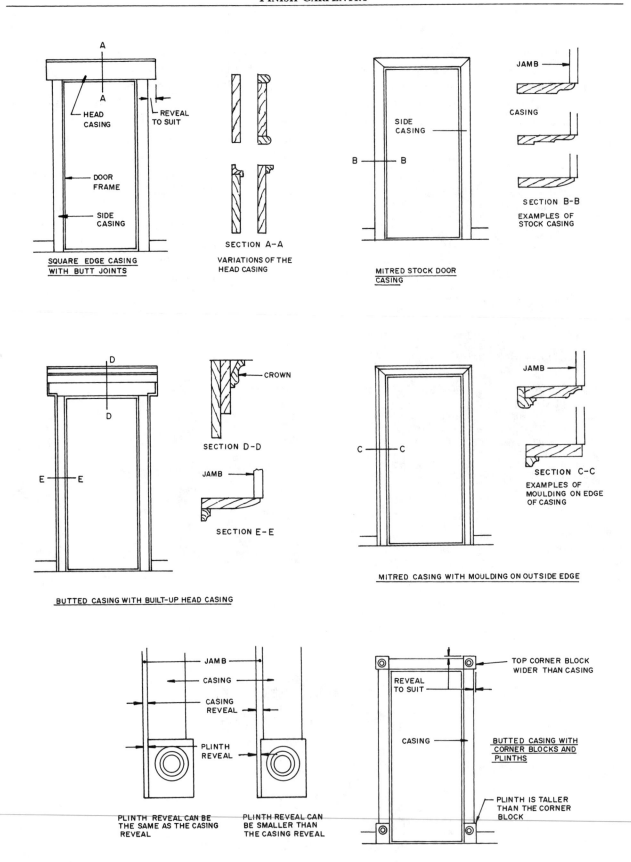

5-31 *Some typical casing techniques used on interior door frames.*

Casing Styles

The style of casings on interior door openings generally is the same as used on the windows. There are exceptions, such as when it is desired to have more elaborate door opening casings which are exposed to view and simpler casing on the windows which are covered with draperies. A few door casing designs are shown in 5-31. The actual design could take many forms. The designer can draw up specifications to match a classic style or devise an original design using standard flat and profiled casings and various mouldings. Custom-designed casings can also be ordered. (Refer to Chapter 4 for additional information on casings and other mouldings.)

Installing Door Casing

The **door casing** is a decorative wood moulding covering the opening between the door frame and the finished wall material. In addition to being attractive, it structurally stiffens the union between the frame and the wall. It should be, therefore, nailed not only to the frame but to the trimmer stud before forming the rough opening (see 5-32). The door casing is set back from the edge of the jamb giving a reveal of 3/16 to 1/4in (4.5 to 6mm); the same reveal is used when casing the windows.

Possibly the mitred casing is the most commonly used style. (The technique for cutting and installing is basically the same as discussed for windows in Chapter 6.) Some finish carpenters prefer to install the mitred top casing first. Mark the reveal on each frame. Measure and cut the top casing for all doors to the same size. Nail it to the frame with 3d or 4d finishing

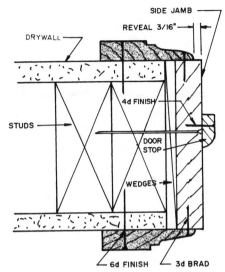

5-32 *Setting casing on an interior door opening.*

nails spaced 8 to 10in (20.3 to 25.4cm) apart. Do not set the nails at this point, because it may be necessary to remove them to adjust the top casing to the side casing.

Cut the side casings to length. Some prefer to cut them about 1/4in (6mm) short of the floor. This allows some room to adjust the side casing as it meets the top casing. The space at the floor will be covered with the carpeting or other finished floor material. Nail the side casings to the door frame. When they are in place with the correct reveal and a tight mitre, nail to the header and studs with 6d or 8d finishing nails. Do not nail too close to the mitre. Instead, toenail the corner to keep it closed. If there is a danger of splitting the casing, drill small holes for each nail. A suggested nailing pattern for a butt joint casing is shown in 5-33.

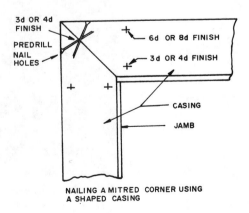

5-33 *Nailing mitre- and butt-casing corner joints.*

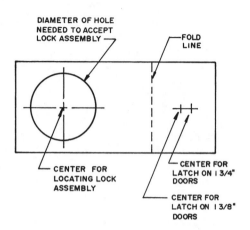

5-34 *A template supplied with each lockset is used to locate the lock on the door.*

Installing a Lockset

Many prehung doors have the holes bored to receive a **lockset**. This eliminates a rather difficult task for the finish carpenter. If the doors are not prebored, it is necessary to locate and bore the holes for the lock. Each set of hardware comes with detailed instructions and a template to be used to locate the centers of the holes. It also specifies the required hole diameters (see **5-34**).

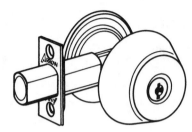

5-37 *A dead bolt.* (Courtesy Arrow Lock Manufacturing Co.)

Generally the center of the lock is located 36in (91.4cm) above the bottom of the door. The amount the center is set back from the edge of the door varies with the type and brand of lock.

Details of a typical lock used on interior and exterior doors are shown in **5-35**. A decorative handle used on entrance doors is shown in **5-36**. A dead bolt is shown in **5-37**.

To install a lock, measure 36in (91.4cm) from the bottom of the door, and make a mark across the end of the door. Using this as a guide, place the centerline of the cardboard template that comes with the lock on this mark. Mark the center for the holes on the face and end of the door (see **5-38**). Bore the holes at the diameter specified.

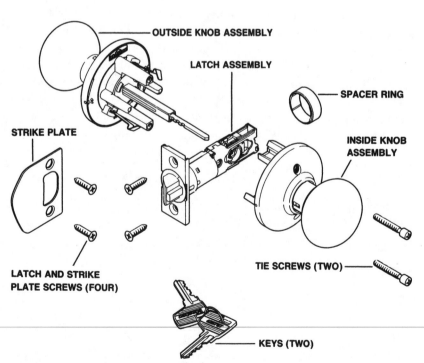

5-35 *Locksets used for interior and exterior doors.* (Courtesy Master Lock Co.)

5-36 *A decorative handle used on front doors in residential work.*

1 MARK HOLES

Mark height line on edge of door 38" from floor. Position center line of template on height line and mark center point of door thickness and center point for 2-1/8" hole.

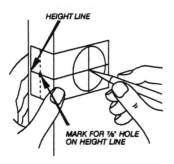

HEIGHT LINE

MARK FOR 7/8" HOLE ON HEIGHT LINE

NOTE: Cylinder Locks of this type are factory assembled half right handed and half left handed unless handedness is specified on order. When this lock is mounted on a door, the key should be in this position as it enters the cylinder.

TO CHANGE HAND OF LOCK
REVERSE CYLINDER AS FOLLOWS:
TO REMOVE KNOB:
1. With outside knob in open position, turn knob clockwise as far as it will go.
2. Insert awl or small pin through sleeve hole, depress knob catch and pull knob from tube.
TO REPLACE KNOB:
3. Rotate knob 180° and push knob back on tube until it hits knob catch (for easier installation, insert key half way and wiggle cylinder).
4. Turn knob clockwise as far as it will go, insert awl of small pin through sleeve hole and depress knob catch. As you depress knob catch, push knob until knob catch clicks into up position.
FOR HOTEL LOCKS, F.LOCK, DC-LOCKS:
REMOVE KNOB:
1. Insert key into cylinder.
2. Insert awl or small pin through sleeve hole and while exerting pressure, slowly turn key in clockwise direction until knob catch depresses, then pull off knob.
REPLACE KNOB:
3. Partially remove key from cylinder, rotate knob 180° and push knob back on tube until it hits knob catch. (For easier installation, wiggle cylinder with key.)
4. Insert key fully into cylinder. Insert awl or small pin through sleeve hole and while exerting pressure, turn key clockwise until knob catch depresses. Then push knob until knob catch clicks into up position.
FOR PROPER INSTALLATION ALL HOLLOW METAL AND STEEL DOORS MUST HAVE LATCH AND LOCK CASE SUPPORT BY THE DOOR MANUFACTURER.

OUTER KNOB SLEEVE HOLE

2 BORING HOLES

Bore the 2-1/8" hole at point marked from both sides of door. Bore 7/8" latch unit hole straight into edge of door at center point on height line. Mortise for latch front and install latch unit.

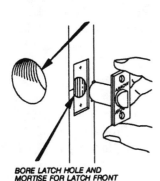

BORE LATCH HOLE AND MORTISE FOR LATCH FRONT

3 REMOVE INSIDE KNOB AND ROSE

Depress knob catch with screw driver. Pull knob off tube. Remove rose and retainer plate.

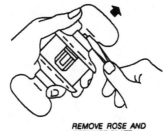

REMOVE ROSE AND RETAINER PLATE

4 ADJUST FOR DOOR THICKNESS

Rotate outside rose to adjust lock for door thickness. Lock will fit any door from 1-3/8" to 1-3/4" thick.

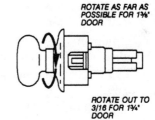

ROTATE AS FAR AS POSSIBLE FOR 1⅜" DOOR

ROTATE OUT TO 3/16 FOR 1¾" DOOR

5 INSTALL MAIN UNIT

Main housing must engage with latch prongs and retractor with latch tailpiece as shown.

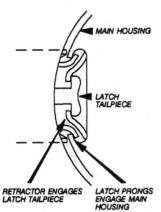

MAIN HOUSING

LATCH TAILPIECE

RETRACTOR ENGAGES LATCH TAILPIECE

LATCH PRONGS ENGAGE MAIN HOUSING

6 ATTACH INSIDE ROSE

Slide on retainer plate; insert and tighten machine screws. Snap rose over retainer plate.

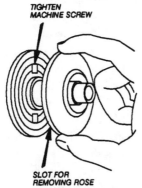

TIGHTEN MACHINE SCREW

SLOT FOR REMOVING ROSE

7 REPLACE INSIDE KNOB

Line up depression in knob sleeve with slot in tube. Slide knob on tube. Depress knob catch and push knob into position.

DEPRESS KNOB LATCH

8 INSTALL STRIKE

Make shallow mortise in door jamb to align with latch face and install strike.

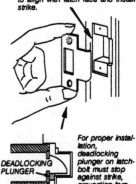

For proper installation, deadlocking plunger on latchbolt must stop against strike, preventing forcing when door is closed.

DEADLOCKING PLUNGER

STRIKE

CAUTION:
Do Not Attempt to Mount Lock Unit with Door Closed.

5-38 *The steps to install a lockset.* (Courtesy Arrow Lock Manufacturing Co.)

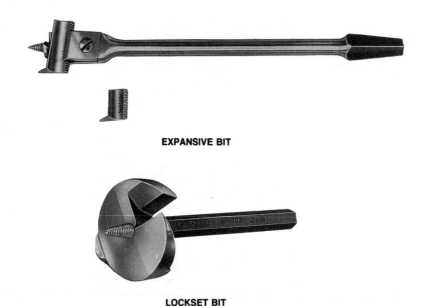

EXPANSIVE BIT

LOCKSET BIT

5-39   *Bits used to bore the large-diameter holes required for installing locksets.* (© 1994 Stanley Tools)

The large-diameter hole can be bored with an expansive bit, lockset bit, or a hole saw (see **5-39**). *Be careful; do not bore all the way through the door.* Bore from one side until the tip of the bit just shows through the other side. Finish boring by coming from the other side. Then bore the smaller hole from the edge of the door.

Install the lock as instructed by the manufacturer's directions.

The strike is installed on the door jamb; locate it opposite the faceplate on the latch. Place the loose strike over the installed latch, and carefully close the door. Hold the strike in place, and mark the top and bottom edges of the jamb. Then draw a line along the edge of the door onto the strike.

Open the door, place the strike on the marks, and draw around it. Chisel the recess so that the strike is flush with the surface of the jamb. Hold the strike in the recess, and mark the hole for the latch to enter the jamb. Bore the hole; then install the strike with the wood screws provided (see **5-40**).

Installing Door Stops

Interior doors have **door stop moulding** nailed to the frame to serve to stop the door as it is closed. Typical door stop moulding is ⁷⁄₁₆in (11mm) thick and from ⅞ to 1⅜in (22 to 35mm) wide. Two types of door stop moulding are available. One has a profiled edge and must be mitred at the corners of the frame. Another type is a rectangular, square-edge moulding that can be butted at the corners.

The door stop is installed after the lockset is in place (see **5-41**). Close the door so that it is held in place by the lockset. Cut the top moulding to length. Place it *lightly* against the closed door, and nail to the top jamb. If there is a danger of damaging the door with the hammer, mark the location of the stop on each end, open the door, and then nail the

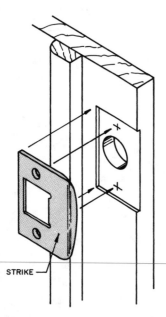

STRIKE

5-40   *Installing a strike plate on the side jamb.*

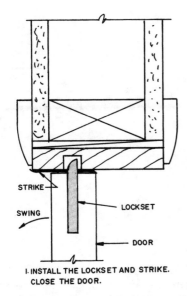

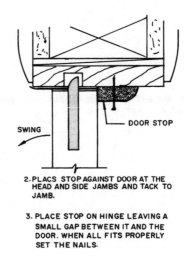

STRIKE

SWING

LOCKSET

DOOR

1. INSTALL THE LOCKSET AND STRIKE.
CLOSE THE DOOR.

SWING

DOOR STOP

2. PLACS STOP AGAINST DOOR AT THE
HEAD AND SIDE JAMBS AND TACK TO
JAMB.

3. PLACE STOP ON HINGE LEAVING A
SMALL GAP BETWEEN IT AND THE
DOOR. WHEN ALL FITS PROPERLY
SET THE NAILS.

5-41   *Wood door-stop moulding positions the door in the frame as the door is closed.*

stop to the head jamb. Do not set the nails, because it may be necessary to move the stop. Now close the door, and see if it is firm against the door. Now cut and nail the stop on the lockset side; this is usually set rather firmly against the closed door to keep the door from rattling. Install the hinge side stop last. It can clear the door by about $\frac{1}{32}$in (0.8mm). Use a piece of cardboard or wood veneer as a spacer between the door stop and the moulding. Check the installation carefully before setting the nails.

6

Installing and Trimming Windows

Windows are an important part of the exterior design of a building. The architectural designer selects types and sizes that suit the architectural style and proportions of the various walls of the building. Windows admit light and also provide ventilation.

The wide variety of window types available are shown in **6-1**. The **double-hung window** has two sashes that slide vertically in separate channels in the side jambs. Some types have the top sash fixed and only the bottom moves. **Casement windows** consist of a sash hinged on one side that swings outwards. **Awning windows** consist of a sash hinged at the top that swings towards the outside. **Hopper windows** are hinged at the bottom and swing into the room. **Sliding windows** have one fixed sash and one sash that slides horizontally in tracks on the header jamb and sill. **Fixed windows** consist of a frame in which a sash is fitted in a fixed position so that it does not open. **Skylights** are fixed-sash windows deigned to be used to let light through a roof. **Roof windows** are similar to skylights, except that they can be opened to provide ventilation. A variety of **fixed decorative windows** are manufactured. These include circle top, elliptical, arch, oval, round, and hexagonal windows. **Bay windows** have three window units. The side windows typically are on an angle of 30, 45, or 90 degrees to the middle sash. They extend outside the building. **Bow windows** also extend outside the building and have four to seven window units that form a curve.

The architectural designer indicates the location and type of window on the floor plan (see **6-2**). The type of window is shown with an architectural symbol, such as the commonly used symbols shown in **6-3**. These symbols only tell the type of window. The size and other specifications are given in the window schedule (see **6-4**). Manufacturers' catalogs give the rough opening size for each of the windows. In some cases, these are not on the working drawings; it is good general practice for the framer to keep manufacturers' catalogs on hand for reference.

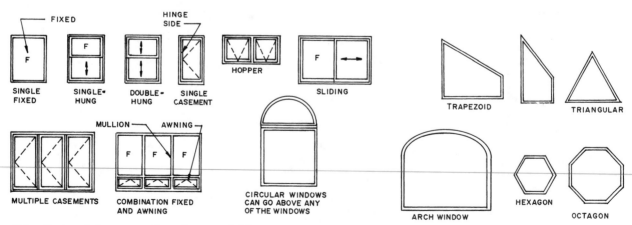

6-1   Some of the types of window available.

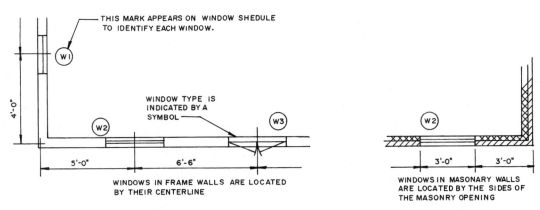

6-2 *Window types and locations are identified on architectural drawings by an identifying symbol and a mark with dimensions.*

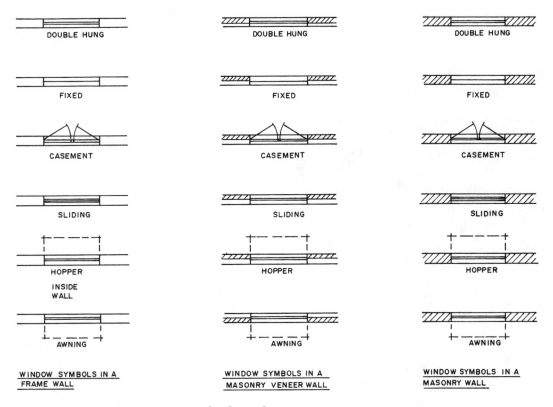

6-3 *Window symbols as they appear on the floor plan.*

WINDOW SCHEDULE						
MARK	UNIT SIZE	ROUGH OPENING	TYPE	MATERIAL	GLAZING	REMARKS
W I	2'-5" X 2'-9"	2'-5" X 2'-10"	FIXED	WOOD	DOUBLE	PLASTIC COVERED COLOR-SAND
W2	5'-5" X 5'-1"	5'-6" X 5'-2"	D.HUNG	DO	DO	DO .
W3	4'-11" X 2'-0"	5'-0" X 2'-05/8"	CASEMENT	DO	DO	DO

DO MEANS DITTO

6-4 *Specific data about the windows to be used is given in an annotated list referred to as the window schedule.*

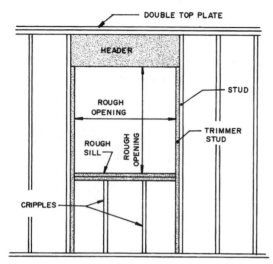

6-5 *The rough opening is framed to the size specified by the window manufacturer.*

6-6 *The rough window opening is wrapped with builder's felt or plastic sheeting before the window is installed.*

When the windows arrive on the job, they are completely assembled. The method for securing any window to the exterior wall is basically the same for all. The most commonly used methods are discussed here.

Installing Wood-Framed Windows

Generally the framers or exterior finish carpenters install the windows. The interior finish carpenter installs the **casing** on the **inside frame.**

Following is a brief description of how to install a window. The framing carpenters prepare a rough opening (see **6-5**). The rough opening should be plumb and square and sized as specified by the window manufacturer. If the opening is not plumb and square, adjustments in the framing will be necessary.

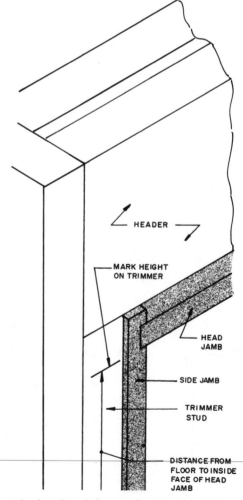

6-7 *The height of the window head jamb is marked on the trimmer stud.*

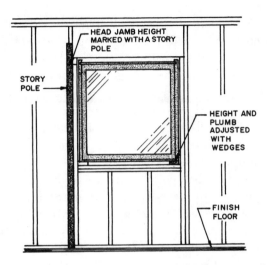

6-8 *The head height can be marked for all windows using a story pole.*

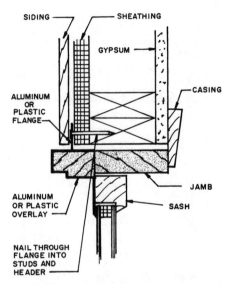

6-9 *This window is nailed through a flange into the studs and header.*

The window opening should be wrapped with builder's felt or plastic sheeting to reduce air infiltration (see **6-6**).

Manufacturers often enclose an instruction sheet with each window explaining how they recommend the window should be installed.

In most cases the designer wants the window heads to line up with the door head jamb. This is usually 6'-8" (2.03m) above the floor. Mark the trimmer stud at each window with the required height (see **6-7**). Frequently a **story pole** is used. A story pole is a straight piece of wood with the desired height marked

on it. It saves time because it locates the height without having to open up a tape rule each time a measurement is required (see **6-8**).

There are two frequently used ways windows are secured to the wall. One uses an aluminum or plastic flange that runs around all sides of the window frame. It has holes punched at evenly spaced intervals for nails (see **6-9**). Another type has a thick wood casing nailed to the frame. The window is nailed to the wall with casing nails driven through this wood casing (see **6-10**).

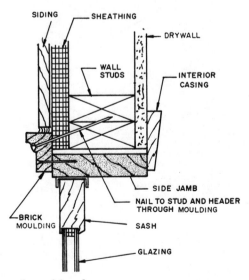

6-10 *This window is nailed through the wood casing to the studs and header.* (Courtesy Senco Products, Inc.)

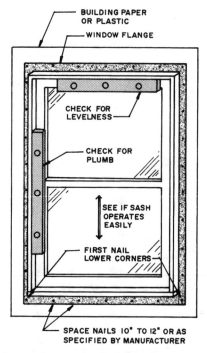

6-11 *The window is checked for plumb and levelness with a carpenter's level.*

To install the window, slide it into the rough opening from the outside of the building. Using wedges on each corner of the bottom, raise it until the head lines up with the mark on the trimmer stud (see **6-8**). Using a level, check the frame to see that it is plumb, and adjust the wedges, if necessary (see **6-11**). Drive a nail through the flange or casing near the bottom of one side, but do not set tightly. Recheck the side jamb for plumb and the sill for levelness. If all is correct, drive a nail on the bottom side opposite the first nail. Next see if the sash moves freely. If it moves easily finish nailing the flange or casing to the studs and header. Space the nails 10 to 12in (approx. 25 to 30cm) apart.

Generally this completes the installation of the window. However, since the side jamb on long win-

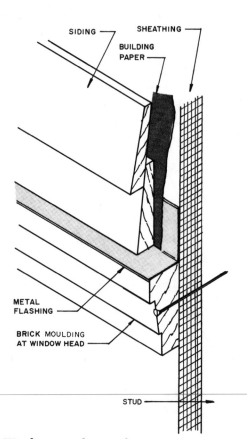

6-12 *Windows with wood exterior casings are flashed at the head.*

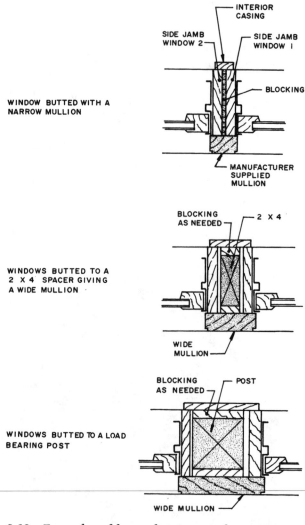

6-13 *Examples of how adjoining window units can be butted. These are generalized examples; follow the manufacturer's directions.*

dows can bow, it is advisable to place **shims** between the frame and trimmer stud, and nail through the window frame and shims into the trimmer stud with casing nails. The number of these used will depend on the length of the window, but a spacing of 16 to 20in (approx. 41 to 51cm) is often used.

The top flange on windows that use flanges for installation serves as the **flashing**. Wood-cased windows require installation of a small aluminum flashing strip as shown in **6-12**. The flashing is covered by the exterior siding material.

When nailing through a casing, use aluminum or galvanized casing nails long enough to go through the casing, sheathing, and penetrate the stud by 1½in (38mm). When nailing flanges, use 1¾in (44mm) or longer galvanized roofing nails. When nailing through soft-foam-type sheathing, it is good practice to cut away a small section where each nail will go, and replace it with wood of equal thickness. This will stiffen the window installation. If you do not do this, be certain to drive the nails until they are firm, but do not overdrive because this could cause them to break through the flange.

Installing Multiple-Window Units

Frequently window units are butted side by side or one on top of the other. Window manufacturers have prescribed ways to install these units and can supply the exterior mullion for some units. The manufacturer gives the sizes of the rough openings for multiple-unit assemblies. Typical details are shown in **6-13**. In one example the side jambs are butted and have a narrow blocking between them. The exterior mullion is narrow. This is done if no structural support is needed and a narrow mullion is wanted for appearance. The other examples show 2 × 4 and larger posts between the two window units. This provides structural support and a wide exterior mullion.

Elliptical and circle top units are installed on top of other windows, such as casement or double hung. They are designed to fit as shown in **6-14**.

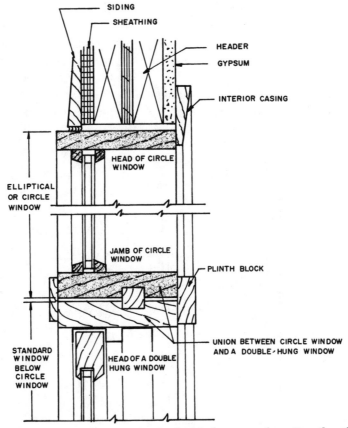

6-14   Generalized details showing a circle window on top of a double-hung window. Details will vary from one manufacturer to another; follow the manufacturer's directions.

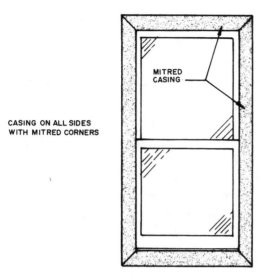

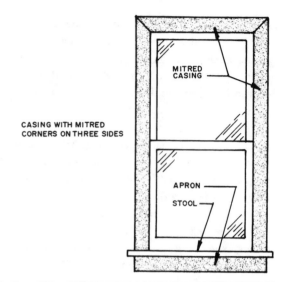

6-15 *Mitred-corner interior window casing installation.*

Styles of Interior Window Trim

Selected profiles for casing materials are discussed and shown in Chapter 2. These may be used in various ways to trim out a window. The decision as to the style to use is made by the designer and owner.

Possibly the most commonly used style is some form of mitred frame. The window can be framed with the casing on all four sides or on three sides with a stool and apron at the bottom (see **6-15**).

Another style uses a rectangular casing and joins the head in a butt joint. A variation of this is made by adding various mouldings. A few examples are shown in **6-16**. One type has a flat head casing extending beyond the side casing. Another type uses some form of moulding to enclose the trim. Corner blocks are typically used when the designer is reproducing a period style of traditional house. The corner blocks are available from various manufacturers. (Refer to Chapter 4 for more on casing designs. As pointed out there, window casing and door casing usually follow the same design.)

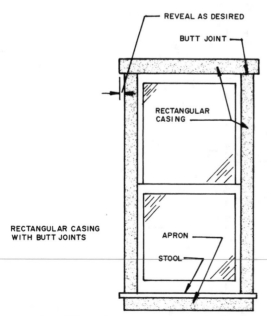

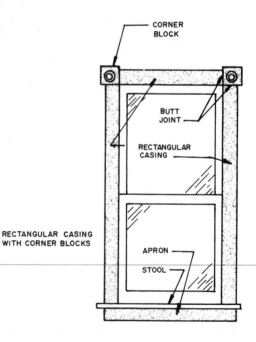

6-16 *Examples of butted-corner interior window casings.*

Preparing to Install the Casing

A mentioned, the interior finish carpenter will most likely not be the one to install the windows. Therefore, before starting to cut and fit trim, it is wise to check the window frame to see that it is plumb, level, and square. This is the time to make corrections. Check to see if the windows open and close smoothly.

If the exterior wall is built using 2×6 studs, the window frame will fall short of extending over the drywall. It is necessary to install **jamb extensions**. Jamb extensions are wood strips added to the frame to bring it flush with the drywall (see **6-17**). Window manufacturers will supply jamb extensions that are to be glued into grooves in the edge of the jamb. They can be firmed up by driving a few finishing nails. Jamb extensions can also be made on the job. White

pine is the recommended wood, because most windows are made from that material. If the extension used is wider than the wall, the width can be marked by drawing a line where it touches the drywall (see **6-18**). The jamb extension is usually glued to the window frame. Narrow extensions can be held by nailing or screwing through them into the frame. Wider extensions may require blocking between them and the trimmer stud, and they are nailed through the extension to the stud. Careful work is required to get a good joint.

Before the casing is installed, **insulation** should be inserted into the space between the frame and the studs and header. Loose insulation can be inserted, but it must be kept loose and fluffy. Expanding foam insulation (looks like shaving cream) is available in small pressurized cans; it is good for filling small cracks. Since it expands greatly, only a very small amount is required.

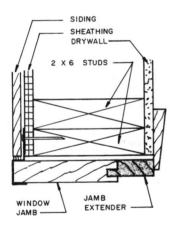

6-17 *Window jambs are made wider by adding jamb extenders.*

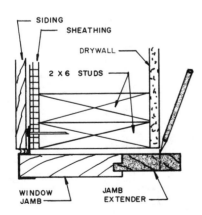

6-18 *Mark the jamb extender, and cut it so that it is flush with the finished interior wall.*

Installing a Wraparound Mitred Casing

Begin by marking the **reveal** on the corners of the casing. Typically a reveal is ³⁄₁₆ or ¼in (5 to 6mm). A reveal is the amount the casing is set back from the edge of the frame. An easy way to do this is to set a combination square with the blade extending out the amount of the reveal. Make a pencil mark on each corner (see **6-19**).

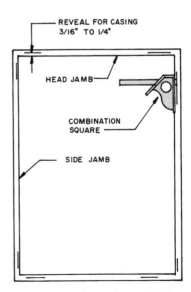

6-19 *The casing reveal can be marked using a combination square.*

HEAD AND SILL CASING LENGTH EQUALS
DISTANCE "A" PLUS TWICE THE REVEAL.

SIDE CASING LENGTH EQUALS DISTANCE "B"
PLUS TWICE THE REVEAL.

6-20 *Finding the casing length for a wraparound mitred casing measured on the short side.*

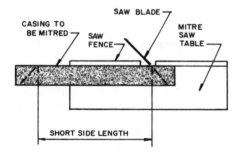

6-21 *To cut the casing place the length marks next to the mitre saw fence. This shows cutting to length when the short-side measurement is used.*

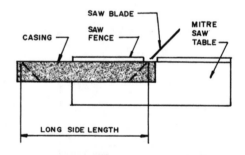

6-23 *How to position the casing on the mitre saw when cutting it to length using the long-side dimension.*

HEAD AND SILL CASING LENGTH EQUALS
TWICE THE CASING WIDTH PLUS TWICE
THE REVEAL PLUS DISTANCE "A".

SIDE CASING LENGTH EQUALS TWICE THE
CASING WIDTH PLUS TWICE THE REVEAL
PLUS DISTANCE "B".

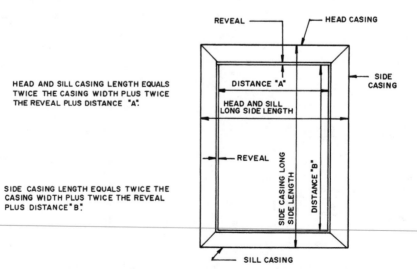

6-22 *Finding the casing length for a wraparound mitred casing measured on the long side.*

A wraparound mitre casing has two lengths of casing. The length of each can be measured on the short or long side of the casing. In **6-20** the lengths are taken to the short side of the casing. This includes the distance inside the jambs plus twice the reveal. When

cutting the mitres, place the edge with the marks next to the fence (see **6-21**).

If you prefer to cut to the long side of the casing, the length will be equal to the width inside the jambs, plus twice the reveal, plus twice the width of the casing material, as shown in **6-22**. It is placed on the mitre saw as shown in **6-23**.

Interior finish carpenters approach the installation of mitred casings in different ways. Following is one suggested procedure. Start the installation by nailing the head casing to the jamb edge with 3d or 4d finishing nails. Do not set the nails firmly, because it may be necessary to adjust the casing to get a tightly closed mitre. Be certain it fits flat to the surface of the drywall. If it does not, it may be necessary to file off some of the drywall or plane a little off the jamb. Be certain the casing lines up with the reveal marks; actually, it should just cover the marks (see **6-24**).

Now install the side casings, being certain that they line up with the reveal marks and that the mitres close. If this is the case, nail them to the frame. Check again to be certain the mitres are closed after nailing. If the mitres do not close, adjust them as described in the next paragraph. Finally, cut and install the sill casing. You can measure the actual length required, or cut a mitre on one end, place the stock across the bottom, and mark the location of the other end. Cut and install the bottom casing. If all mitres are closed, finish nailing by placing nails about 8 to 10in (approx. 20 to 25cm) apart along the edge on the frame. Then using 6d or 8d finishing nails, nail the thick side of the casing to the header or stud. Suggested nailing patterns are shown in **6-25**.

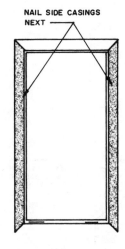

1. NAIL HEAD CASING. LINE UP WITH REVEAL MARKS.

NAIL HEAD CASING FIRST

SIDE JAMB

REVEAL MARKS

NAIL SIDE CASINGS NEXT

2. LIGHTLY TACK SIDE CASING IN PLACE. THIS PERMITS THEM TO BE MOVED IF NECESSARY TO FIT THE SILL CASING.

3. LIGHTLY TACK SILL CASING IN PLACE. ADJUST SIDE AND SILL CASINGS TO GET A TIGHT MITRE BEFORE FINAL NAILING.

NAIL SILL CASING

6-24 *A suggested sequence for installing wraparound mitred casing.*

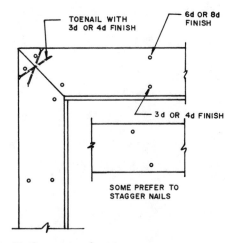

TOENAIL WITH 3d OR 4d FINISH

6d OR 8d FINISH

3d OR 4d FINISH

SOME PREFER TO STAGGER NAILS

6-25 *Nailing mitred casing.*

The mitres will not always fit tightly on the first try, and the casing will have to be removed and the mitre adjusted. In **6-26** are the types of corrections that will need to be made. The top drawing shows a mitre that has no gaps and is square. This is how all mitres *should* appear, but, because of variances in the wall surface or the window frame, some adjustments to the mitre often need to be made. The casing must always keep the reveal uniform on all sides of the window.

The second drawing in **6-26** shows a mitre with the toe touching, but open at the heel. The third shows the mitre touching at the heel and open at the toe. In these drawings the amount of gap is greatly exaggerated; in actual practice the gap will be much smaller. Usually the gap is in the range of 1/64 to 1/32in (0.4 to 0.8mm).

Closing a Gap in a Mitre

The gap in a mitre may be closed by removing wood from one side of the mitre. This may be done several ways. One way is to place the casing on the mitre saw, place a small wedge between the casing and the fence, and make a very fine cut across the mitre. All you will get will be some sawdust off of the end to be lowered (see **6-27**). The amount to remove is judged by examining the joint and observing the size of the gap. Usually a thin piece of cardboard gives enough change in the angle of the mitre to close the joint. Check the joint after cutting, and remove more, if needed.

Another way to lightly trim a mitre is to use a block plane, as shown in **6-28**. Plane "down the slope." Slant the plane a little across the surface, and move it with a slicing motion. Take very light cuts, and be certain the plane is very sharp. Caution must be exercised to

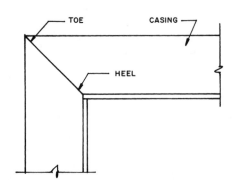

I. A PROPER MITRE IS CLOSED AT THE TOE AND HEEL.

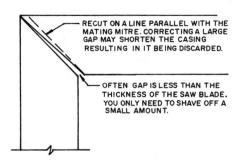

2. THIS MITRE TOUCHES AT THE TOE AND IS OPEN AT THE HEEL.

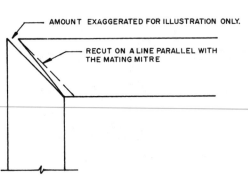

3. THIS MITRE TOUCHES AT THE HEEL AND IS OPEN AT THE TOE.

6-26 *How mitres need to be adjusted.*

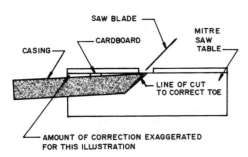

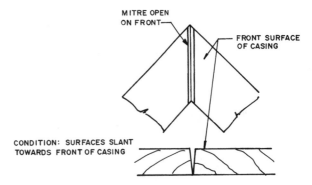

6-27   *Cardboard wedges can be placed between the casing and mitre saw fence to slant the mitre for a corrective cut.*

6-29   *When mitred surfaces slope towards the front of the casing, the mitre will be open even if it is cut clearly on a 45-degree angle.*

keep the surface square with the front of the casing. Never slant the surface to the front; however, it can be slanted a little to the back surface. This will actually help close the mitre. Often a mitre will have parallel edges, but will not close. This is an indication that the surfaces of the mitre slant towards the front. Remove some wood off the back edge until the mitre closes, as shown in **6-29**.

Some finish carpenters use files to correct mitres. While files do remove material, it is difficult to keep a surface flat or straight. Filing tends to round the surface, which, if it occurs, will keep the mitre from closing. Wood chisels and multiblade forming tools also can be used.

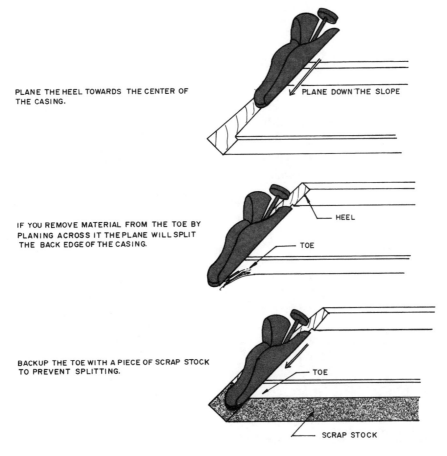

6-28   *A mitre can be adjusted by carefully removing stock with a block plane.*

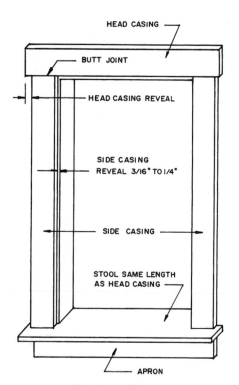

6-30 *A square-edge, butted casing with a stool and apron.*

Installing Casing with a Stool and Apron

A butted casing with a **stool** and **apron** is shown in **6-30**. Often the head casing and side casings are the same width. In this case, the head casing usually overhangs the side casing so that its length is equal to the length of the stool. This is typically ½ to ¾ in (12 to 18mm). However, the head casing may be wider and have various mouldings applied to it.

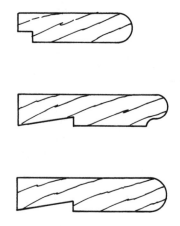

6-31 *Typical stock stools.*

Typical stool profiles are shown in **6-31**. They are available as stock material from building materials suppliers. In some cases the window manufacturers have stool material for their specific window units available. A stool with an angled bottom surface is used on windows made with a sloping sill (see **6-32**).

Fitting the Stool

First cut the stool to its finish length. This includes the width between the window jambs, plus two times the reveal, plus two times the width of the casing, plus two times the length of the horn. Check the distance between them to verify it is the same as the distance between the side jambs. Then measure the window unit to see how deep a notch is needed to form each horn, and lay this out on the stool. Cut the horn notches, and fit the stool to the window frame. Trim

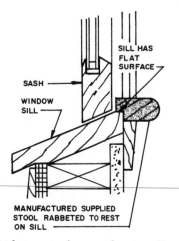

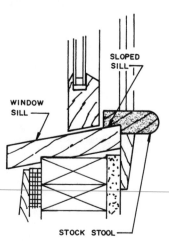

6-32 *These window units have a sloping sill on which the stool must rest.*

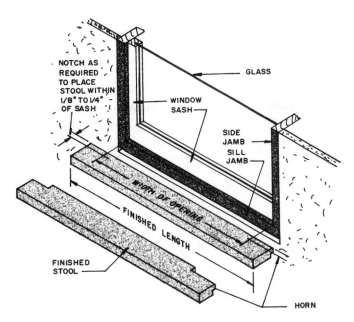

6-33 *Notch the stool at the horns so that it overlaps the sill and butts the window sash.*

and adjust, as necessary, to get the required fit as shown in **6-33**. Be certain the stool is level. If it is not, it may be necessary to shim it.

If the window needs a jamb extension, some carpenters prefer to install the stool first and then add the jamb extension. Others prefer to add the jamb extension and cut the stool to them (see **6-34**).

After you are satisfied with the fit of the stool, consider shaping the ends of the horn. They can be left square, as cut, if you sand out the saw marks. Some finish carpenters prefer to round the horn or shape a profile on it, as shown in **6-35**.

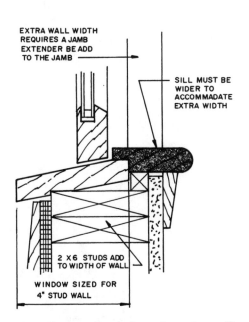

6-34 *The sill must be wider when the wall width requires that jamb extenders be added.*

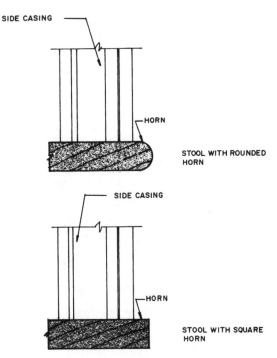

6-35 *The stool horn may be left square or rounded.*

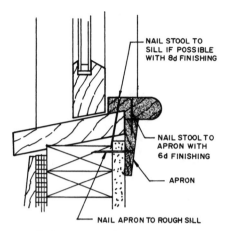

NAIL STOOL TO
SILL IF POSSIBLE
WITH 8d FINISHING

NAIL STOOL TO
APRON WITH
6d FINISHING

APRON

NAIL APRON TO ROUGH SILL

6-36 How to nail the stool and apron to the window and wall.

Now nail the stool in place. Nail through the stool into the rough sill (if possible) using 8d finishing nails. After the apron is installed, nail the stool to it with 6d finishing nails (see **6-36**). Since the actual design of window frames varies, the stool may have to be nailed into the sill below it. On some stock windows, it is not possible to install a stool.

Installing the Apron

The apron is usually made from the same material used to trim the window. It is placed below the stool and covers any opening between the sill and the drywall. It is placed with the thick edge up against the stool (see **6-36**).

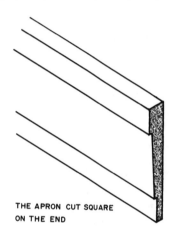

THE APRON CUT SQUARE
ON THE END

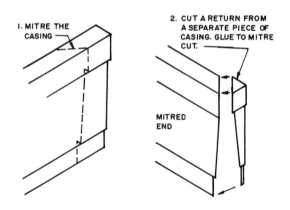

1. MITRE THE CASING

2. CUT A RETURN FROM A SEPARATE PIECE OF CASING. GLUE TO MITRE CUT.

MITRED END

THE APRON WITH A RETURNED END

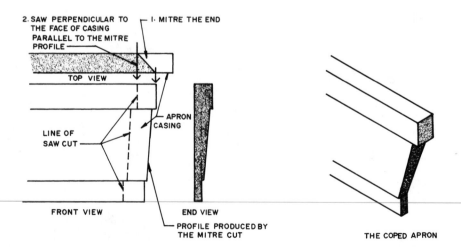

2. SAW PERPENDICULAR TO THE FACE OF CASING PARALLEL TO THE MITRE PROFILE

1. MITRE THE END

TOP VIEW

APRON CASING

LINE OF
SAW CUT

FRONT VIEW

END VIEW

PROFILE PRODUCED BY THE MITRE CUT

THE COPED APRON

6-37 Various ways to finish the ends of the apron.

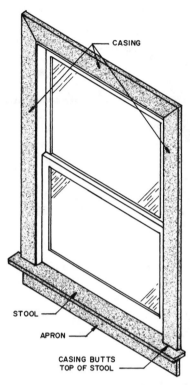

6-38   *Installing mitred casing with a stool and apron.*

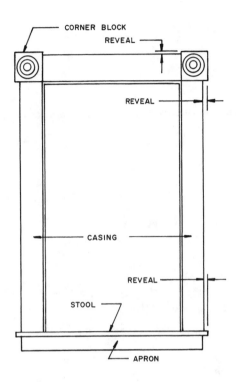

6-39   *This square casing uses corner blocks.*

The length of the apron is usually made the same as the overall width from one side of the window casing to the other. This permits the stool horn to extend beyond the apron.

The ends of the apron may be finished in several ways, as shown in **6-37**. The easiest is to cut them square. Another is to cut them square, and then with a coping saw to cut the profile of the face design around the end. Another is to mitre the ends and glue a return.

Installing the Casings

The casing with mitred corners is installed in the same manner described for installing a wraparound mitred casing. The only difference is that after installing the head casing, the side casing is mitred on one end and cut square on the other, so that it butts against the stool (see **6-38**).

The butted window casing is installed by first cutting the side casings to length. Both ends are cut square. The top end should touch the reveal marks. Be certain that the end butting the stool has a tight, closed joint when the casing is in line with the reveal marks. If not, you will have to trim the butt end as

described for correcting mitres. Once the side casings are correct, nail in place temporarily. Now cut the head casing to length with square ends. It should be the same length as the stool. This provides the same overhang of the casing at the head as occurs at the stool. Locate the head casing with equal extensions beyond the casing, and nail in place. A finished installation is shown in **6-30**.

Corner Blocks

Butted casings on some traditional houses use **corner blocks.** The corner blocks are available from building materials suppliers. They are typically wider than the casing, and overhang the casing the same amount as the horn on the sill.

Begin by installing the stool and apron. Then install the side casings as described for butted casings. Next tack the corner blocks on top of each side casing, carefully measuring the overhang, which, as mentioned, is usually the same as the horn of the stool. Measure the distance between the corner blocks and cut the head casing. It must butt tightly against each corner block. Usually some minor adjustments are needed to get the tight joints desired. In all cases keep the reveals uniform (see **6-39**).

101

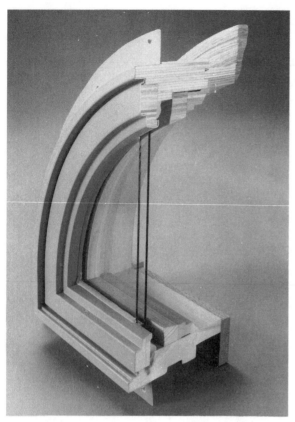

6-40 *A section through a circular window shows its construction and the curved finished casing provided.* (Courtesy Andersen Windows, Inc.)

Circle and Elliptical Head Casing

The manufacturers of circle top windows also supply the necessary casing cut to fit the unit (see **6-40**). Usually several casing styles are available. They also

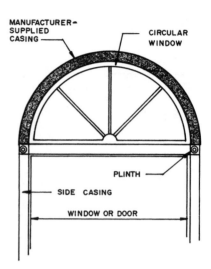

6-41 *Casing a circular head window.*

supply **plinth blocks,** which the curved casing and the horizontal casing below the window join in a butt joint (see **6-41**).

Special Head Casing Designs

The designer may copy an ornate traditional head casing or prepare an original design. Each situation may have particular requirements so that detailed drawings are necessary to allow the finish carpenter to build exactly what is specified. Special casings could also be built at a cabinetmaking or millwork shop, and delivered to the job site assembled. Details for installation are the same as described in the earlier parts of this chapter.

7

Installing Base, Crown, and Other Mouldings

Interior base and other mouldings should not be installed until after the walls are finished. The drywall should be taped and thoroughly dry. If the walls are of plaster, it must be completely dry and the rooms free of moisture. The wood moulding will absorb moisture and warp, if installed in an area of high humidity. Actually the moulding should not be brought into the building until the atmosphere is at normal humidity levels for that region. Plastic moulding is not affected by moisture.

Building Codes

Under most building codes used for residential construction, interior trim such as baseboard, shoe moulding, window casing, picture moulding, chair rails, and ceiling moulding can be wood. This will not violate restrictions pertaining to fire regulations. Foam plastic interior trim may be used if it meets a series of specifications in the code and does not cover more than a specified percentage of the wall or ceiling area. A 10 percent maximum coverage is typically specified.

Preliminary Work

Before installing the baseboard, check to see that the walls are plumb and straight. See if the floors are level or have an irregular surface. Any of these conditions will make it difficult to do a good job of installing the base and may call for some corrective action before you start to cut and install the base.

In some cases the corners of a room will not be 90 degrees or will have excess drywall compound that changes the angle. This occurs on both inside and outside corners.

Verify that proper backing for nailing wide baseboards was installed. Baseboards under 5in (127mm) wide can be nailed to the studs and bottom plate. If baseboards wider than 5in (127mm) are used, the framers should have installed backing boards as shown in 7-1. Correcting these and other defects is discussed later in this chapter.

Baseboards are installed after the door and window casings are in place and after the wainscoting, panelling, and drywall are installed. Check the plans to be certain the interior is finished and ready for the base.

Find out what type of finished floor is to be used and whether a shoe moulding is specified. Some carpenters install the base ¼in (6mm) above the subfloor. This helps avoid most irregularities in the floor. If vinyl floor covering is used, a shoe moulding covers

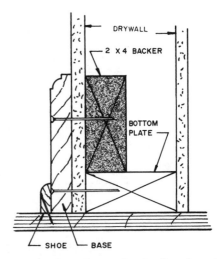

7-1 Wide baseboards need a backer board nailed between the studs.

103

the space at the floor. When carpet is used, shoe moulding is generally omitted, and the carpet butts the base. If hardwood flooring is specified, it is best if it can be installed before the base. If this is not the case, use pieces of the flooring below the base as spacers to allow the clearance needed for the floor to be installed. The hardwood floor may go under the base, not butt it. Since wood expands when exposed to moisture, the floor could buckle if expansion space is not left around the wall. The shoe covers this space at the base (see **7-2**).

Finally, check the moulding received. Select the best pieces for use on the walls that are most visible. Less desirable pieces may be used where short runs

are needed and defects can be cut away, or they can be used in closets and other areas where they are seldom seen.

Corner Joints

The base meets at inside corners and outside corners as shown in **7-3**. Outside corners are formed by cutting a 45-degree mitre. Inside corners can be formed by cutting a mitre or coping the moulding. Coping is preferred because, if the joint does open up over time, it will not be noticeable. A square base can use a butt joint at inside corners.

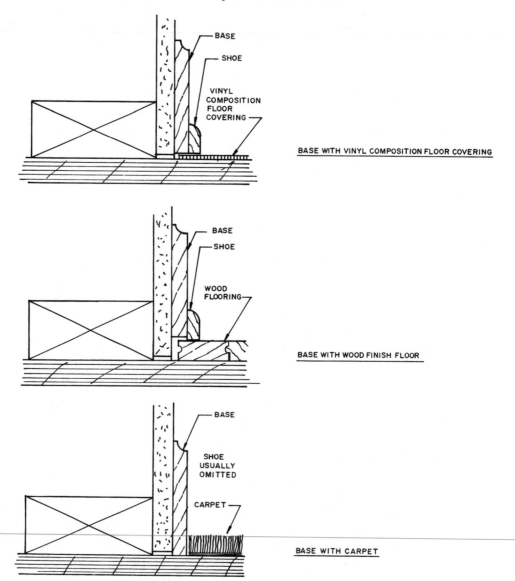

7-2   Base installation with various types of finish floors.

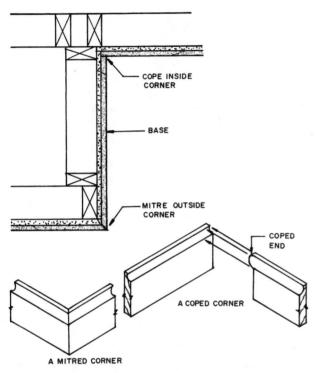

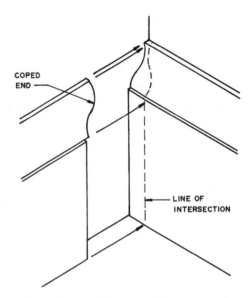

7-4 *A typical coped base moulding.*

7-3 Joints used to form inside and outside corners with the base and shoe moulding.

Cutting a Coped Joint

The **coped joint** is used on **base, shoe, crown,** and other mouldings where they form inside corners. It is more time-consuming to make than a mitre, but it makes openings in the joint that occur as the moulding shrinks and swells with changes in humidity less noticeable. The cope is cut on one of the two mould-

ings forming the corner. The coped profile butts against the other base, forming the inside corner.

To cope a moulding (see **7-4**):

1. Mitre the end of the moulding so that the length of the moulding is slightly longer than required. This provides some wood so that the saw can get started and cut on the waste side of the line forming the profile. The mitre should slope in the same direction as it would if an inside mitre were cut.

2. Cut the profile using a coping saw. The edge formed by the mitre is the line of the profile to be cut (see **7-5**).

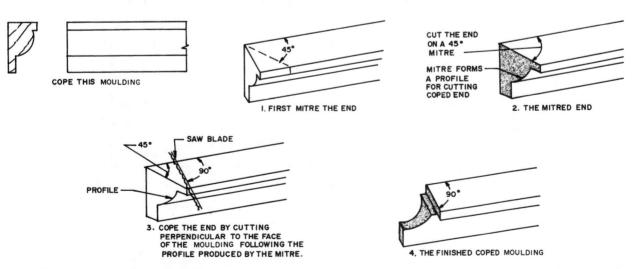

7-5 The steps in coping a moulding.

3. Keep the coping saw perpendicular to the front of the moulding and saw following the curved profile formed by the mitre.

4. Test the joint by placing the coped end against the butting moulding. Use a file to smooth the cope and alter the shape until a close joint is developed.

5. Some carpenters will angle the cope so that the back edge is slightly behind the front. This back-cut leaves the front edge firmly touching the butting moulding.

6. The coped joint is not glued. Since it contains end grain the glue would not give any special strength or help hold it closed.

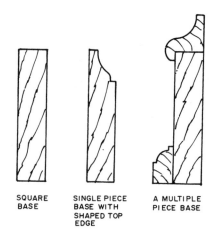

SQUARE BASE   SINGLE PIECE BASE WITH SHAPED TOP EDGE   A MULTIPLE PIECE BASE

7-6 *Several forms of base commonly used.*

Installing the Base

Finish carpenters develop their own favorite procedures for installing base. The following are commonly used techniques. The procedures include installing single-piece square base, single-piece base with a shaped top edge, and multipiece base (see **7-6**).

Begin by planning the order of installation of each piece in the room. Generally the first piece installed is the one on the longest wall (see **7-7**). This piece can be cut with square ends and butted to each wall. While some prefer to cut it about ⅛in (3mm) longer than the wall length to get a tight fit, others prefer to

cut it to the exact length or even a bit short. If a base fits too tightly and the moisture content increases, it will warp and buckle away from the wall.

Some carpenters prefer to cut the next pieces following the walls to their left and others go to the right. The direction to proceed is simply a matter of habit or personal preference. In **7-7** it was decided to work to the left. The longest piece, No. 1, was butted wall to wall. The adjoining pieces are coped and mitered as shown. Notice that the base butts the door casing, is coped at inside corners, and is mitred at

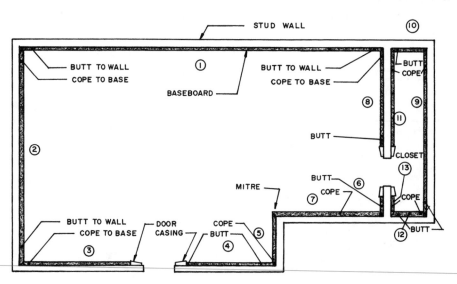

NUMBERS INDICATE THE ORDER IN THE BASE IS CUT AND INSTALLED

7-7 *A suggested way to fit and install base moulding.*

outside corners. It can be mitred at inside corners instead of being coped, but, since walls seldom are at right angles, mitres tend to open. Coping tends to hide imperfections in the corner.

Correcting Defects in Floors and Walls

Sometimes the floor will have a slight bulge causing the base to rock on it and making it difficult to get it level or form good joints. If these defects are small, they can be compensated for by planing a small amount of the subfloor and scribing the bulge on the base to plane off some of it. One way to scribe the bulge onto the base is shown in **7-8**. Plane the base until you get near the line, then place the moulding on the floor to check it. Continue removing small amounts, until the fit is satisfactory. Generally it is helpful to remove some from both the floor and the base rather than trying to take it all from one or the other.

Another problem arises when the base butts a wall that is not plumb. Before cutting the base to its finished length, place one end against the wall, and scribe the slope on the base as shown in **7-9**. Cut to this scribed line. A flat carpenter's pencil is an excellent tool to use to scribe the line.

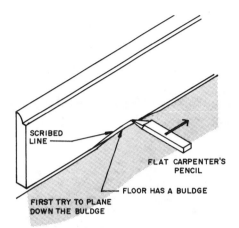

7-8 *To scribe a floor bulge on the base, hold the base level while sliding a pencil along the floor marking the bulge on the base.*

If a corner is not square, it may be possible to cut a mitre that is not 90 degrees. To do this, measure the actual angle of the corner with a T-bevel (see **7-10**). Find the number of degrees between the handle and blade with a protractor. Divide this angle in two and use it to set the mitre saw. You can also cut the corner on a 45-degree angle, and by then, by trial and error, lightly trim the mitred surfaces until a good fit is achieved. This will require you to leave a little extra length to allow for the additional trimming.

Sometimes an inside or outside corner is out of square because extra drywall compound was applied on the corner. If this is only a small amount, the excess compound can be removed with a Surform tool, wide wood chisel, or coarse sandpaper wrapped around a wood block.

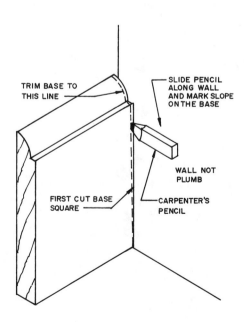

7-9 *One way to scribe a base to butt a wall that is out of plumb.*

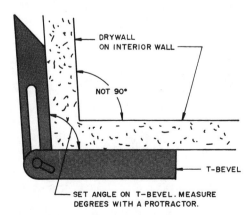

7-10 *Use a T-bevel to find the angle of corners that are other than 90 degrees.*

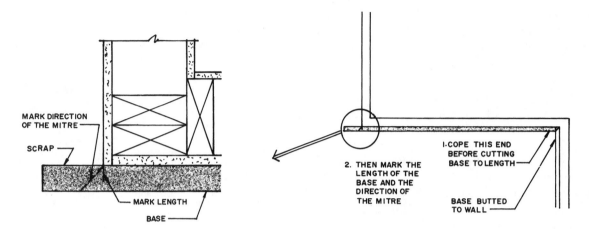

7-11   *Cope the end to butt the base on an inside corner before marking and cutting the mitre at an outside corner.*

Cutting Mitres

Mitres can be cut with a hand or power mitre saw. Both produce a straight, smooth cut. The piece to have the mitre may have the other end coped or cut for a butt joint. In any case it is necessary to mark the exact length from that end to the corner of the wall where the outside mitre will occur. To do this, first cut and fit the coped or butted end. Then place the base along the wall, and mark the length from the corner (see **7-11**). Mark the direction of angle on top of the moulding so that the mitre is cut in the correct direction. If the corner is square and the wall plumb, cutting each piece this way will form a tight mitre. Often, however, this is not the case, and the mitre has to be adjusted out of plumb just a little.

If the mitre opens at the top, it will have to be trimmed a little at the bottom (see **7-12**). If it opens at the bottom, the top will have to be trimmed. Many carpenters do this by placing a thin piece of cardboard on the table of the mitre saw, and then taking a light cut from the edge to be lowered. The cut should remove just a fine layer of sawdust. Try the pieces at the corner until the joint closes. This same technique can be done with a sharp plane. It is advisable to remove a little from each piece rather than trying to take it all from one piece.

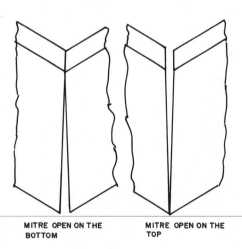

7-12   *Mitres that open on the top or bottom need to be trimmed to close.*

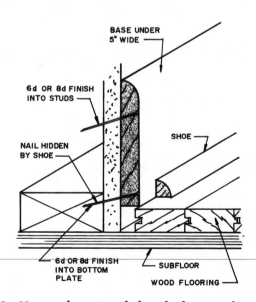

7-13   *Narrow base is nailed to the bottom plate and each stud.*

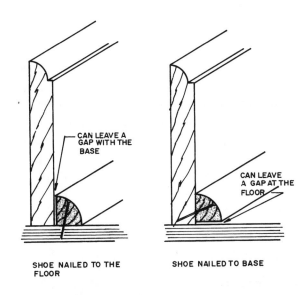

SHOE NAILED TO THE FLOOR

CAN LEAVE A GAP WITH THE BASE

CAN LEAVE A GAP AT THE FLOOR

SHOE NAILED TO BASE

7-14 *Two ways to nail a shoe moulding.*

Nailing the Base, Shoe, and Cap Moulding

Softwood base can be installed by nailing through the finish wall material into the studs with two finish nails long enough to give good penetration into the stud and plate. Usually 6d or 8d finishing nails are adequate. Place one nail about ½in (12mm) from the bottom into the bottom wall plate (see **7-13**). This will be covered with the shoe moulding or carpet. The other nails will have to be set, and the holes filled. Nail near the ends of each piece to help stabilize the joint. If splitting is a problem, drill small holes for the nails. The procedure for nailing wide base is shown in **7-1**. Hardwoods often require that the nails have predrilled holes. This helps prevent splitting and bent nails.

When nailing, there are several things to consider. One is that the base and other mouldings can be pulled tight against a wall surface having small waviness in the surface. This can be accomplished when there is adequate backing to nail into. Another consideration is the determination of the best way to nail shoe and cap mouldings. Some prefer to nail the shoe moulding to the floor (see **7-14**). When this is done the base can move vertically without exposing a gap at the floor; the shoe moulding keeps any gap covered. However, when this movement occurs the line of paint between the base and shoe will break, and unfinished base will be exposed. If the shoe is nailed to the base, they will move vertically together, but will leave a gap at the floor. Carpenters generally will use

7-15 *Installing base using a power nailer is fast and less likely to split the wood than hand nailing. (Courtesy Hitachi Power Tools)*

the procedure that they believe has caused them the least trouble.

If the shoe moulding is placed on top of wood flooring that has not been sanded and finished, lightly tack it in place. The floor finishers will want to remove it so that they may sand closer to the baseboard. The shoe moulding is nailed in place *after* the floor is finished. When prefinished wood flooring has been installed, the shoe can be permanently nailed as it is cut and fit.

The cap moulding is usually nailed into the top of the base and moves with it.

Many finish carpenters prefer to use power nailers to install mouldings. These are fast and do a good job. Power nailers have thinner nails available for trim work and therefore tend not to split the wood as often (see **7-15**).

109

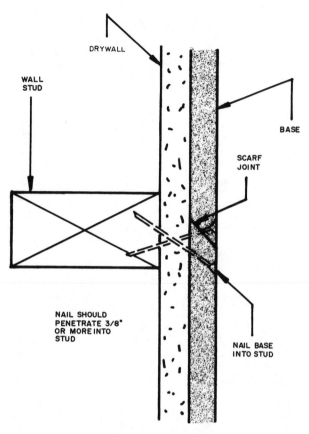

Splicing Moulding

When moulding has to be spliced to span a long wall, it is cut on a 45-degree angle to form a **scarf joint.** This joint should be located at a stud so that there is adequate nailing surface to close and hold the joint. A typical situation that arises when base is being installed is shown in **7-16**. The one side is nailed to the stud. The other is nailed through the joint into the studs. Use two nails in each piece. Some carpenters glue the joint.

7-16 *Splice the base at a stud with a scarf joint so that a nailing surface is available.*

Installing Square-Edge Base

Square-edge base is installed as shown in **7-17**. The exterior corners are mitred. The interior corners are often butted, but can be mitred. If it has shoe and base cap moulding installed, they will be coped.

Installing Single-Piece Shaped Base

Single-piece shaped base has the exterior corners mitred and the interior corners either mitred or, better still, coped. (Refer to **7-7** for specific details.)

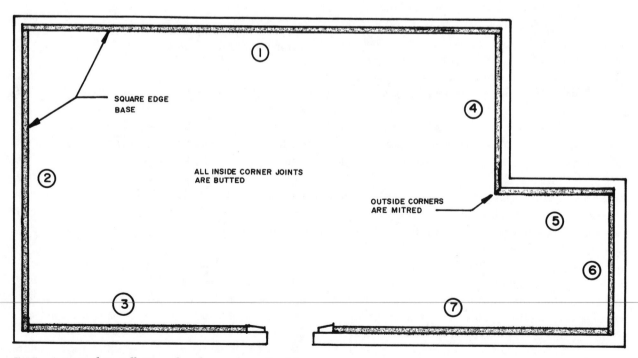

7-17 *A typical installation plan for square-edged base.*

Installing Multipiece Base

Multipiece baseboards usually are built around square edge stock. The base is installed as described for square edge base. The shoe and top moulding are then cut and fit. They are mitred at exterior corners and usually coped at interior corners (see **7-18**).

Mitreless Base Installation

This wood product eliminates the need for mitres by supplying internal and corner pieces. After these are installed by nailing and gluing to the wall, the base is cut to length at 90 degrees on each end and fitted between the end pieces. The nails are countersunk and filled. The base can be stained, painted, or varnished (see **7-19**).

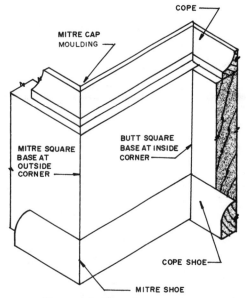

7-18   *Installing multipiece base.*

7-19   *The internal and external corner pieces are installed and the base cut to length and butted against each corner piece.* (Courtesy Ornamental® Mouldings)

111

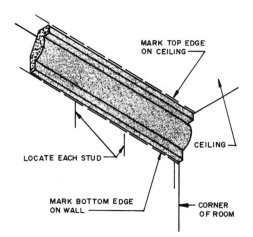

7-20   *Locate the bottom and top edges of the plastic moulding and each stud.*

Installing Moulded-Plastic Mouldings

Following is a recommended way to install moulded plastic mouldings.

1. Hold the moulding in place on the wall, and mark the top and bottom projections. A line can be drawn from one end to the other to give an accurate mark for installation. Also mark the location of each stud below the bottom edge mark (see **7-20**).

2. Measure and cut as described previously for wood moulding, using a hand or power mitre saw. Cut the pieces slightly longer than required. Allow about ⅛in (3mm) per 5ft (approx. 1.5m) of length. Corners can be coped or mitred.

   When cutting the mouldings try to cut so that the pattern repeats uninterrupted. If the pattern must be broken, let this occur in a place in the room where it is the least noticeable as you enter

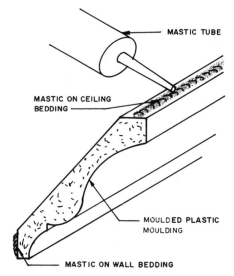

7-22   *Apply mastic to the wall and ceiling beddings.*

the room (see **7-21**). Cut the moulding with the bottom side up. Joints must fall over a stud or backer board.

   End joints are made by cutting the moulding square and bonding the ends with mastic. Test match the pieces for thickness before bonding, and shave off the back when necessary.

3. Before applying the mastic, fit the pieces to the wall, and check the joint for thickness. Shave off the back until the faces of the butting pieces are flush. If a piece is too low, it can be shimmed. The face surfaces can be lightly sanded, if necessary.

4. Apply the mastic recommended by the manufacturer to the top and bottom bedding edges of the mouldings (see **7-22**).

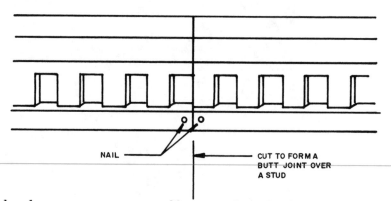

7-21   *Plan joints so that the pattern can repeat, and have a stud or other backing to permit nailing.*

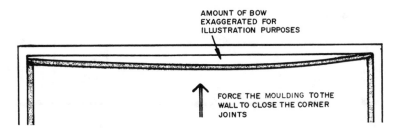

7-23 The moulding is cut slightly long to permit extra pressure to be applied to close the joints.

5. Press the moulding in place on the wall. Since it was cut slightly longer it will bow and have to be forced against the wall. This is necessary to get a tight end joint (see **7-23**). When the piece of moulding does not reach the full length between two walls, nail an end block to the wall so that the moulding can be sprung into place. Such an end block is simply some form of carpenter-made blocking, as shown in **7-24**. This is needed to get good corner and butt joints on a long wall.

6. Drive a finishing nail into each stud or backer board at least every 16in (approx. 41cm). Narrow moldings can be nailed into each stud. Wide mouldings should be nailed to a backer board installed behind the gypsum drywall.

7. Begin the installation from the most conspicuous outside corner, and work around the room. Plan to end in the most inconspicuous corner. Many moulded-plastic mouldings have decorative patterns and any mismatch will be less noticeable if it occurs on an inside corner.

8. Countersink the nails, and cover with spackling. Apply a manufacturer-supplied vinyl patching compound over the filled nail holes and any sanded areas. Gaps at the ceiling can be filled with caulking.

9. Allow the installation to set for 48 hours before applying the paint or stain finish coats.

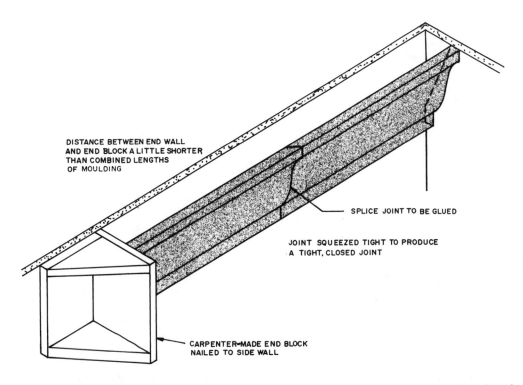

7-24 An end block can be used to put the moulding under compression and produce a tight, closed joint.

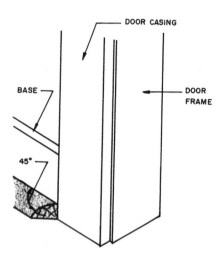

7-25 *The shoe moulding can be mitred where it meets a door casing.*

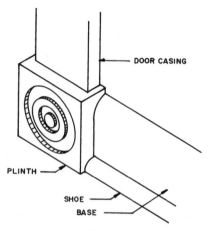

7-26 *The intersection between casing, plinth, and shoe moulding.*

Special Situations

Often when a shoe moulding is used, it will stick out beyond the casing at the doors. In this case the shoe is cut on a **45-degree bevel** (see **7-25**).

Some traditional interiors use **plinth blocks** and **rosettes** on the door openings. The casing and base butt against these blocks. Plinth blocks and rosettes of various designs are available from companies that manufacturer mouldings. While there is no hard and fast rule, the block is often wider than the casing and higher than the base (see **7-26**). It should be thicker

than both so that it has a reveal on the sides where moulding butts it.

If a base has a moulding applied to the top that is wider than the base, it will stick beyond the casing. Where it meets the casing, the moulding is notched around the casing and smoothed to produce a finished return (see **7-27**).

If the base ends along a wall in a location where it does not terminate in a casing or butt the wall, the exposed end should be finished by coping it or mitring and cutting a return. A coped end is shown in **7-28**. A mitred end is formed as shown in **7-29**. The

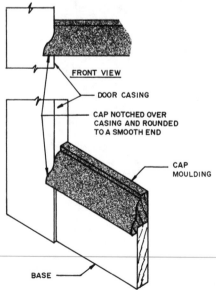

7-27 *One way to end an overhanging base cap moulding at the door casing.*

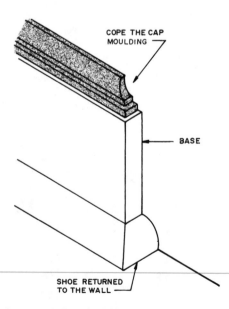

7-28 *The exposed end of base can be coped to produce a decorative finish.*

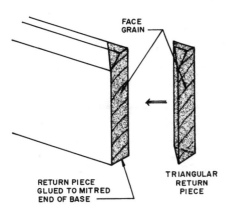

7-29 *Exposed end grain of a base can be covered with a mitred return piece.*

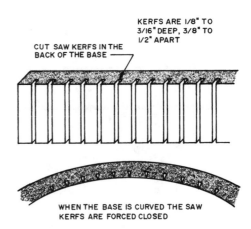

7-30 *Base can be installed on a curved wall by cutting saw kerfs in the back side.*

end is cut on a 45-degree angle. Cut the return piece from the end of another piece of moulding. Glue the return to the base. If an attempt is made to nail it, the danger of splitting is so great that the nail hole should be predrilled. Use a smaller-diameter wire brad.

If wood base must be installed along a curved wall, it will have to have saw kerfs cut in the back. Cut the kerfs about ⅛ to ³⁄₁₆in (3 to 4.5mm) deep and ⅜ to ½in (10 to 13mm) apart. Use good-quality, straight-grained stock. The kerfs will be visible on the top of the base (see 7-30). If it is to be painted, they can be filled and the top sanded smooth. A better solution is to plan to use a base having a small, separate, moulding nailed to the top. This will bend around the curve easily to cover the saw kerfs. Another solution is to use moulded plastic base for the job. It is easily made to follow curved walls without the need for notching.

Sometimes an electric outlet box falls in the area to be covered by the base. This is especially true in

traditional-style homes having very wide baseboards. The location of the outlet box must be on the back of the base. One way to do this is to cut and fit the base to the wall. Then rub chalk on the edges of the outlet box. Place the base against the wall and press against the box to produce a chalk outline on the back of the base. Drill holes through the base at each corner, and then cut from hole to hole with a sabre saw (see 7-31).

While most heat registers used with hot-air heat are now placed in the floor, some are still installed to open through the wall at the floor. They are usually higher than the baseboard. Therefore the baseboard can be butted to the sides of the register. If a more pleasing appearance is desired, cope moulding from the top of the base and mitre around the register, as shown in 7-32. If the moulding is separate from the base, it is simply a matter of cutting and fitting it around the register. If it is a one-piece shaped base, the top shaped portion can be cut from a piece of base and mitred around the register.

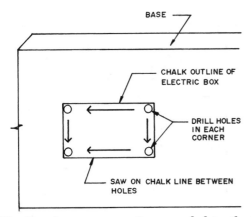

7-31 *Openings are sometimes needed in the base, such as for a previously existing electrical outlet.*

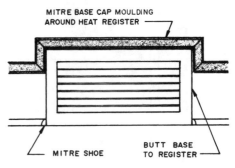

7-32 *Base cap moulding can be mitred around a heat register or other wall protrusions.*

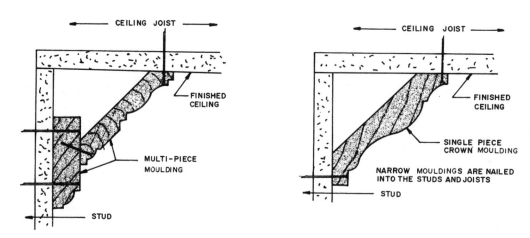

7-33   *Crown mouldings are used to decorate the union of the wall and ceiling.*

Crown Moulding

Crown moulding is available in wood or plastic. Much that has been described earlier in this chapter also applies to the installation of crown moulding. Crown moulding is installed to cover or decorate the joint formed where the interior wall and ceiling meet. While the crown moulding is a single-shaped moulding, it is often combined with other moldings to form a large ceiling moulding (see **7-33**), which is sometimes referred to as an **interior cornice**.

If the ceiling moulding has flat members, they are installed in the same manner as baseboards. Be certain they are level. Any gaps between the ceiling and flat moulding will be covered with the crown moulding.

Crown mouldings up to about 4in (102mm) wide may be nailed to the studs and ceiling joists. Nail through the flats on the top and bottom edges. Wider mouldings or wider multipieced ceiling mouldings re-

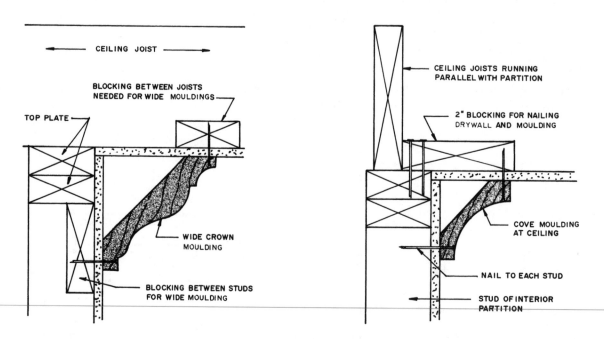

7-34   *Blocking between studs and joists is required when wide crown mouldings are to be used.*

7-35   *Blocking on partitions running parallel with the joists is needed to give a nailing surface.*

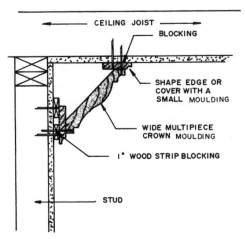

7-36 *Surface-mounted wood strips can be used to mount wide crown moulding when blocking is not placed between the studs.*

7-37 *This crown moulding is being power-nailed to a surface-mounted moulding.* (Courtesy Senco Products, Inc.)

quire blocking to be installed by the framing carpenter between the studs and possibly between ceiling joists (see **7-34**). On walls running parallel with ceiling joists, blocking should be nailed to the top plate and cantilevered out beyond the top plate. This is done to provide nailing for the drywall. It would have to be wider for holding crown moulding (see **7-35**). If this blocking has not been installed, it is still possible to install a wood backing on the outside of the drywall, and then nail the ceiling moulding to this. The moulding must be designed to cover this backing board, as shown in **7-36**. Notice in **7-37** that the crown moulding is nailed to a surface-mounted moulding that provides the nailing base.

Joinery

Crown moulding is mitered at outside corners and can be mitred or coped at inside corners. Since most walls do not meet at exactly right angles, the mitre usually has to have considerable adjustment, as explained for mitring base moulding. Also, if there is any movement in the wall, the mitre will open, producing a gap that is plainly visible. It is best to cope the joints at inside corners, as explained for base moulding.

The big difference in coping crown moulding is that the mitre cut must be made with the moulding placed on the saw able *upside down and backwards* from the way it will rest on the wall. It will have one inside face flat against the fence and the other flat against the saw table (see **7-38**). This produces the

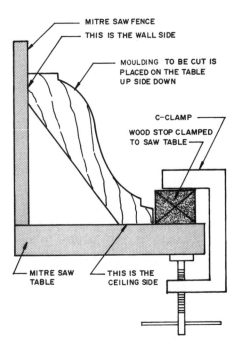

7-38 *How to position crown moulding on the mitre saw.*

required mitre cut needed to cope the end of the moulding. The mitre on the end to be coped must slant towards the wall. It is difficult to hold the crown moulding firmly in place when cutting the mitre. To help hold it, some carpenters clamp a wood strip to the saw table to serve as a stop.

117

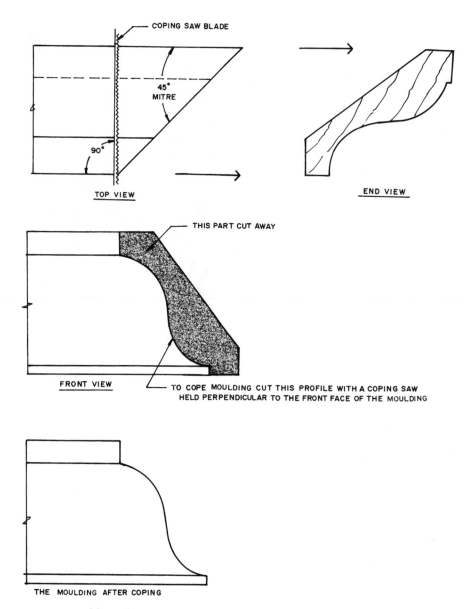

COPING SAW BLADE

45°
MITRE

90°

TOP VIEW

END VIEW

THIS PART CUT AWAY

FRONT VIEW

TO COPE MOULDING CUT THIS PROFILE WITH A COPING SAW
HELD PERPENDICULAR TO THE FRONT FACE OF THE MOULDING

THE MOULDING AFTER COPING

7-39   *How to cope crown moulding.*

After the mitre has been cut, cope to the line produced by the cut, as shown in **7-39**. Cut perpendicular to the face of the moulding. Trim and fit to the butting moulding using a file.

Installing Crown Moulding

Finish carpenters have their own techniques and procedures for accomplishing this difficult task. There are any number of ways that the various problems and procedures may be handled. Following are some that are used.

1. Find and mark the studs and ceiling joists. Mark with a light, soft-leaded pencil. Do not use ballpoint pens, because it is very difficult to cover the ink marks with paint.

   To find the studs and joists, use a stud finder or look for the rows of nails covered by drywall compound. To get the exact location, nail through the drywall and hit each member. Do this in an area where it will be covered by the moulding.

2. Check to see whether the ceiling is flat and level. This can be done a number of ways. One is to measure a fixed distance from the floor, such as

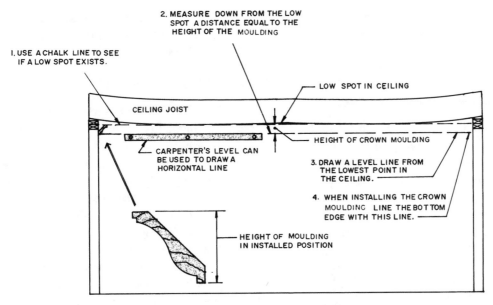

7-40   *How to position the crown moulding when the ceiling is out of plumb.*

8ft, in each corner and run a chalk line. The variance in the ceiling can then be marked. If a ceiling is not flat, it is most likely to bow slightly in the center. Mark the low spot, if one exists, as shown in **7-40**. Then measure down from the low point a distance equal to the height of the moulding in its installed position. Run a level line through this point from wall to wall. When installing the crown moulding, place its bottom edge on this line.

If things are going well, the gap between the ceiling and the moulding will be small. The top edge of the moulding is sometimes relieved (sloped a little to the back). This helps disguise a small gap. If the gap is too large to let go, the drywall contractor can feather a layer of compound to reduce the size of the gap (see **7-41**).

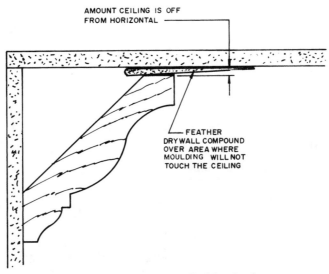

7-41   *Gaps between the crown moulding and the ceiling can be filled by feathering the drywall compound in the low areas.*

3. Plan the layout of the crown mouldings. As was recommended for the installation of base, run one piece on the longest wall and butt to each wall. One suggested plan is shown in **7-42**. Doors and windows are not shown, because they do not interrupt the run of the moulding.

4. Cut and install the first piece. Cut it to the exact length or a bit short. If cut too long and the moulding absorbs moisture from a period of high humidity, it may buckle. Any tiny gap at the wall is covered by the adjoining moulding. Align the bottom of the moulding with the mark, and nail through the flats at the top and bottom of the moulding. The nail should be long enough to give good penetration into the studs and joists. Sometimes the moulding can be pulled to the wall a little. However, too much pull will produce a wavy result. If the wall or ceiling are out of plane quite a bit, it may be necessary to place wood shims between the wallboard and moulding to keep the moulding flat and straight.

5. Continue to cut, fit, cope, and butt each piece as you proceed around the room. You can work to the left or right, as desired.

Mitring Outside Corners

It is difficult to make tight outside mitre joints with crown moulding. After the mitres are cut, it usually takes some adjusting to get the joint to close. Whenever possible the moulding containing an outside mitre on one end should butt the wall on the other end. As the mitre is adjusted, the butted end may clear the wall a little but this is covered by the coped moulding that will butt it. The length of the moulding can be measured by finding the distance from the wall to the edge of the outside corner, as shown in **7-43**. If a moulding has to have a coped end and a mitred end, some carpenters prefer to cut the coped end first, then mark the length to the bottom corner of the mitre and cut the mitre. Cut the mitre a bit long so that it can be trimmed to fit the butting mitre. Nail the moulding in place, but drive the nails only par-

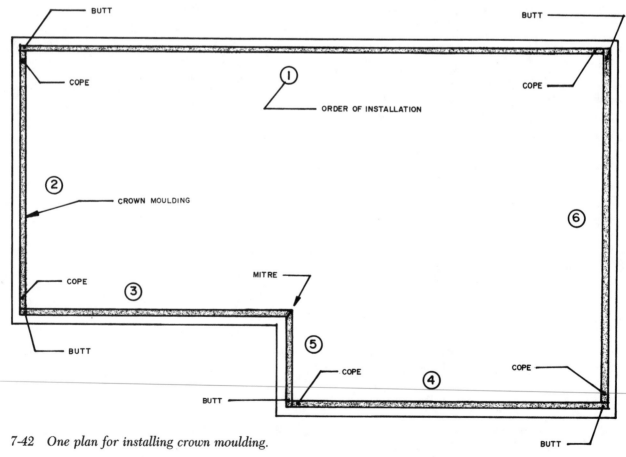

7-42 *One plan for installing crown moulding.*

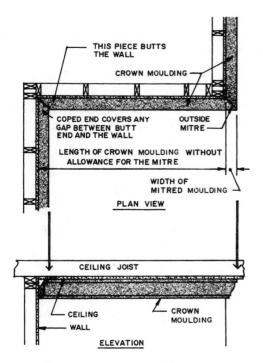

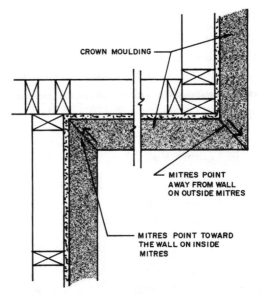

7-43 *The length of crown moulding having an out-side mitre equals the length of the wall plus the width of the mitred moulding.*

7-44 *Be certain to get the mitres pointing in the right direction before outlining the moulding.*

tially in so that the moulding can be removed if the mitre needs additional adjustment. Do not set any nails until the moulding has a perfect fit on both ends.

Remember, when cutting mitres, that the point must face away from the wall. This will help keep you from cutting the mitre in the wrong direction. Inside corner mitres point towards the wall (see **7-44**).

Outside mitres are glued and nailed. It is impor-tant that the nails do not break out the front or back of the moulding. The continued closure of the joint depends on a good nailing job.

Probably the most commonly occurring problem with an outside mitre joint is when it has a parallel open outside gap. When this occurs, change the angle of the cut by a few degrees to remove wood from the back side of the mitre. If there is a gap and it tapers, remove a fine amount from the high side of the face of the mitre (see **7-45**).

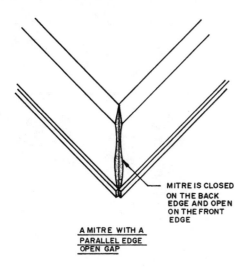

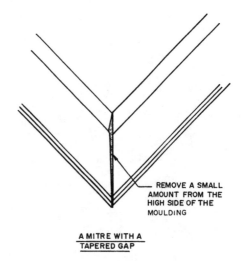

7-45 *When a mitre opens on the front, a small amount must be removed from the back edge of the mitre to close it.*

Mitreless Crown Moulding

This wood product eliminates the need for mitres by supplying internal and external corner blocks. The crown moulding is cut to length with square ends and butts these corner pieces, as shown in **7-46**. The moulding and corners are glued and nailed to the wall.

Installing Chair Rail Mouldings

The design and height of the **chair rail moulding** above the floor will be specified on the working drawings. If these are not available, it is necessary to contact the owner or designer. Normally chair rail is placed 32 to 36in (81.3 to 91.4cm) above the floor (see **7-47**). The chair rail serves to keep furniture from scraping the wall, and originally it was used in dining rooms. It can be used almost anywhere, and now serves as a divider between two different wall finishes. For example, the area below the chair rail, called the **dado,** may have panelling and the area above, called the **frieze,** may be covered with wallpaper (see **7-48**). Chair rail can be a one-piece moulding or built up from several pieces. A typical built-up installation over plywood wall panelling is shown in **7-49**.

Chair rail is installed as described for base. The corners are mitred and coped in the same manner. For best results, it is recommended that a 1×4 wood member be let in the studs to provide a solid backing for nailing the chair rail or 2×4 blocking be nailed between the studs (see **7-47**).

When a chair rail meets a casing at a door or window, it can be butted if it is thinner than the casing. If it is thicker, it can have a mitred return or be notched to overlap the casing, as shown in **7-50**.

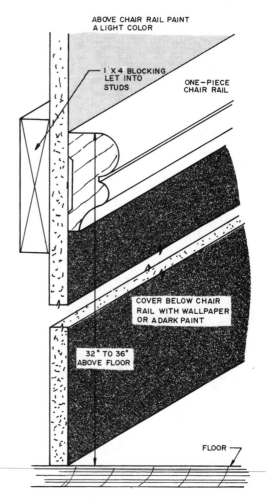

7-46 *This crown molding butts internal and external corner blocks, eliminating the need to cut mitres.* (Courtesy Ornamental® Mouldings)

7-47 *Chair rail mouldings permit the use of different wall finishes above and below the rail.*

7-48 *This beautifully cased door opening is butted by a double chair rail. Notice the difference in wall finish above and below the chair rail. (Courtesy Ornamental® Mouldings)*

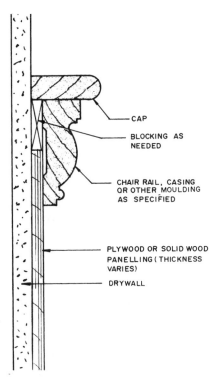

CAP

BLOCKING AS NEEDED

CHAIR RAIL, CASING OR OTHER MOULDING AS SPECIFIED

PLYWOOD OR SOLID WOOD PANELLING (THICKNESS VARIES)

DRYWALL

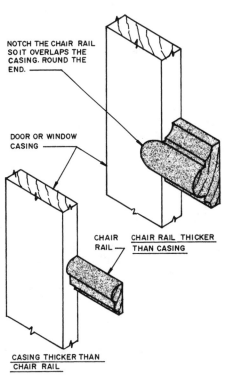

NOTCH THE CHAIR RAIL SO IT OVERLAPS THE CASING. ROUND THE END.

DOOR OR WINDOW CASING

CHAIR RAIL THICKER THAN CASING

CHAIR RAIL

CASING THICKER THAN CHAIR RAIL

7-49 *A multipiece chair rail over wood panelling.*

7-50 *Several ways to butt a chair rail to a casing.*

It is important that the chair rail be absolutely level. The height can be measured on each end and a chalk line snapped, giving a level line. This usually represents the bottom edge of the moulding.

The rail should fit tightly against the wall. It can usually be pulled some when nailing. If the wall is too wavy, the drywall contractor may have to come back and add additional compound. Some prefer to glue it and nail it in place. Generally 8d finish nails are used.

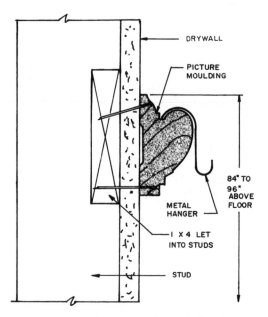

7-51 *Picture moulding must be nailed to blocking set between the studs.*

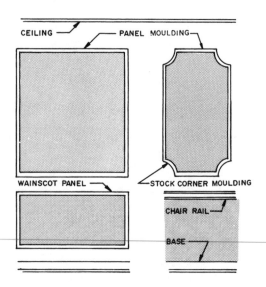

7-52 *Typical wall panel installations.*

Installing Picture Mouldings

Picture mouldings are shaped to hold metal clips which hold long cords secured to the rear of picture frames (see **7-51**). They are installed 84 to 96 inches (2.1 to 2.4m) above the floor. At the 96in (2.4m) level they form a ceiling moulding of rooms with 8ft (2.4m) ceilings. Installation is the same as described for chair rails. Since they may have to support heavy pictures, they need to be securely nailed or screwed into the studs and backing strip. Screws with oval heads may be left exposed. Flathead screws should be set below the surface and plugged.

Installing Panel Moulding

Panel mouldings are used to produce decorative panels. Often the area inside the panel created has a different finish from the rest of the wall, as shown in **7-52**. The design of panel mouldings can include single-piece stock, special machine material, or can be made up by combining several mouldings. The size and location is determined by the designer and should appear on the working drawings.

The key to success is careful layout of the exact location as specified on the plan. The sides must be vertical and the top and bottom members horizontal. These can be levelled with a long carpenter's level, and marked on the wall with a soft lead pencil. Prior to installing the finish wall material, such as gypsum drywall, provision should be made to install blocking to which the moulding can be nailed. Joints are mitred.

Estimating Trim Quantities

Base, shoe moulding, ceiling moulding, and chair rail quantities are determined by finding the lineal feet in the perimeter of the room plus any related areas, such as closets. Make no allowances for doors; this will give a little extra for waste. Some add 10 percent for waste.

Panel moulding quantities are determined by calculating the lineal feet around the perimeter of each panel and adding 10 percent for waste. In order to avoid splicing the moulding, some carpenters determine what they can get from a standard length. Study the panels shown in **7-53**. They require six pieces 24in, two pieces 33in, and four pieces 50in with no allowance for cutting mitres. Assuming you can buy the panel moulding in 10ft lengths, and adding 2in to

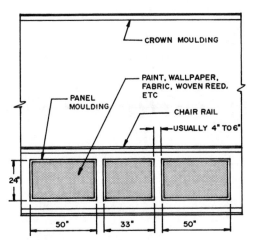

7-53 *A panel layout from which quantities of mould-ing required may be estimated.*

| 10'-0" (120") STOCK PANEL MOULDING |

52"	26"	26"	16"
52"	26"	35"	7"
52"	26"	35"	7"
52"	26"	26"	16"

WASTE—

7-54 *One possible cutting plan for the panel mould-ing layout shown in 7-53.*

each length for mitring, they could be cut from four 10ft pieces. If you figure the perimeter, which is 460 lineal inches including the waste factor, this indicates that four 10ft pieces would be required (see **7-54**). This could be refigured with other lengths to see whether the waste could be reduced. Perhaps there is

a computer estimating program that will assist you in figuring the most economical lengths. Either way, you will, on large quantities of moulding, get very close to the same result. This method does assume that the carpenter also takes the time to try to figure out the most economical way to cut the stock lengths.

Quantities of door and window casing can be figured by calculating the lineal feet around each opening and then adding 20 percent for waste. Many manufacturers supply these in precut lengths as sets. You can order a set for each opening.

8

Wainscoting and Panelling

Wainscoting is a decorative and protective facing applied to the lower part, the dado, of an interior wall. Typically it is solid wood, plywood, hardboard, or some other bump-resistant facing material (see **8-1**). The top edge is covered with some type of wainscot cap. It can be used in almost any room and in halls. It is typically 36 to 40in (91.4 to 101.6cm) high.

    Panelling uses the same materials described for wainscoting. However, it runs from the floor to the ceiling. One difference is that wainscoting has the top edge covered with a wainscot cap and panelling usually has some form of moulding called a **cornice,** at the ceiling (see **8-2**). The ceiling moulding can be crown, bed, cove, or some form of flat moulding.

Building Codes

Interior wall and ceiling finish materials are regulated by local building codes. The finish carpenter and the designer must consider these code specifications in the selection of materials and how they are installed.

    Solid-wood and plywood wainscoting and panelling are acceptable for most residential applications. Exposed foam-plastic surface materials are generally not acceptable.

    Typically codes require plywood or hardboard panelling under ¼in (6mm) thick to be installed over a fire-resistant backing, such as gypsum drywall. The drywall is applied to the studs and the panelling ap-

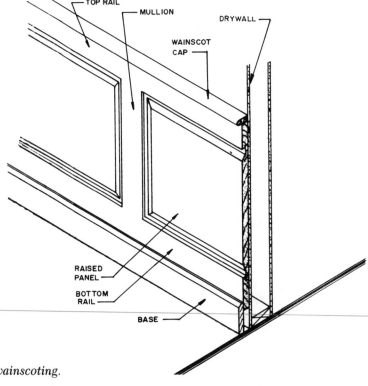

8-1   A raised-panel wainscoting.

126

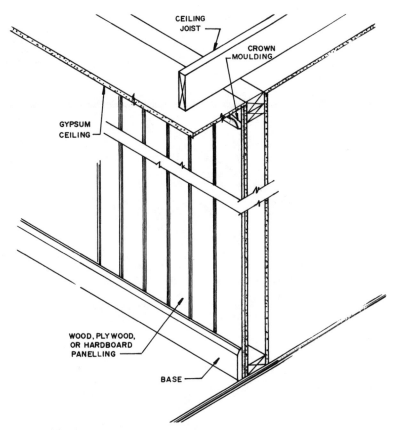

8-2   *Panelling covers the wall from the floor to the ceiling.*

plied over it. Gypsum drywall can also be used under solid-wood panelling, when a fire-resistant backing is required behind it.

Storage

Panelling should not be brought into a building until all operations that might create high humidity have been furnished and the humidity level returns to normal. This includes letting the drywall compound thoroughly cure and plaster set and cure. Keep the panelling stored flat so that it will not twist or warp. If it is to be in the area for a while, some carpenters prefer to place 1 × 2 wood spacers between the layers to permit air to circulate.

Plywood panelling can be stored in a vertical position with the long side on the floor or stored flat. Again, wood spacers are recommended if it is to be in storage for a long time. In both cases great care must be taken to prevent scratching or otherwise damaging the visible face (see **8-3**). Solid-wood panelling should be stored flat.

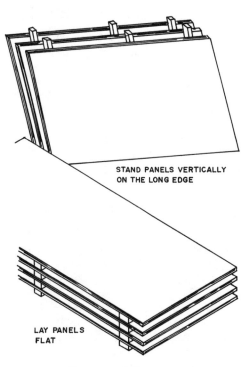

8-3   *Store panelling carefully to avoid warping and scratching.*

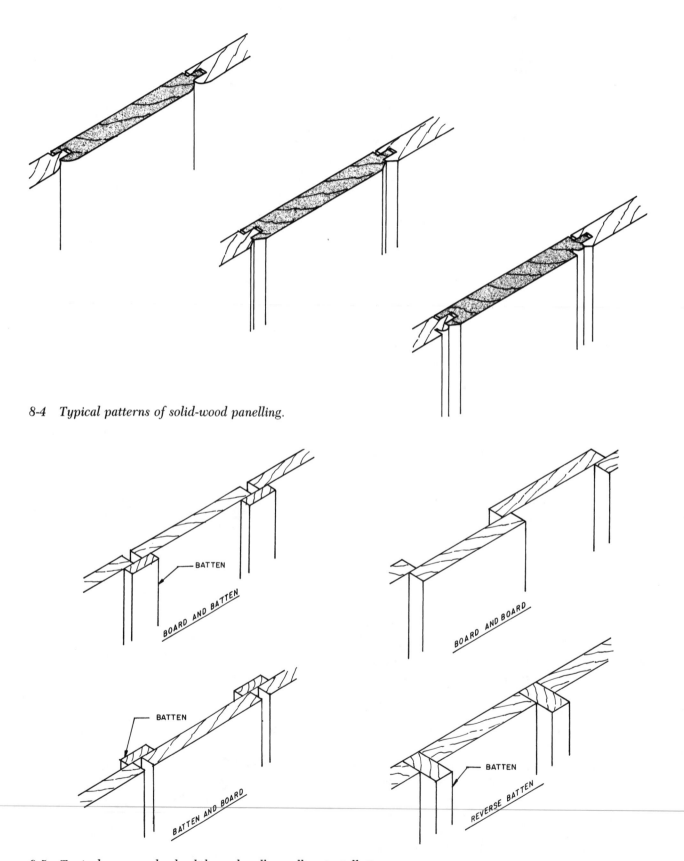

8-4 *Typical patterns of solid-wood panelling.*

8-5 *Typical square-edged solid-wood wall panelling installations.*

Solid-Wood Panelling

Various types of solid-wood panelling are available. Perhaps the most commonly used is some form of **tongue-and-groove panelling.** It is available in various widths and profiles (see **8-4**). **Square-edge panelling** is also used. It can take several forms as shown in **8-5**. Often rough sawn boards are used for these types of installations.

Panelling should be ⅜in (9mm) thick for 16in (40.6cm) O.C. (on center) framing, ½in (12.7mm) thick for 20in (50.8cm) O.C. framing, and ⅝in (16mm) thick for 24in (61cm) O.C. framing. It must have been kiln dried to 8 percent moisture.

Wood panelling is usually manufactured in 4 to 8in (102 to 203mm) widths. Wider stock tends to cup and may require extra blocking and nailing.

Installing Solid-Wood Wainscoting

Before installing any wood panelling, check local building codes to see whether the wood panelling can be applied directly to the studs. As already mentioned, it is often the case that gypsum drywall is required under the wood to meet fire requirements.

Blocking is required behind the top edge of the wainscoting and often about halfway between the top and the floor. This can be 2×4 (38×101mm) blocking nailed between studs of 1×4 (25×101mm) stock let into the studs (see **8-6**).

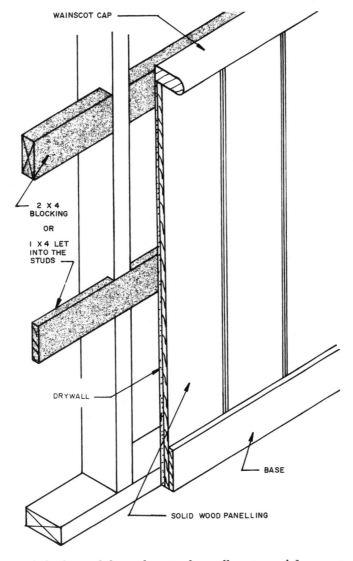

8-6 *Blocking is recommended when solid-wood vertical panelling is used for a wainscot.*

To begin a wainscoting, measure the desired height from the floor to one end. Run a chalk line that is perfectly horizontal to the other wall and snap a line on the wall (see 8-7). Plan to allow the panelling to have a small gap at the floor.

Next, check the first wall for plumb with a level. If it is out of plumb, measure out a distance equal to the width of one board, and draw a plumb line. Measure the distance from the wall to the line at the top and bottom. Plane a little off the edge of the panelling that will butt this wall.

Now install pieces of panelling across the wall. Every now and then measure the distance to the other wall. If the top and bottom measurements are close to the same, continue on across the wall. If it appears that a large difference is developing, plane a very slight taper on each piece of panelling, thus reducing the size of the angle that will be needed on the last piece. This is not an easy thing to do and takes some experience. If the last piece has some slope on the butting end in an inside corner, it might be left because this is not too noticeable.

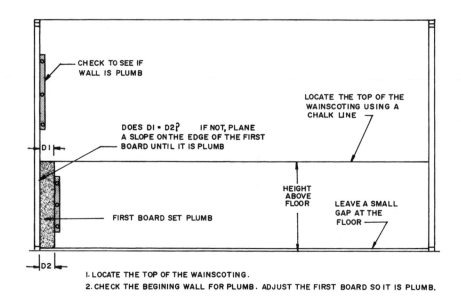

CHECK TO SEE IF WALL IS PLUMB

LOCATE THE TOP OF THE WAINSCOTING USING A CHALK LINE

DOES D1 = D2? IF NOT, PLANE A SLOPE ON THE EDGE OF THE FIRST BOARD UNTIL IT IS PLUMB

D1

FIRST BOARD SET PLUMB

HEIGHT ABOVE FLOOR

LEAVE A SMALL GAP AT THE FLOOR

D2

1. LOCATE THE TOP OF THE WAINSCOTING.
2. CHECK THE BEGINING WALL FOR PLUMB. ADJUST THE FIRST BOARD SO IT IS PLUMB.

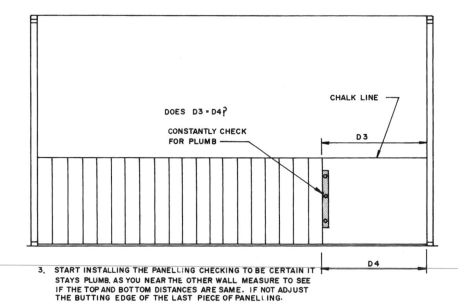

DOES D3 = D4?

CONSTANTLY CHECK FOR PLUMB

CHALK LINE

D3

D4

3. START INSTALLING THE PANELLING CHECKING TO BE CERTAIN IT STAYS PLUMB. AS YOU NEAR THE OTHER WALL MEASURE TO SEE IF THE TOP AND BOTTOM DISTANCES ARE SAME. IF NOT ADJUST THE BUTTING EDGE OF THE LAST PIECE OF PANELLING.

8-7 *The steps to lay out and install vertical wood wainscoting.*

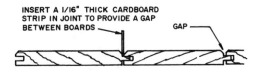

8-8 *Provide a small gap between boards at each joint to allow for expansion.*

Do not force the tongue all the way into the groove. Leave a small gap of around ¹⁄₁₆in (1.5mm) to allow for expansion. This will help prevent the panelling from buckling if the humidity should increase a great deal. The gap can also be adjusted to help keep the boards plumb (see **8-8**). This gap can be established by placing a piece of wood veneer, plastic laminate, or other thin hard material in the joint as it is being closed.

Another thing to check and determine is the width of the last panel. As you proceed across the wall you can measure the distance remaining and, knowing the width of the panelling used, can determine the exposed width of the last panel. The makeup of the corner also influences this width. If the difference is not great, it can be left. If it is great and a near full-width panel is desired on the end, it will be necessary

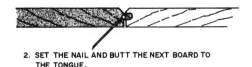

8-9 *Blind-nail the wainscoting boards through the tongue.*

to plane a small amount off the grooved edge. It may be necessary to rebevel the edge to match the original design.

The panelling is nailed through the tongue into the backing boards. Use finishing nails long enough to get good penetration in the backing material. The last board will have to be face-nailed (see **8-9**).

The inside corner can be made as shown in **8-10**. If the butting wall is a little out of plumb, it will be necessary to scribe the last piece and cut it on a slight taper to form a closed joint. Cut it a little too wide, and get a close fit by smoothing the edge with a hand plane, power plane, or jointer. The jointer will give the straightest edge. An exaggerated illustration is shown in **8-11**. If the work is carefully done, the actual taper will be small. Outside corners also are shown in **8-10**.

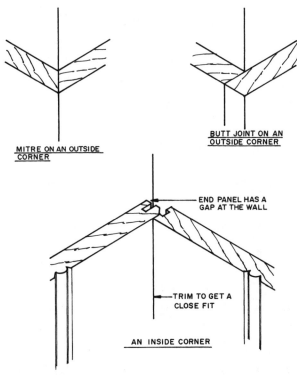

8-10 *Leave a gap at the corner to allow for expansion.*

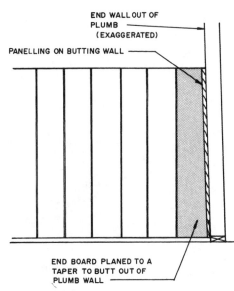

8-11 *When necessary, scribe and plane the last board to a taper so that it butts the end wall.*

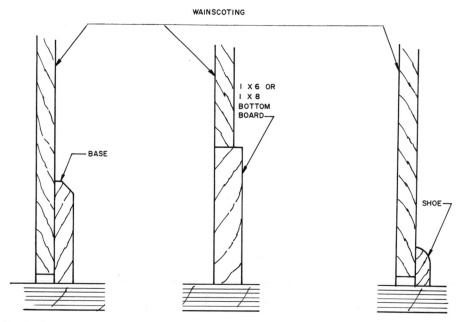

8-12   *Ways to finish the wainscoting at the floor.*

At the floor the wainscoting can be covered with a base or can butt a 1×6 (25×150mm) or 1×8 (25×200mm) board which may have a shoe moulding at the floor (see **8-12**).

When the wainscoting meets the door or window casing, it can butt it as shown in **8-13**. The casing should be thicker than the panelling so that a slight reveal is exposed. The casing can be the same thickness as the panelling, but this is not as attractive.

There are two ways to install panelling at a window. If the window has the casing on all four sides (no stool), butt the panelling to the casing, as shown in **8-13**. The casing chosen should be thicker than the panelling so that a slight reveal is exposed. The pan-

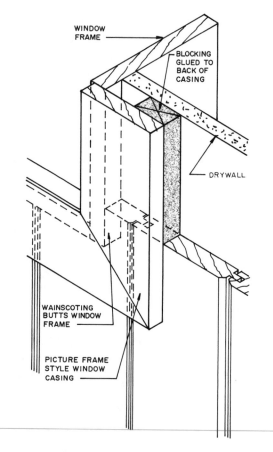

8-14   *If the wainscoting butts the window frame, blocking is needed behind the casing on all sides of the window.*

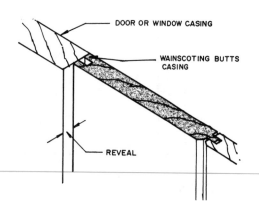

8-13   *The wainscoting can butt the door and window casing.*

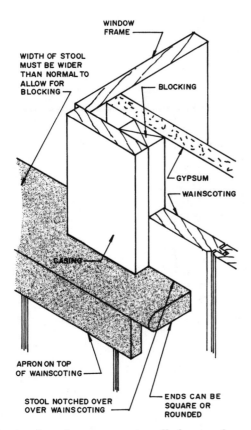

8-15 *Stool and apron are installed over the wainscoting.*

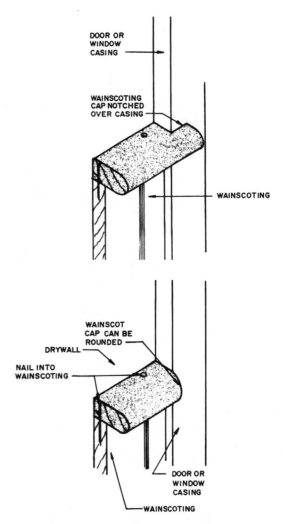

8-16 *The wainscoting cap can be notched around the casing or butted and rounded or bevelled on the extended end.*

elling can be installed before the casing is applied and overlap the window frame. The casing is then applied on top of the panelling. This requires that blocking be installed behind the casing above the panelling to fill the void that is created by the thickness of the panelling. This can be nailed to the window frame or glued and nailed to the rear of the casing. This permits the use of thinner casing (see **8-14**).

If the window has a stool, generally the wainscoting is installed before the casing is applied. Then cut and install the stool, notching it over the casing. The casing and apron are nailed over the panelling (see **8-15**).

The wainscoting cap is usually notched over the door or window casing, as shown in **8-16**. It could be bevelled or rounded, but the notched end is most attractive. The wainscoting cap can be specially milled to the specifications of the designer or made up of stock mouldings (see **8-17**). The wainscoting cap is nailed through the top of the cap into the top edge of the panelling. The baseboard is installed over the panelling in the normal manner.

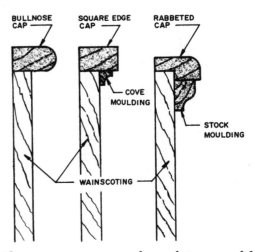

8-17 *The wainscoting cap can be made in many different ways.*

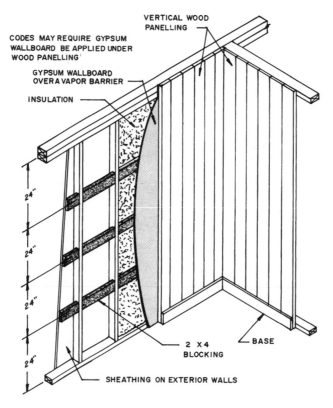

VERTICAL WOOD PANELLING

CODES MAY REQUIRE GYPSUM WALLBOARD BE APPLIED UNDER WOOD PANELLING

GYPSUM WALLBOARD OVER A VAPOR BARRIER

INSULATION

24"

24"

24"

24"

2 X 4 BLOCKING

BASE

SHEATHING ON EXTERIOR WALLS

8-18   *Details for installing vertical solid-wood panelling.*

Installing Vertical Solid-Wood Panelling

Solid-wood panelling may be installed horizontally or vertically. The same basic techniques apply to both. Usually blocking is installed between the studs when it is applied vertically (see **8-18**). When installed on an exterior wall, the insulation is in place and a vapor barrier is stapled over it. Usually 6d finishing nails are used, and the panels are nailed to the block and studs. Boards six inches wide require two nails. One is blind-nailed through the tongue, and the other is face-nailed. Boards eight inches wide require one blind nail and two face nails. The face nails are set and covered with a filler, as shown in **8-19**.

Plan how you will proceed (see **8-20**). Some car-penters prefer to start at outside corners and work towards inside corners. The outside corner is more visible; beginning there will give full-width boards until you get to the inside corner. The final board may have to be narrower; this is less noticeable at the inside corner. The outside corner can be mitred or butted (see **8-10**). Since it is a long joint, it is very difficult to mitre.

If there are no outside corners, begin at inside corners, and work towards doors and windows and other inside corners.

SET AND FILL

USE 6d FINISH NAILS

8" BOARD

6" BOARD

8-19   *Nailing solid-wood vertical panelling.*

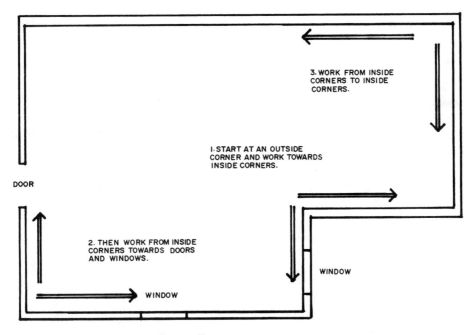

8-20 A plan for installing vertical wall panelling.

Vertical wall panelling is installed in the same manner as described for wainscoting. The first piece is scribed to the butting wall, set plumb, and nailed. Additional pieces are installed, and checked for plumb. When necessary, adjustments are made to keep the boards plumb (see **8-21**). The last piece is scribed to the other end wall and face-nailed to the backing.

The baseboard is installed on top of the panelling unless the panelling is butted to a wider board at the floor (see **8-12**). Ceiling moulding is used to conceal the joint between the panelling and ceiling (see **8-22**).

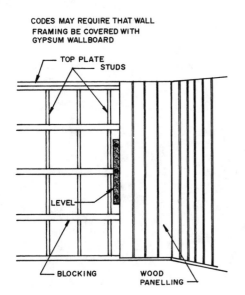

8-21 When installing vertical wood panelling, check frequently to see that it is plumb.

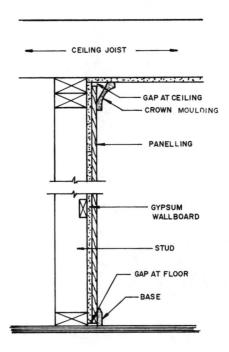

8-22 Crown moulding is often used to conceal the joint between the panelling and the ceiling.

Installing Horizontal Solid-Wood Panelling

Horizontal wood panelling is nailed directly to the studs. Begin by installing the first row at the floor. Leave a small gap between the board and subfloor. Be certain the first row is level (see **8-23**). As additional layers of boards are installed, constantly check to be certain they remain level. If it is tongue-and-groove panelling, leave a $\frac{1}{16}$in (1.5mm) open space between the end of the tongue and the bottom of the groove. Outside corners are mitred, and inside corners are butted. Tongue-and-groove panelling is blind-nailed, as explained for vertical panelling. Square-edge panelling is face-nailed. Ceiling moulding is used, and baseboard is installed in the usual manner.

Panelled Wainscoting and Walls

The procedure for installing panelled wainscoting and walls is much like that described for solid-wood pan-

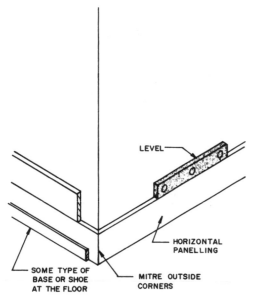

8-23   *Begin installing horizontal wood panelling by levelling the first piece at the floor.*

8-24   *This attractive wainscot was designed to flow into the cabinet base units.*
(Courtesy Ornamental® Mouldings)

136

elling (see **8-24**). Panelled wainscoting and wall panels are fabricated by machining solid-wood raised panels to fit into solid-wood frames. Some are made by skilled cabinetmakers or finish carpenters with the highest woodworking skills and good wordworking equipment. The working drawings should show an **elevation** (a projection of the structure or an object onto a vertical plane) of each wall to be panelled and give **sections** through the panels to show the profiles required and construction details. A typical example is shown in **8-25**. Before starting to make the panels, the carpenter or cabinetmaker must go to the job site, and measure the actual distances the panels will cover.

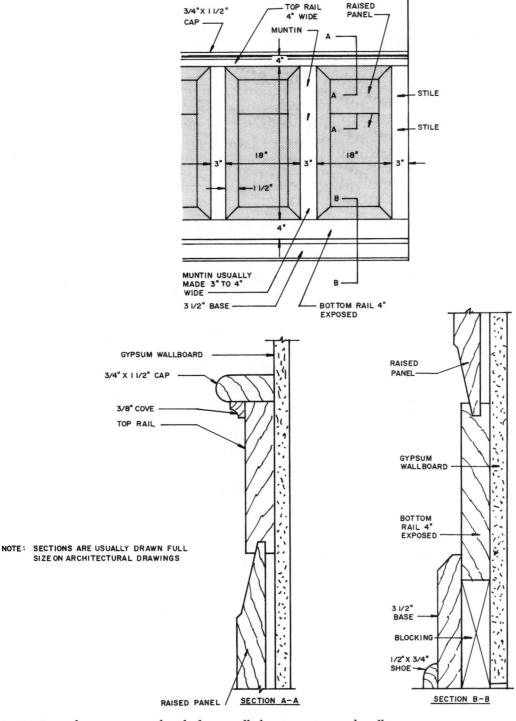

8-25 *Typical construction details for panelled wainscoting and walls.*

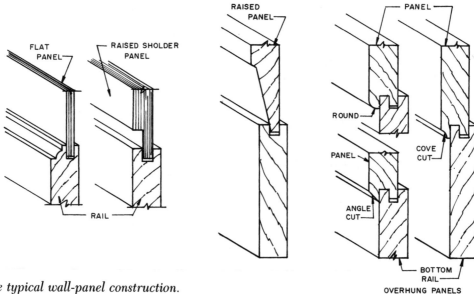

8-26 *Some typical wall-panel construction.*

The design of wall panels can take many forms. A few are shown in **8-26**. It is desirable that outside corners be mitred, since these panels are of high-quality woods, usually hardwoods, and the very best joinery is expected. A butt joint would be satisfactory if the exposed edge grain is not considered objectionable. Inside corners should be designed so that the exposed stile on the butting panels is the same width. Since the panels are designed for a particular space, the let-in panels can be adjusted in size as the unit is made to allow the **stiles** and **muntins** to be the same size. The inside corner could be a butt joint, but a better job is had if a tongue-and-groove joint is cut. Examples are shown in **8-27**.

The method of joining the stiles, muntins, and **rails** may be specified by the designer. This is commonly done using dowels, mortise and tenons, or oval biscuits also called plates installed with a biscuit joiner. These are shown in **8-28**.

Installing Panelled Wainscoting and Wall Panels
This procedure is much the same as that described for wood panelling, except that the panelled units are long and heavy. Measure in one corner the desired height of the panel. Snap a chalk line across the wall, producing a level line for the top of the panel. Allow room so that the bottom of the panel will clear the floor. Set the first panel in place. Which panel will be

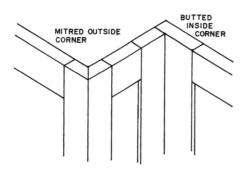

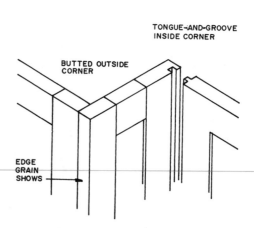

8-27 *How to form corners when installing panel units.*

138

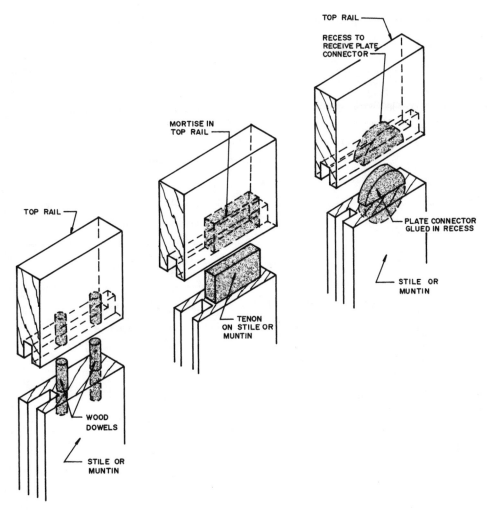

8-28 *Ways to join panel frames.*

"first" depends on how the joints at the corners were designed. The panel with the wider stiles for inside corners must be installed first.

Check the walls that the panel will butt for plumb. It may be necessary to plane a little off the stile, if the wall is out of plumb.

To set the panel, place it on the wood blocks to allow the floor gap desired. Nail through the top rail into the studs. If all goes well, these nails will be covered by wainscoting cap or ceiling moulding. Nail through the bottom rail into the bottom plate about every 16in (approx. 41cm). These nails should be covered by the baseboard. The end stiles can be face-nailed into the corner studs. These can be set and filled for paint-grade work. If it is hardwood with a stained or natural finish, the nails can be set and covered with colored fillers as used on furniture construction. Wood screws could be used. They can be

set in a counterbore and covered with wood plugs cut from the same wood used to make the panels (see 8-29).

Once the panels are installed, the baseboard, ceiling moulding, and wainscoting cap are installed, if required.

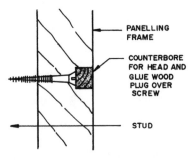

8-29 *Wood screws can be covered with wood plugs.*

Estimating Solid-Wood Panelling

The following is based on the plan shown in **8-30**.

1. Calculate the area of the walls to be covered. This is the length times the height of each wall.

    $20 \times 8 \times 2$ walls $= 320$ sq ft
    $14 \times 8 \times 2$ walls $= \underline{126 \text{ sq ft}}$
    446 sq ft Total

2. Subtract door and window areas. Assume the following

    1 door, $3 \times 7 \qquad = 21$ sq ft
    2 windows, $3 \times 4 \times 2 = \underline{24 \text{ sq ft}}$
    45 sq ft

    Other wall-covering objects, such as fireplaces, and cabinets, can also be subtracted.

3. Total wall area is $446 - 45 = 401$ sq ft.

4. Multiply the number of square feet by the area factor for the type of panelling. The area factor is found by dividing the nominal width by the face size, as given in **8-31**. If you plan to use 1×6 tongue-and-groove panelling, the area factor is

1.19. Therefore we need $401 \times 1.19 = 478$ board feet of panelling.

5. Some add a 5 percent or 10 percent waste factor. At 5 percent, the total would be $478 + 24 = 502$ board feet of panelling.

Plywood Panelling

Plywood panelling is available in a large variety of wood veneers. Typical thicknesses are $5/32$, $1/4$, $5/16$, and $7/16$ in (3.9, 6.4, 7.9, and 11mm). The most commonly used panel is 4×8ft (1.2×2.4m). Most panelling is prefinished; so it must be handled with care (see **8-32**).

The thickness of plywood panelling to use depends on the spacing of the studs (see **8-33**).

The humidity in the room must be at normal levels. All drywall compound and plaster must be thoroughly cured. Panels should be stored in the room 48 hours before installing so that their moisture content equalizes with the surrounding area.

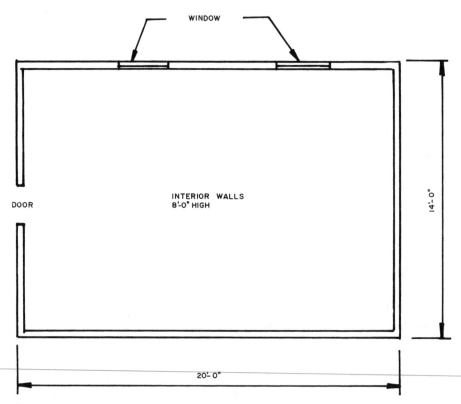

8-30 This room will require 502 board feet of solid-wood tongue-and-groove panelling to cover the walls to the ceiling.

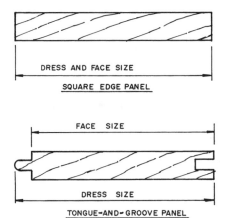

Coverage factors for solid-wood panelling (inches).

	Panelling Width		
	Nominal size	Dress Size	Face Size
Tongue-and-Groove Panelling	1 × 6	5⁷⁄₁₆″	5¹⁄₁₆″
	1 × 8	7⅛″	6¹³⁄₁₆″
	1 × 10	9⅛″	8¹³⁄₁₆″
Square-Edge Panelling	1 × 6	5¼″	5¼″
	1 × 8	7¼″	7¼″
	1 × 10	9¼″	9¼″

8-31   *Use the nominal size divided by the face size to obtain an area factor for calculating the board feet of panelling needed.*

Lean the panels up along the walls and examine them for color and grain. Place them so that they are in a harmonious arrangement; avoid putting a very dark panel directly next to a lighter panel. By moving panels around, the appearance of the room may be improved.

8-33   *Minimum plywood panelling thicknesses for various stud spacings.*

Stud Spacing	Minimum Thickness
16″ O.C.	¼″
20″ O.C.	⅜″
24″ O.C.	½″

8-32   *This dining room has plywood-panelled walls, giving the room a warm, pleasant atmosphere. (Courtesy Georgia-Pacific Corp.)*

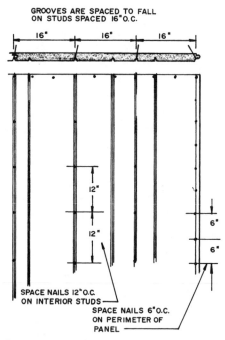

8-34 *The proper nailing pattern for installing plywood panelling.*

Generally the panels must be installed over a solid backing, which is usually gypsum drywall. They are installed with 5d finishing nails. Nails may be set and covered with colored putty, which is available in stick form. Nails with the heads painted to match the color of the panels are also used and are not set. The nails are spaced 6in (approx. 15cm) apart on the edges and 12in (approx. 30cm) apart on the interior of the panel (see **8-34**). Do not nail closer than ⅜in (9.5mm) to the edge of the panel. While panels appear to have randomly spaced grooves, there is a groove every 16in (40.6cm). If the first panel is properly set, a groove will fall on each stud. Nail to the stud, putting the nails in the groove; this helps hide them.

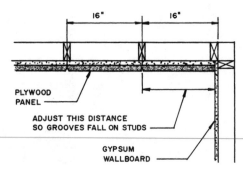

8-36 *Adjust the first panel so that the grooves fall on the studs to allow the nails to be hidden in the grooves.*

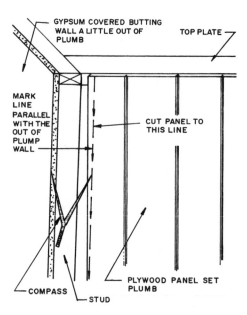

8-35 *Use a compass to scribe a line on the edge of the panel that is parallel to the out-of-plumb wall.*

Installing Plywood Panelling
Begin by marking the location of each stud. Make a mark on the ceiling and floor indicating the stud locations.

It is important to get the first panel absolutely plumb. Since the wall it will butt may not be plumb, the edge of the panel must be scribed to it. Usually this is only a very small amount. Place the panel on the wall, and push it up to the butting wall. Using a level, set it plumb. If the butting edge leaves a gap that will not be covered when the adjoining wall is panelled, scribe a line on the edge parallel with the wall (see **8-35**). Cut or plane the edge to this line. If the panelling has V-grooves 16in O.C. check to see that they fall on a stud. If not, adjust the width of the first panel so that this occurs (see **8-36**).

Now the first panel is ready to be nailed to the studs. Set it so that it is a little above the subfloor. Before nailing, spray-paint a strip of dark color down the face of the gypsum over the stud where the two panels will meet. Since the butting panels must be spaced ¹⁄₃₂in (0.8mm) apart to allow for expansion, this hides the white gypsum drywall that is visible. Keep the bottom of the panel above the floor about ⅜ to ½in (9.5 to 12.5mm).

Continue installing panels across the wall. Measure the width needed for the last panel. Also note whether the butting wall is plumb, and scribe to it, if

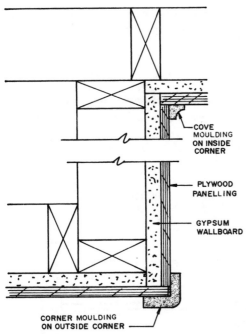

8-37 *Mouldings are often used to finish corners when plywood panelling is used.*

necessary. Since plywood panelling is thin, it is difficult to get tightly butted inside and outside corners. To handle this, some type of molding, such as cove moulding, is often used on inside corners and corner moulding is used on outside corners (see 8-37).

The panels can butt door and window casings. To do this requires careful measuring and cutting so that a gap does not occur. Baseboard is usually nailed over the panelling at the floor.

Installing Plywood Panelling with Adhesives

Plywood panelling can be bonded to studs, gypsum drywall, or any other sound wall surface with adhesives recommended by the plywood manufacturer. After the panel as been scribed and filled, apply adhesives to all four edges and to the line of studs on the interior panel as shown in 8-38. Place a strip of wood on the subfloor, and rest the bottom of the panel on it. Then press the panel against the wall. Tap over the glue lines using a wood block covered with cloth until you get a good bond between the panel and the backing material. Some adhesives require that the panel be pressed against the wall, but pulled away again for a few minutes to let the solvent evaporate rapidly, and then pressed back, and tapped until it is firm. Some recommend placing nails at the top and bottom where they will be covered by moulding or base. Some place a few nails within the panel to hold it as the adhesive sets (see 8-39).

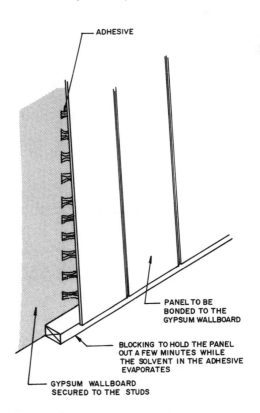

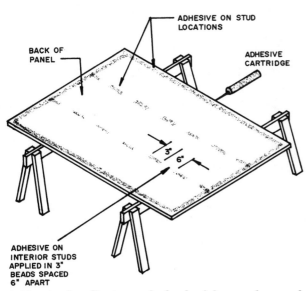

8-38 *Apply adhesive to the back of the panel around the perimeter and at the location of each stud.*

8-39 *Some adhesives require a few minutes' exposure to the air to allow solvent to evaporate before the panel is pressed against the wall.*

Hardboard Panelling

Hardboard panelling is available in a wide range of simulated wood grains and colors. Most panels are ¼in (6mm) thick and 4 × 8ft (1.2 × 2.4m) in size. Other products, such as hardboard planks, are available.

They are installed following the same procedures given for plywood panelling.

Estimating the Numbers of Panels Needed

The following is based on the plan shown in **8-40**.

1. Determine the lineal feet of wall around the room. For this example, this equals 20 + 16 + 20 + 16, or 72 ft.

2. Divide 72 by 4 (4ft per panel), which equals 18 panels.

3. Some estimators deduct the following for doors and windows:
   Doors—deduct ½ panel.
   Windows—deduct ¼ panel.

You can also deduct for other things such as wall and base cabinets and fireplaces.

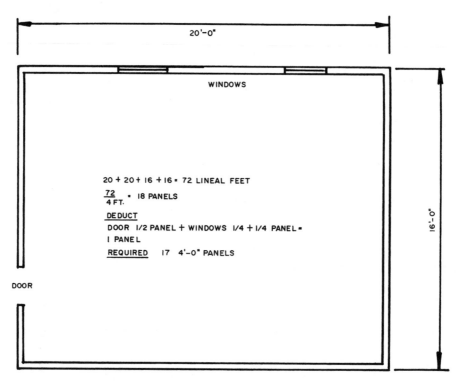

8-40 Estimating the number of 4 × 8ft plywood panels that are needed to panel a room.

9

Installing Wood Flooring

Wood flooring is available in hardwoods and softwoods, in a variety of species. The most commonly used hardwoods are oak and maple, although beech, birch, and pecan are also used. The most frequently used softwoods are yellow pine and Douglas fir (see **9-1**).

9-1   This hardwood flooring comprises varying-width planks. (Courtesy Harris-Tarkett, Inc.)

Grades of Wood Flooring

The various grades of wood flooring are established by various manufacturers' associations. Such grades are shown in **9-2**. The grade determines the appearance of the exposed surface. All grades are equally strong and can be used with confidence of structural integrity. Wood flooring is available unfinished or with a factory-applied finish.

Storing on the Site

Solid-wood flooring should not be delivered to the job site until the structure is weather-tight and concrete work, drywall, plaster, and other humidity-raising installations are dry. The subfloor and framing members must have a moisture content below about 12 to 14 percent before the flooring is delivered. In the winter the building should be heated to 65 to 70°F (18 to 21°C) for five days before the flooring is delivered and maintained until it is installed and finished. In the summer the interior of the building should be well ventilated to reduce moisture, and temperature kept in the vicinity of 70°F (21°C). Operation of the air-conditioning unit is helpful to control temperature and moisture. Various types of laminated wood flooring have even more restrictive requirements. Consult the manufacturer's specifications for proper storage and installation temperature and humidity requirements.

It helps if the area below the floor, such as a basement or crawl space, is dry and well ventilated. The bare ground in a crawl space must be covered with a 6-mil polyethylene vapor barrier.

9-2   *Flooring grades for oak, maple, and Southern pine.*

Hardwood flooring grades of the National Oak Flooring Manufacturers' Association			
Unfinished Oak Flooring	**Beech, Birch, and Hard Maple**	**Pecan**	**Prefinished Oak Flooring**
Clear Plain or Clear Quartered—best appearance	First Grade White Hard Maple—face all bright sapwood	First Grade Red—face all heartwood	Prime—excellent
Select and Better—mix of Clear and Select	First Grade Red Beech—face all red heartwood	First Grade White—face all bright sapwood	Standard and Better—mix of Standard and Prime
Select Plain or Select Quartered—excellent appearance	First Grade—best	First Grade—excellent	Standard—variegated
	Second and Better—excellent	Second Grade Red—face all heartwood	Tavern and Better—mix of Prime, Standard, and Tavern
No. 1 Common—variegated	Second—variegated	Second Grade—variegated	Tavern—rustic
No. 2 Common—rustic	Third and Better—mix of First, Second, and Third	Third Grade—rustic	
Softwood flooring grades of the Southern Pine Inspection Bureau		**Maple flooring grades of the Maple Flooring Manufacturers' Association**	
Grades		**Grades**	
B and Btr—best quality C and Btr—mix of B and Btr and C C—good quality, some defects D—good economy flooring No. 2—defects but serviceable		First—highest quality Second and Better—mix of First and Second Second—good quality, some imperfections Third and Better—mix of First, Second, and Third Third—good economy flooring	

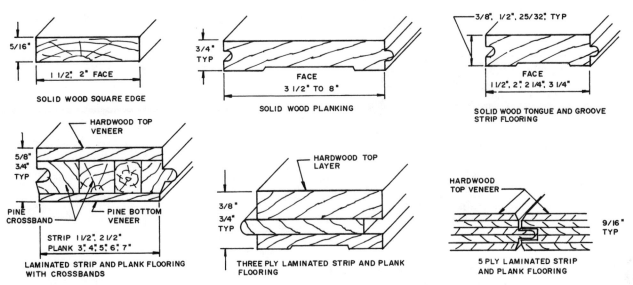

9-3 *Wood flooring is available in solid-wood and laminated strips and planks.*

The bundles of unfinished flooring should be broken open and spread about in the rooms in which they are to be installed. Flooring material should be laid flat on the subfloor and stored in this manner at least three days before the start of installation so that it can adjust to the temperature and humidity in the building.

Some types of prefinished flooring are shipped shrink-wrapped in plastic and are therefore protected from moisture. The shrink wrap should be kept intact until the flooring is installed; it is not necessary to have any on-site acclimation time. Consult the manufacturer's directions that usually accompany each shipment.

Protection after Installation

To assure years of satisfactory use of the hardwood flooring, the flooring contractor should be certain that the general contractor provides a permanent, controlled atmosphere to protect the flooring. The building should be built so that the basement crawl space will remain dry. This can be assured by waterproofing the foundation, sloping the soil away from the building, installing drain tile around the inside of the foundation, and providing lots of ventilation for the area under the floor. In addition the installed flooring must be protected from excess heat generated by a furnace below the floor or by uninsulated heating ducts. One solution is to install ½in (12mm) or thicker insulation board between the joists. Anything installed over a furnace must, of course, be a nonflammable material.

Types of Wood Flooring

Wood flooring is available as **solid-wood strip and plank flooring, laminated strip and plank flooring,** and **parquet wood blocks.**

Strip and Plank Flooring

Examples of typical sizes and construction of strip and plank floor are shown in **9-3.** Strip flooring is available in widths from 1½ to 3¼in (38 to 82mm) and plank flooring is from 3½ to 8in (89 to 203mm). These are laid over the subfloor at right angles to the joists. They have tongue-and-grooved edges and are end-matched with a tongue-and-groove as shown in **9-4.**

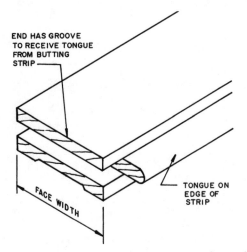

9-4 *Strip and plank wood flooring are end-matched.*

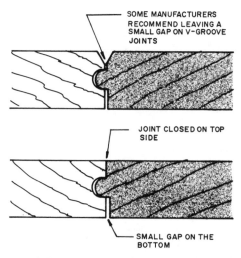

9-5 *Wood flooring edge joints are machined so that the top joint can be closed leaving a small gap at the bottom.*

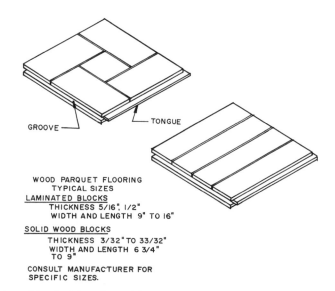

WOOD PARQUET FLOORING
TYPICAL SIZES

LAMINATED BLOCKS
    THICKNESS 5/16", 1/2"
    WIDTH AND LENGTH 9" TO 16"

SOLID WOOD BLOCKS
    THICKNESS 3/32" TO 33/32"
    WIDTH AND LENGTH 6 3/4"
    TO 9"

CONSULT MANUFACTURER FOR
SPECIFIC SIZES.

9-6 *Typical wood parquet flooring blocks.*

9-7 *Wood parquet floor.* (Courtesy Harris-Tarkett, Inc.)

9-8 *Sweep the subfloor so that it is absolutely clean.* (Courtesy National Oak Flooring Manufacturers' Association)

The boards vary in length from 2 to 16ft (0.6 to 2.4m). They are available in several thicknesses. The face is slightly wider than the back so that, when the joints are pulled up tight, the top edges close and the bottom edges have a slight gap (see **9-5**). Some flooring manufacturers recommend leaving a very small gap between strips if the flooring edge butts with a V-groove. Consult the manufacturer's installation instructions before proceeding.

Parquet Blocks

Parquet blocks may be made from solid wood or laminated veneers, much like plywood. The solid-wood blocks are made from pieces of strip flooring bonded along the edges. The exposed edges are tongue-and-grooved to facilitate installation and produce a tight joint. The laminated blocks are bonded with a moisture-resistant adhesive. Parquet blocks are available in a wide range of sizes from 3×9in (76×228mm) to 12×12in (305×305mm), as shown in **9-6**. They have a variety of patterns on the exposed face (see **9-7**).

Laying Strip Flooring

Be certain the subfloor is securely fastened to the joists. If it has any bounce, this must be corrected. Also examine it for damage. Often it is subject to rain before the roof is on the structure. This sometimes causes parts of the top veneer to swell, bulge, and

even split. Repair these defects. If necessary, sand the subfloor to remove any uneven spots. Sweep the subfloor so that it is free of all debris (see **9-8**). Then cover the subfloor with 15-pound asphalt-saturated building paper, lapped 4 to 6in (100 to 152mm) on the side and end seams. This helps keep out dust and serves as a moisture barrier (see **9-9**).

Locate and mark the position of each floor joist on the builder's felt so that the nails are certain to penetrate into them. This can be done by snapping a chalk line at each joist.

9-9 *After sweeping the subfloor, cover it with 15-pound asphalt-saturated building paper.* (Courtesy National Oak Flooring Manufacturers' Association)

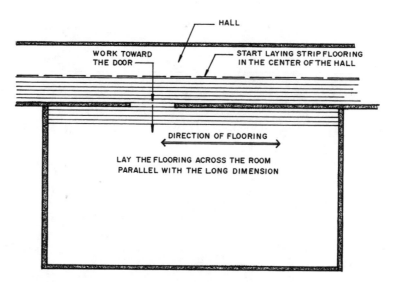

9-10   *When the flooring is also in the hall, start in the center of the hall and lay the flooring into the room.*

Strip flooring gives the best appearance if it runs parallel with the longest wall of the room, and it is best if it runs perpendicular to the floor joists so that it can be nailed through the subfloor into the joist. However, if the long wall runs parallel with the joists, the strip flooring can be nailed to the subfloor alone if it is ¾in (18mm) plywood. If the subfloor is ½in (12mm) plywood, the strip flooring must be nailed into the joists and have a nail in between the joists.

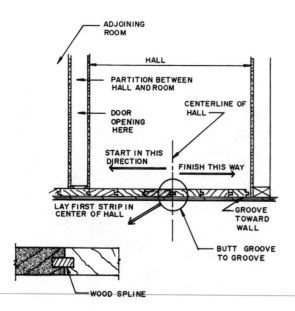

9-11   *Use a wood spline in the groove of the starting strip as a tongue for working the tongue-and-groove flooring towards the other wall.*

Also you must consider how the direction of the flooring may affect the floor in a hall or other room opening onto it. Plan for the strip flooring to work through a door and into a hall when the hall is also to have strip flooring (see **9-10**). If the hall parallels the long dimension of the room and the flooring is installed parallel with the long dimension, start by installing the flooring in the middle of the hall and working towards the door of the room. Snap a chalk line down the middle of the hall to get started. Place the groove in the flooring towards the centerline. Lay the flooring across the hall, through the door, and into the room. To finish the hall insert a spline in the groove, and lay the flooring to the other wall (see **9-11**).

If it is desired to change the direction of the flooring in an abutting room, it can butt a wood sill made from flooring or a marble sill (see **9-12**). Cut off the groove or tongue so that the flooring butts a solid, square edge. Face-nail each piece to the subfloor.

Starting to Lay Strip Flooring
The first strip should be placed ½ to ¾in (12 to 19mm) from the wall, with the groove towards the wall (see **9-13**). The gap allows for expansion of the floor and will be covered by the base and shoe moulding.

1. Begin by measuring ½ to ¾in (12 to 19mm) in from the wall on each end of the room. Snap a chalk line from one end of the room to the other (see **9-14**).

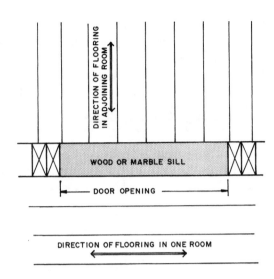

9-12 Use a sill at the door when the flooring changes directions from one adjoining room to another.

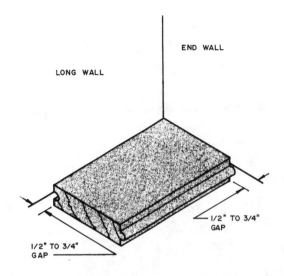

9-13 The wood flooring is set away from the walls to allow for expansion.

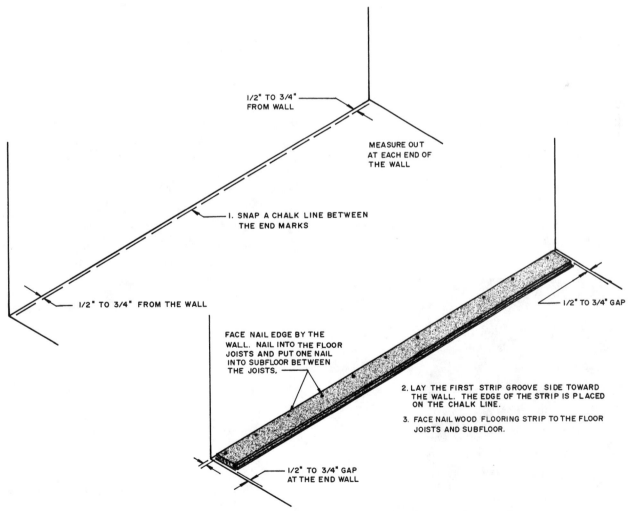

9-14 Install the first strip parallel with the wall and ½in to ¾in (12mm to 19mm) away from it.

151

9-15 *Face-nail the first strip into the floor joists.* (Courtesy National Oak Flooring Manufacturers' Association)

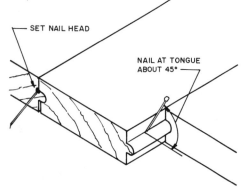

9-16 *Blind-nail the rest of the strips through the tongue into the floor joists.*

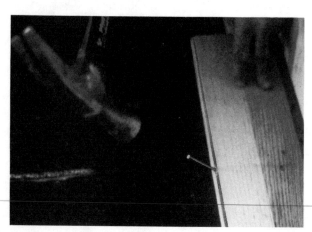

9-17 *Drive the nail through the tongue.* (Courtesy National Oak Flooring Manufacturers' Association)

2. Place the first strip with the edge along the chalk line. Be certain it is parallel with the wall. Face-nail into the floor joists, and place one nail between joists using 8d finish nails. If there is a danger of splitting the wood, predrill each hole. These nails should be close enough to the edge to be covered with the shoe moulding (see **9-15**).

3. Blind-nail through the tongue into the subfloor and floor joist, as shown in **9-16**. The nail is driven just above the tongue and on about a 45-degree angle.

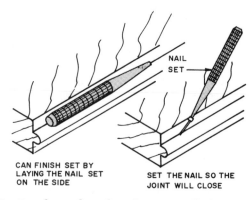

9-18 *Set the nail so that the joint will close.*

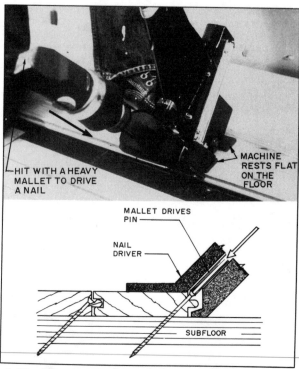

9-19 *Flooring can be nailed using a nailing machine.* (Courtesy National Oak Flooring Manufacturers' Association)

Do not try to drive the nail flush with a hammer, because you will most likely damage the edge of the flooring (see **9-17**). The nail can be set using a nail set or, if it is driven in far enough, the nail set can be laid on the tongue and struck to set the nail (see **9-18**). A nailing machine can also be used; the plate rests on top of the floor, and the plunger is hit with a mallet (see **9-19**). These usually use special nails for installing flooring.

4. Select the proper nails. A suggested nailing schedule is shown in **9-20**.

9-20 A suggested nailing schedule for solid-wood flooring. (Courtesy National Oak Flooring Manufacturers' Association)

NOFMA Hardwood Flooring must be installed over a Proper Subfloor Tongue & Grooved **MUST** be **Blind-Nailed** **Square Edge** must be Face-Nailed		
A slab with screeds 12″ O.C. does not always require a subfloor.		
Strip T & G Size Flooring	**Size Nail to be Used**	**Blind-Nail Spacing along the length of strips. Minimum 2 nails per piece near the ends (1″–3″)**
¾ × 1½″, 2¼″, & 3¼″	2″ serrated edge barbed fastener, 7d or 8d screw or cut nail, 2″ 15 gauge staples with ½″ crown. On slab with ¾″ plywood subfloor use 1½″ barbed fastener.	In addition—10–12″ apart—8–10″ preferred ½″ plywood subfloor with joists a maximum 16″ O.C., fasten into each joist with additional fastening between, or 8″ apart
MUST install on a Subfloor		
½ × 1½″ & 2″	1½″ serrated edge barbed fastener, 5d screw, cut steel, or wire casing nail.	10″ apart ½″ flooring must be installed over a MINIMUM ⅝″ thick plywood subfloor.
⅜ × 1½″ & 2″	1¼″ serrated edge barbed fastener 4d bright wire casing nail	8″ apart
Square-edge Flooring ⁵⁄₁₆ × 1½″ & 2″ ⁵⁄₁₆ × 1⅓″	1″ 15 gauge fully barbed flooring brad 1″ 15 gauge fully barbed flooring brad	2 nails every 7″ 1 nail every 5″ on alternate sides of strip
Plank ¾ × 3″ to 8″	2″ serrated edge barbed fastener, 7d or 8d screw, or cut nail. Use 1½″ length with ¾″ plywood subfloor on slab.	8″ apart
Follow Manufacturer's instructions for installing Plank Flooring		
Widths 4″ and over must be installed on a Subfloor of ⅝″ or thicker plywood or ¾″ boards. On slab use ¾″ or thicker plywood.		

For additional information—write to: National Oak Flooring Manufacturers' Association, P.O. Box 3009, Memphis, TN 38173-0009

9-21 *Lay out several rows of flooring and arrange so that the joints fall as required.* (Courtesy National Oak Flooring Manufacturers' Association)

5. Next lay out several rows of flooring. Select long pieces, and arrange them so that the end butt joints are at least 6in (152mm) apart. It is recommended that they be farther apart than this when possible (see **9-21**). Fit the second strip to the first, and position the end ½in (12mm) from the wall. Drive the piece tightly against the first strip, being certain the joint closes. To close the joint place a piece of scrap flooring next to it, and hammer on the scrap so as to not damage the piece (see **9-22**). The joint can also be closed by tapping a ripping bar into the subfloor and using it as a pry (see **9-23**). Once the second piece is in place, blind-nail it through the tongue. Space the nails as shown in the nailing schedule.

6. Continue working across the room, being careful to space the end joints so that the overall appearance is attractive. Avoid bunching up end joints or several short pieces. Keep short pieces of flooring for use in closets. As you get to the other side of the room, remember to allow a ½in (13mm) gap along the wall. This may require that the last piece be ripped to width to fit the space remaining.

Installing Prefinished Flooring

Manufacturers of prefinished hardwood flooring recommend a 6-mil polyethylene-film vapor barrier be laid on the subfloor with no adhesive. A ⅛in (3mm) thick resilient, closed-cell polyethylene, high-density

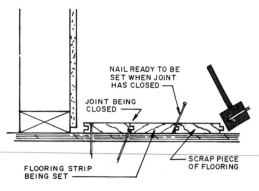

9-22 *A joint between strips can be closed by driving it in place with a scrap block and a mallet.*

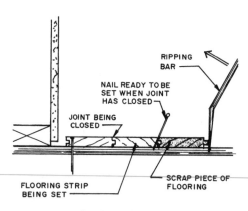

9-23 *Joints can be forced to close by prying with a ripping bar.*

foam underlayment is laid on top also with no adhesive. The hardwood flooring has a polyvinyl acetate adhesive applied to the bottom side and to the groove side and end groove. The strips are positioned on the floor as described earlier.

Prefinished flooring can also be installed by gluing without the foam underlayment and can also be nailed to the wood subfloor as described for unfinished strip flooring.

Installing Plank Flooring

Plank flooring is normally wider than strip flooring, running as wide as 8in (203mm). It is installed by blind-nailing or with wood screws set in counterbores and covered with wood plugs (see **9-24** and **9-25**). The plugs are furnished by the flooring manufacturer. It is installed in the same manner as described for strip flooring. Usually it is made up of planks of several widths. Start the first row with the narrowest boards; then use the next widest, etc. After one row of each width has been laid, repeat the pattern. Manufacturers provide instructions on how they want their product installed.

Use 1in (25mm) screws for flooring laid over ¾in (19mm) plywood on a concrete slab and 1 or 1½in (25 or 38mm) screws for flooring laid over plywood subfloor or on screeds bonded to a concrete slab. Screws should be spaced as recommended by the manufacturer. A finished plank floor is shown in **9-1**.

9-24 *Plank flooring is often installed with screws which are counterbored and have a wood plug glued over them.* (Courtesy National Oak Flooring Manufacturers' Association)

9-25 *Wood plugs are glued over the counterbored screws.* (Courtesy National Oak Flooring Manufacturers' Association)

Installing Strip and Planks over a Concrete Slab

It is vital that any installation over a concrete slab have a polyethylene vapor barrier on the ground below the slab and on top of the slab below the flooring. Moisture from the earth can penetrate a concrete slab, causing swelling and buckling of the wood floor.

Test the Slab for Moisture

The concrete slab must be tested for moisture before attempting to install wood flooring over it. If it fails the test, either some provision must be made to correct the moisture problem or wood flooring should not be installed over it. The following tests are recommended by the Oak Flooring Institute of the National Oak Flooring Manufacturers' Association.

1. **The Rubber Mat Test.** Lay a flat, noncorrugated rubber mat on the slab, place a weight on top to prevent moisture from escaping, and allow the mat to remain overnight. If there is "trapped" moisture in the concrete, the covered area will show water marks when the mat is removed. Note that this test is worthless if the slab surface is other than light in color originally.

2. **The Polyethylene Film Test.** Tape a one-foot square of heavy, clear polyethylene film to the slab, sealing all edges with plastic packaging tape. If, after 24 hours, there is no "clouding" or drops of moisture on the underside of the film, the slab can be considered dry enough to install wood floors.

3. **The Calcium Chloride Test.** Place one-quarter teaspoonful of dry (anhydrous) calcium chloride crystals (available at drugstores) inside a 3in (76mm) diameter putty ring on the slab. Cover with a glass so that the crystals are totally sealed from the air. If the crystals dissolve within 12 hours, the slab is too wet for a hardwood flooring installation.

4. **The Phenolphthalein Test.** Put several drops of 3-percent phenolphthalein solution in grain alcohol at various spots on the slab. If a red color develops in a few minutes, there is a moist alkaline substance present; it would be best not to install hardwood flooring. (This solution is available at drug- or chemical stores).

Preparing the Concrete Slab

There are two ways to prepare the slab to receive residential wood flooring: the **plywood-on-slab** method and a method using **wood screeds**. There are other procedures recommended for installation of wood flooring in commercial construction that will not be discussed.

The plywood-on-slab method involves placing a 6-mil polyethylene plastic film over the slab, lapping all edges 4 to 6in (100 to 150mm), as shown in **9-26**. It is laid on the slab and not bonded with a mastic. The ¾in (19mm) plywood subfloor is laid on top of the polyethylene film and secured to the slab with powder-actuated concrete nails. Start nailing the panel in the middle, and work out towards the edges. Use at least nine nails per panel. Additional nails will help assure that it will stay flat.

Arrange the panels so that the end joints are staggered every 4ft (1.2m). Leave a ½in (12.5mm) space at the walls and a ¼in (6mm) space between the edges and ends of the panels. At places where there will not be base or shoe, such as at a door opening, cut the plywood to fit within ⅛in (3mm) of the space.

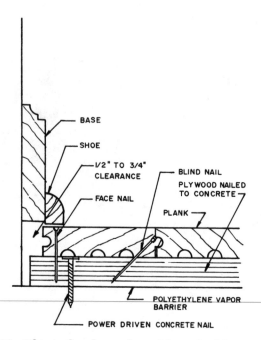

9-26 *This is the plywood-on-slab method for installing wood flooring.*

9-27 *The screed method for installing wood flooring over a concrete slab involves embedding wood screeds in a bed of hot asphalt mastic.* (Courtesy National Oak Flooring Manufacturers' Association)

The screed method involves coating the concrete slab with an asphalt primer, and allowing it to dry. Then hot or cold asphalt mastic is applied where each screed is to be located. Wood 2×4 (51×102mm) screeds 18 to 48in (457 to 1220mm) long are embedded in the mastic. The ends of the screeds are lapped 4in (102mm) and the ends at the walls have a ¾in (19mm) gap. Space the screeds 12 to 16in (305 to 406mm) O.C. The wood screeds should be pressure-treated, but creosote should not be used (see **9-27**).

Next spread a 6-mil polyethylene-film vapor barrier over the screeds. Lap the edges and ends at least 6in (152mm). Do not nail or staple the film in place, because this will put holes in it, reducing its moisture-resisting purpose (see **9-28**). A vapor barrier should be placed below the slab.

The strip or plank flooring is nailed to the screeds, as discussed earlier. It may be necessary to use a 5d nail, rather than the usual 6d, if there is a danger that they may hit the concrete below the screed. This obstruction would make it difficult to set the nail and to get a tight fit.

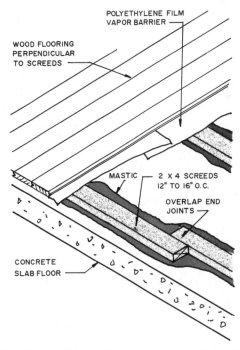

9-28 *The screed method secures wood flooring to wood screeds bonded to the concrete slab.*

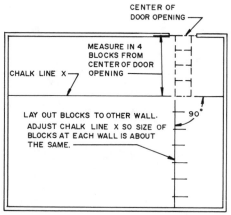

1. MEASURE IN 4 BLOCKS FROM THE CENTER OF THE DOOR.
2. RUN CHALK LINE X PARALLEL WITH THE WALL.
3. LAY OUT BLOCKS TO OTHER WALL.

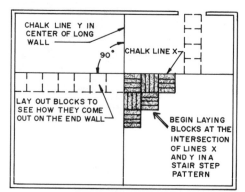

4. RUN CHALK LINE Y PERPENDICULAR TO CHALK LINE X IN THE CENTER OF THE ROOM.
5. LAY OUT BLOCKS ALONG CHALK LINE X TO SEE HOW THEY WORK OUT ON THE END WALLS. ADJUST LINE Y SO SIZE OF BLOCKS AT END WALLS IS ABOUT THE SAME.
6. BEGIN LAYING BLOCKS AT THE INTERSECTION OF THE CHALK LINES.

9-29   *The steps to lay out a square pattern for parquet blocks.*

Installing Parquet Flooring

The procedures for installing parquet flooring vary somewhat depending on the manufacturer. Instructions accompany the flooring when it is delivered to the job. Basically the same procedures as described for strip floor, unfinished and prefinished, are used.

An important factor with parquet flooring is the planning of the preliminary layout. Procedures will

differ somewhat depending on the circumstances. The following sections cite some of the things that must be considered.

Lay Out a Parquet Floor on a Square Pattern
This discussion relates to laying out a parquet floor with the blocks parallel with the long wall of the room (refer to **9-7**). There are two ways this is done. One method, shown in **9-29**, recommends snapping a chalk

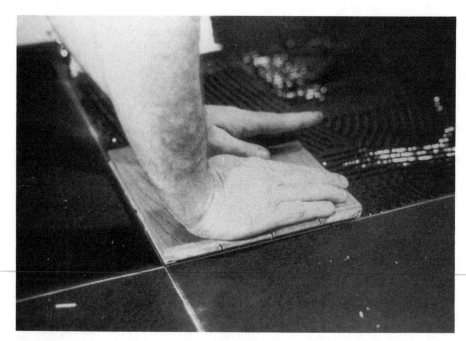

9-30   *Install the first block at the intersection of the lines in the center of the room. (Courtesy National Oak Flooring Manufacturers' Association)*

9-31 *Lay the blocks in a stair-step fashion.* (Courtesy National Oak Flooring Manufacturers' Association)

line four or five blocks from the wall containing the major entrance to the room. This distance is measured from the middle of the doorway. This line is identified as line X in **9-29**. Then find the middle of the room measuring along line X. Snap a chalk line perpendicular to line X through the center point (line Y) and 90 degrees to it. Before laying the first block, check the distance to the other wall to see how the blocks will work out. If the last block is reasonably near a full block, the pattern will be satisfactory. If, however, the last block is just a narrow piece, some carpenters prefer to move line X (see **9-29**) away from or closer to the wall to get the edge blocks closer to the same size. You will have to see how this move changes the size of the block that covers the area in the doorway and include this in your final layout decision.

Once the layout is established, lay the first block at the intersection of the two lines (see **9-30**), and build them in a **stair-step pattern,** as shown in **9-31**. Do not lay parquet flooring in rows. The stair-step procedure helps prevent small inaccuracies of size in the blocks from producing the appearance of misalignment. Complete the installation in one quadrant of the room, leaving any cutting and fitting at the walls until later. Then proceed to fill each quadrant using the stair-step method.

Cut the blocks to fill in the edges leaving a ¾in (19mm) gap, which is covered by the base and shoe moulding. Place wood blocks around the edges in this ¾in (19mm) gap to help keep the blocks from moving. Some recommend placing cork blocks in the gap and leaving them, because they will compress and allow the floor to expand. If wood spacers are used, remove them after the adhesive has set (see **9-32**).

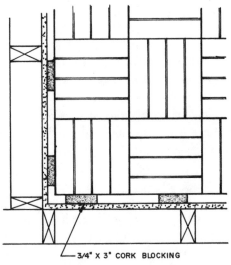

3/4" X 3" CORK BLOCKING

9-32 *Cork blocking can be used to space out parquet blocks from the wall.*

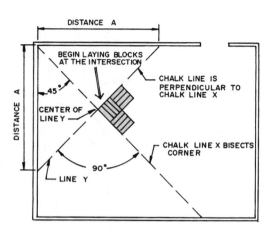

1. MEASURE ANY CONVENIENT DISTANCE (A) FROM THE CORNER ALONG EACH WALL.

2. RUN A CHALK LINE FROM THESE POINTS FORMING LINE Y.

3. MEASURE TO THE CENTER OF LINE Y AND RUN CHALK LINE X THROUGH IT FROM THE CORNER OF THE ROOM.

4. START LAYING BLOCKS AT THE INTERSECTION OF THESE LINES IN A STAIR STEP FASHION.

9-33   How to lay out the room to begin laying parquet blocks on a diagonal.

When laying parquet with adhesive, the blocks tend to slide if sidewise pressure is applied. To help avoid moving them after they are laid, you can lay plywood panels over the laid area, and use these as kneeling boards so that direct pressure is not on individual blocks.

Laying Out Parquet Flooring on a Diagonal
Lay out a diagonal line on a 45-degree angle from a corner of the room, as shown in **9-33**. One way to do this is to measure equal distances right and left from the corner. Connect the ends of these, and measure to find the center of the diagonal. Snap a chalk line from the corner of the room through this center. It will be at 90 degrees to the base line. Lay the first block at the intersection of the lines, and fill in each area using the stair-step method. This requires cutting triangular blocks along the wall. Maintain the ¾in (19mm) gap on all walls.

Securing Parquet Flooring
Parquet flooring is secured in the same ways described for strip and plank flooring. Again, manufacturers will supply instructions for doing several different types of installation, such as blind-nailing, direct-gluing to the subfloor, and bonding to foam plastic underlayment.

Surfacing the Floor

After unfinished hardwood flooring is installed, a floor finishing crew sands it and prepares it for the application of the finish coating. However, there is usually a little more interior work to be completed after the floor is installed; so do not sand it until all the other

trades have finished. Protect the floors from damage by other trades.

Before starting to sand, be certain any exposed nail heads are set below the surface. The opening produced will be filled later. Since dust is created it is best to seal off other rooms and seal heating-duct openings and cold-air returns. If there are cabinets in the room, cover them with plastic drop cloths, and protect surfaces that may be damaged with a covering of heavy corrugated cardboard. Finally sweep the floor to remove all wood scraps and other debris.

Using the Drum Sander
The floor is made flat and ready to finish with a flooring drum sander (see **9-34**). Although the sander has a dust bag which collects much of the wood dust produced, some does escape into the air. It is also a noisy machine. Therefore the operator should wear an ear-protection device and some form of dust mask. The abrasive paper is on a drum at the front of the machine. It pulls the sander forward so the operator must keep firm control.

Following are some things to observe as the drum sander is used.

1. Sand in the direction that the flooring is laid. In other words, sand with the grain of the wood. If there is a spot that is unusually uneven, it can be sanded *briefly* on a 45-degree angle, but leave enough wood to finish sanding with the grain.

2. Keep the sander moving whenever the drum is touching the floor. If it sits still for even a second or two, it will cut a concave depression in the floor.

9-34 *Unfinished wood flooring is sanded with a drum-type sander. (Courtesy National Oak Flooring Manufacturers' Association)*

3. Start the drum sander next to the right side wall and about in the middle of that wall. The drum should be clear of the floor. This is done by tilting the sander backwards. When the drum has reached full speed, slowly lower it to the floor, and move it forward to the end wall.

4. Just before it reaches the end wall, gradually raise the drum off the floor. This produces a tapered or "feathered" cut at the wall. Then move the sander back towards the center of the room, lowering the drum to sand the floor on the return cut.

5. Lift the drum off the floor and move the sander to the left, letting it overlap the first cut by about half the width of the drum. Repeat the above sweep to the wall and back to the middle of the room. Repeat these sweeps until the width of the floor on one end has been sanded. Then sand from the middle to the other end (see **9-35**).

6. When sanding hardwood floors, start with a coarse abrasive, such as a 36 grit, for the first sweep. Then use fine paper, such as 40 grit, followed by an 80 grit, and a final sweep with 100-grit abrasive on the drum. Finer abrasive, such as a 120 grit, can be used if an even smoother finish is desired. When sanding softer woods such as pine, start with a 50-grit abrasive. Remove all wood dust by vacuuming the floor between each sanding.

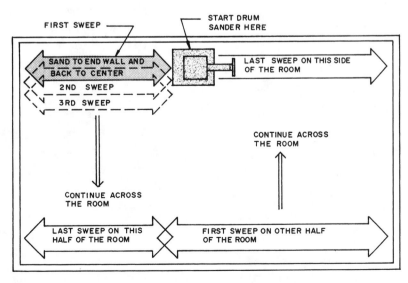

9-35 *A recommended procedure for sanding wood floors with the drum sander.*

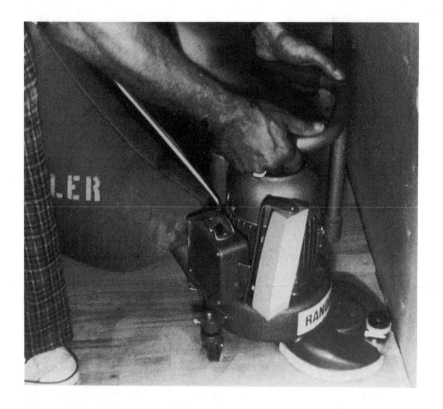

9-36 *A disc sander is used to sand along the wall where the drum sander cannot reach.* (Courtesy National Oak Flooring Manufacturers' Association)

Using the Disc Sander

After the main area of the floor has been rough-sanded, the edge next to the wall is rough-sanded with a disc sander. Usually the disc sander will use an abrasive the same grit as on the drum or one grade finer. After the main floor area has been sanded with the next-finest grit abrasive, the edges are also sanded. This continues until the finest-grit abrasive has been used (see 9-36).

Following are some things to observe as the disc sander is used:

1. Place the sander on the floor. Tilt it back or adjust the rollers so that the disc is clear of the floor.

2. Hold the sander by the handles, and turn the switch on.

3. When the sander reaches full speed, lower the disc to the floor and immediately begin moving it along the edge.

4. Move the sander back and forth in a slow sweeping motion of about 15 to 18in (approx. 38 to 46cm).

5. Begin sanding in a left-hand corner as you face the wall. Move the sander along the wall to the right (see 9-37). Remember to keep the sander moving

while the disc is turning; this avoids creating an unwanted depression that occurs if the machine remains in one spot while sanding.

6. Allow the weight of the sander to apply pressure on the abrasive disc. Do not push down on it to try to speed up the cut.

7. When it is necessary to shut off the sander, tilt it back so that the disc is clear of the floor, and then turn off the switch. Remember to empty the dust-collection bag frequently. Never leave dust in the

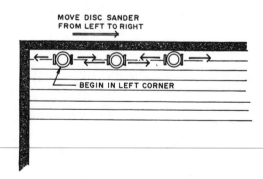

9-37 *Start sanding with the disc sander in the left corner and move to the right.*

9-38 *A small finish sander*. (Courtesy Porter-Cable Corporation)

sander bag overnight, because it can catch fire through spontaneous combustion. Always empty the dust bag before leaving the job at the end of the day.

Finishing the Sanding
The disc sander may leave some marks where it overlaps the drum-sanded area. These marks may be removed using a handheld power sander having a random orbital or straight-line motion (see **9-38**). Areas such as in a corner, where no sander can reach, may be smoothed with a hand scraper and hand-sanded (see **9-39**).

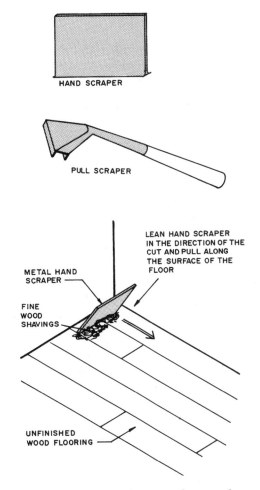

9-39 *Scrapers can be used to smooth areas that cannot be reached with sanders.*

10

Stairs

When the framing carpenters finish their work, they should leave stairwell openings framed as shown in **10-1**. Notice that the header and trimmer joists are doubled.

Stairs can be laid out and cut by the carpenter; or they can be bought completely cut to size, and then assembled and installed by the finish carpenter. If the carpenter builds stairs which are to be carpeted, they often have structurally sound softwood treads cut and fitted. If exposed, finished hardwood treads are required. These are usually bought from a building materials supplier and cut and fitted on the job. They are unfinished but completely machined, ready to install.

Types of Stairs

The commonly used types of stairs are **straight,** stairs with **landings** (**straight**, **L-shaped**, and **U-shaped**), and stairs with **winders**.

The straight stair is perhaps the most frequently used type. It consists of a straight run from one level to another (see **10-2**). Codes typically require stairs with a rise above a specified vertical distance, such as 12ft (3.6m), to place a landing about halfway up. Its purpose is to provide a break in the climb, giving a place to rest (see **10-3**). Landings are also used to change the direction of a stair as shown for the

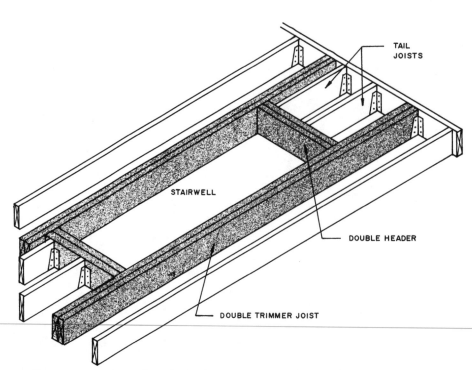

10-1   The stairwell opening is framed with double headers and stringers.

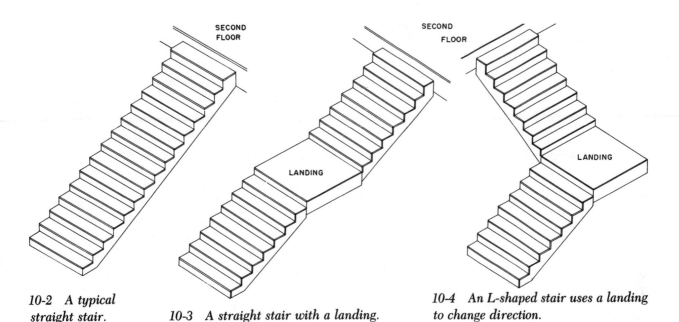

10-2 A typical straight stair.

10-3 A straight stair with a landing.

10-4 An L-shaped stair uses a landing to change direction.

10-5 An L-shaped stair using winders to turn the corner.

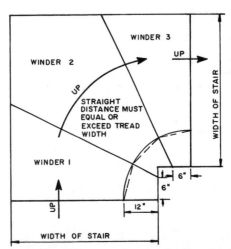

10-6 Typical winder specifications as found in building codes.

L-shape stairs in **10-4** and **10-5**. Since landings take considerable floor space, winders are sometimes used instead when space is tight. Winders, however, are difficult to use and are avoided whenever possible. The design of winders, as always, must meet local codes. A typical example is shown in **10-6**. U-shaped stairs are shown in **10-7**. This configuration requires the most floor space but permits the stairs to reverse direction.

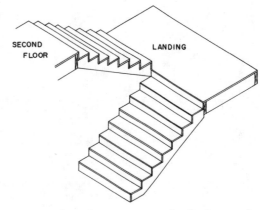

10-7 A U-shaped stair permits the direction of travel to be reversed.

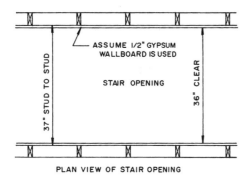

10-8 *Stair width is regulated by local building code.*

Building Codes

Often the stair design is detailed on the working drawings by the designer. It must be designed to meet local building codes. Sometimes the specifications for the stairs are not available on the drawing, and the owner relies on the carpenter to design and build them. Therefore it is important that the carpenter know the requirements specified for the stairs in the code and be able to consult the code for any changes or updates.

Following are examples of *typical* requirements. As always, consult your local code.

1. **Stair Width**—36in (914mm) is required if the occupant load is 50 occupants or less. In private, single-family dwellings the 36in (914mm) width is also the minimum. The width is defined as the clear distance inside the finished wall. To get clear 36in (914mm) width, the stairwell, must be framed wide enough to allow for the finish wall (see **10-8**).

2. **Handrail**—This is required on one side of a stair in single-family dwellings. If a stair has less than three risers, no handrail is required. The handrail can project a maximum of 3½in (89mm) from each side of the stair. The handrail must be continuous for the full length of the stair and extend 6in (15.2cm) beyond the top and bottom risers. It must be at least 30in (762mm) but not more than 34in (863mm) above the tread nosing. The handrail should be 1½ to 2in (38 to 50mm) in diameter and have at least a 1½in (38mm) space between the handrail and the wall.

3. **Railings**—36in (914mm) high for single-family dwelling units (see **10-9**).

4. **Head Room**—For single-family dwellings, there must be a 6'-8" (2032mm) clearance on major stairs. Some codes permit 6'-6" (1982mm) on minor stairs, such as basement stairs.

5. **Landings**—The dimension in the direction of travel must be equal to the width of the stair but not exceed 4'-0" (1220mm) on straight-run stairs. The vertical distance between landings should not be more than 12ft (3.6m) unless a landing is placed halfway up the stairs.

10-9 *Railings are required on stairs and landings and, as always, must meet code specifications.*

6. **Treads and Risers**—Single-family dwellings with less than 10 occupants can have a riser of not less then 4in (101mm) or more than 7 to 7¾in (178 to 196mm). The minimum tread depth is 9 to 11in (229 to 279mm) depending on the code used. All the risers should be the same size, and all treads should be the same size. Any variation can cause accidents. These requirements vary from one local code to another. Again, check your local building code.

The width of winders 12in (305mm) from the narrow side of the tread must equal the specified tread width, as shown in **10-6**. No part of the tread should be less than 6in (152mm) wide.

Parts of a Stair

The parts of a typical stair are shown in **10-10**. The names of the parts vary sometimes in different sections of the country. The **stringer** (also called a **carriage**) is the main structural member and should be of quality stock and free of large knots and other defects. The **kicker** is nailed to the subfloor and resists movement at the bottom of the stair. The **tread** is the horizontal board on which you step. The **riser** is a vertical board that encloses the stair.

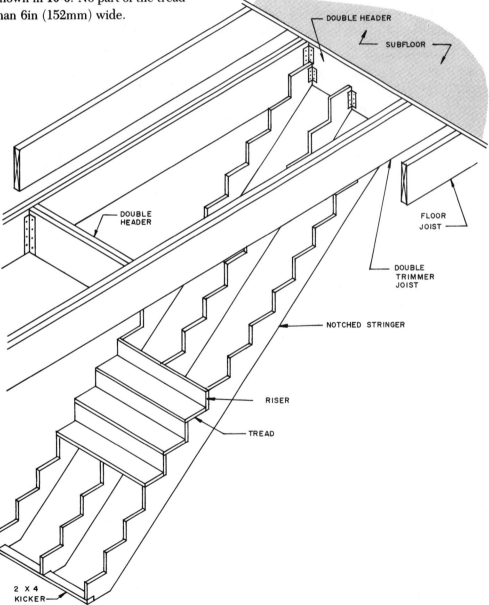

10-10 The parts of a straight stair.

A Typical Stair Working Design Drawing

The drawing in **10-11** is typical of what is found on working design drawings. It gives all the information needed by the carpenter to build the stairs. Factory-manufactured stairs sometimes have instructions sent with them to assist the carpenter. The drawing shows the plan view and a side view giving total rise, total run, and tread and riser data. Notice that there is one less tread than riser. This is because the floor at the top of the stair replaces one tread.

A typical working drawing for a stair with one side open is shown in **10-12**.

Occasionally the stair is designed with the top tread flush with the second floor as shown in **10-13**. When this is done, the stair stringer will have the same number of treads as risers and the total run will be longer because of the extra tread.

Figuring Treads and Risers

If the working drawings do not give the tread and riser data, then they must be calculated. The restrictions set by the building code, as always, must be observed. Begin by measuring the actual total rise as shown in **10-11**. Be certain to measure the *actual distance* on the job rather than relying on the distance given on the drawing. Select the rise, such as 7in (178mm). For this example, divide the total rise by 7in (178mm). This will give the number of risers. Usually it does not work out to a whole number. In **10-11** the total rise was 107in and, when divided by

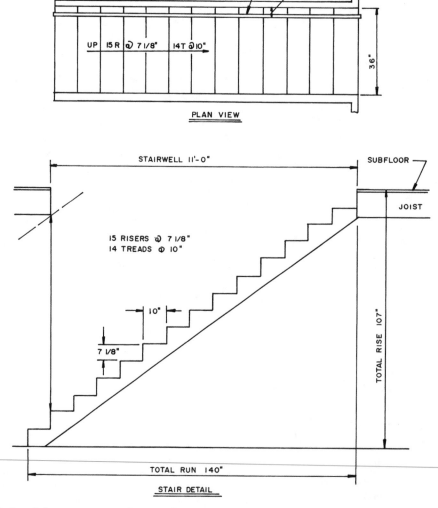

10-11   A typical detail drawing giving basic information for a stair to be built between two walls.

the riser, $107 \div 7$, gave 15.28 risers; to get a whole number of risers, try the whole numbers above and below the fractional number to see what rise they would require. Dividing 107 by 15 risers gives a rise of 7.13in; dividing 107 by 16 risers gives a rise of 6.68in. Most likely, 15 risers at 7.13in (7⅛in or 181mm) would be used. Since you have 15 risers you will have 14 treads. If the specified tread size is 10in (254mm) the total run will be 14 treads × 10in (254mm) or 140in (3556mm).

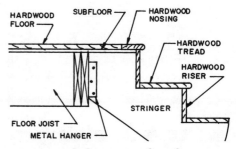

10-13 *A stair with the top tread on the stringer flush with the floor.*

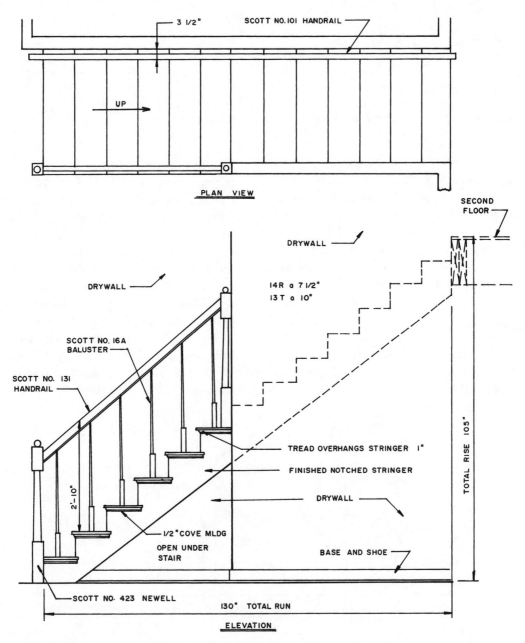

10-12 *A working drawing for a straight stair with one side open partway up.*

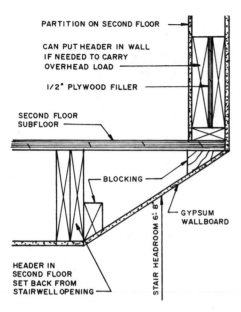

10-14   One way to provide needed headroom.

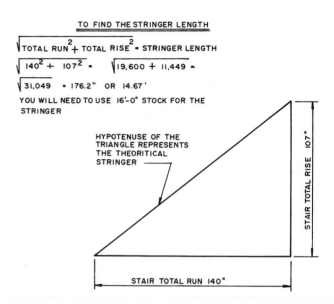

TO FIND THE STRINGER LENGTH

$\sqrt{\text{TOTAL RUN}^2 + \text{TOTAL RISE}^2} = \text{STRINGER LENGTH}$

$\sqrt{140^2 + 107^2} = \sqrt{19,600 + 11,449} =$

$\sqrt{31,049} = 176.2''$ OR 14.67'

YOU WILL NEED TO USE 16'-0" STOCK FOR THE STRINGER

10-15   How to calculate the approximate length of the stringer.

Now check to be certain you have the required headroom. Measure from the double header to a distance equal to the height of the tread directly below it, as shown in **10-11**. If all is going well, the clearance will be greater than the minimum 6'-8" (2032mm). If it is not possible to open the stairwell enough to get the required headroom, the header can be set back and the edge sloped, as shown in **10-14**.

Laying Out the Stringer

First it is necessary to calculate the approximate length of the stringer so that stock of the proper length can be secured. This is done by using the Pythagorean theorem, which is used to find the hypotenuse of a triangle (study **10-15**). To find the hypotenuse you take the square root of the sum of the squares of the other two sides of the triangle. Any pocket calculator will have a square root key to enable you to do this operation. In our example, the hypotenuse (carriage) was 14.68ft so you need 16ft stock. It is always best to get stock a little long, because so often the ends have splits that must be cut away. Douglas fir and yellow pine are strong and suitable for this.

To lay out the stringer, use a framing square. Put **stair gauges** on the riser and tread sizes, as shown in **10-16**. Stair gauges are small clamp-like devices fastened to the framing square. Begin the layout at the

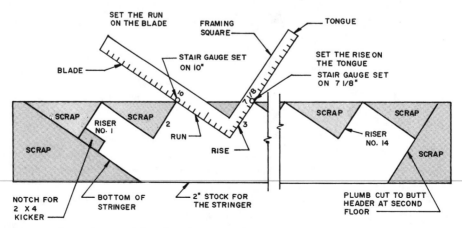

10-16   How to lay out the stringer with a framing square.

170

bottom by marking the bottom cut, then move the square and mark the next riser and tread. Continue up the stock until all have been marked. Lay out the kicker notch at the bottom side. This is usually a 2 × 4 (1½ × 3½in or 39 × 89mm) notch.

Most codes require that the stringer have 3½in (89mm) of uncut stock between the back edge of the carriage and the finish cut.

Dropping the Stringer

Before cutting the stringer, it is necessary to consider if and how much the carriage will need to be lowered to allow for conditions at the subfloor (study **10-17**).

Part 1 of 10-17 shows the stringer as laid out and cut. It is resting on the subfloor. The first rise must be reduced by an amount equal to the thickness of the tread board. If this were not done, the total rise for the first step would be 7in (178mm) plus the thickness of the tread. This makes the first rise greater than the rest and is *not acceptable*.

Part 2 shows the stringer shortened by a distance equal to the thickness of the tread board.

Part 3 shows the stringer on the subfloor with ¾in (19mm) thick finished wood flooring butting it. The stringer must be shortened by a distance equal to the thickness of the tread board minus the thickness of the finished wood flooring.

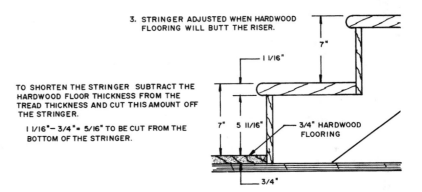

3. STRINGER ADJUSTED WHEN HARDWOOD FLOORING WILL BUTT THE RISER.

TO SHORTEN THE STRINGER SUBTRACT THE HARDWOOD FLOOR THICKNESS FROM THE TREAD THICKNESS AND CUT THIS AMOUNT OFF THE STRINGER.

1 1/16" - 3/4" = 5/16" TO BE CUT FROM THE BOTTOM OF THE STRINGER.

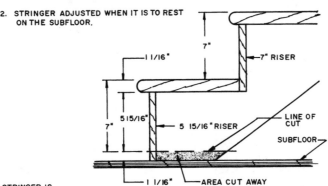

2. STRINGER ADJUSTED WHEN IT IS TO REST ON THE SUBFLOOR.

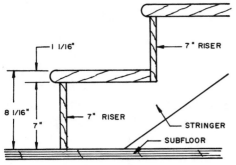

1. THE SITUATION BEFORE THE STRINGER IS ADJUSTED FOR FLOOR CONDITIONS.

NOTICE THE RISE OF THE FIRST TREAD, IF NOT CORRECTED, WOULD BE 8 1/16"

10-17 *How to figure the amount that the stringer needs to be shortened.*

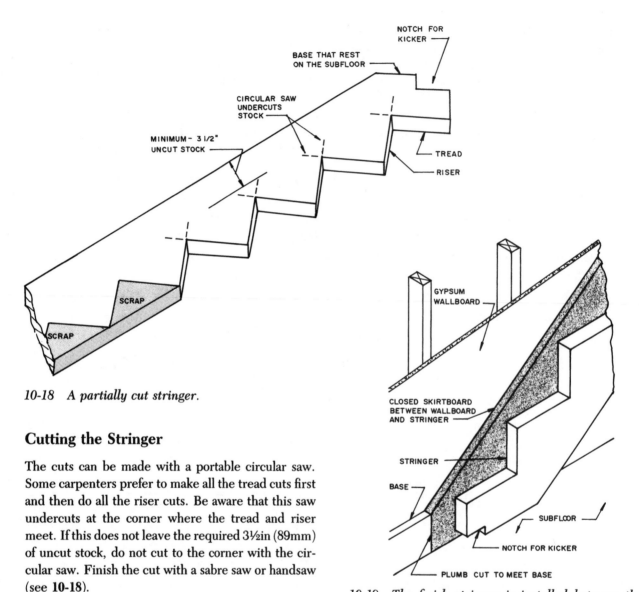

10-18 *A partially cut stringer.*

10-19 *The finish stringer is installed between the drywall and the stringer.*

Cutting the Stringer

The cuts can be made with a portable circular saw. Some carpenters prefer to make all the tread cuts first and then do all the riser cuts. Be aware that this saw undercuts at the corner where the tread and riser meet. If this does not leave the required 3½in (89mm) of uncut stock, do not cut to the corner with the circular saw. Finish the cut with a sabre saw or handsaw (see **10-18**).

Considerations Before Installing Stringers

Usually a stair will butt one or possibly two walls. These walls will eventually be covered with drywall or some other finish material. To protect the finish wall from damage, a notched or open **skirt board** is installed on each wall. The notched or open skirt board not only protects the wall from damage but covers the joint between the wall and stringer.

A closed skirtboard is shown in **10-19**. The skirt board fits between the drywall and the stringer and is nailed to the studs. The top edge of the closed skirt board is placed about 3 to 4in (approx. 7 to 10cm) above the stair tread nosing. The end of the skirt board at the floor is plumb-cut to butt the base.

The installation of such a construction often proceeds by installing the stringers long before any drywall is in place. The stringer is spaced away from the studs a distance needed to install drywall and the closed skirt board at a later date. Usually a 1½in (3.8cm) space is adequate for ½in (13mm) drywall plus a ¾in (19mm) closed skirt board (see **10-20**). The stringers are needed early during the construction to provide access to the second floor. Temporary treads of 2in (51mm) stock are nailed in place. These are removed after the drywall is in place and the finish carpenter is ready to install the closed skirt board, treads, and risers.

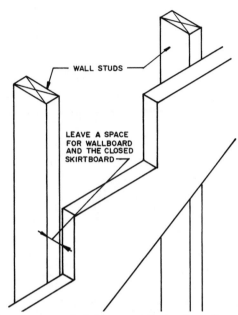

10-20   *A space is left between the studs and stringer for drywall and the finish stringer.*

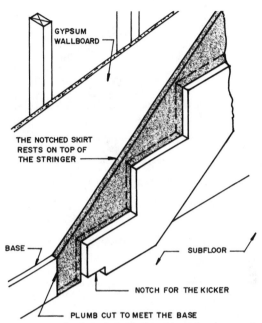

10-21   *A notched skirt board is placed on top of the stringer.*

Another technique is to use a notched skirt board which sits on top of the stringer as shown in **10-21**. A gap for the drywall is left between the studs and the stringer next to the wall. A gap of ¾in (19mm) is adequate for ½in (13mm) drywall. Adjust to suit other thicknesses of finish wall material.

Installing the Stringers

Generally the stringer is designed to butt the double header on the stairwell opening and drop down a distance equal to one riser (see **10-22**). If the second floor

is to have a wood flooring over the subfloor, this drop would have to allow for that even though the finished wood flooring has not yet been installed.

There are a number of ways to install the stringers. One method uses metal joist hanger straps that are nailed to the header and to the back edge of the stringer (see **10-23**). The strap is usually 18 to 24in (approx. 46 to 61cm) long. Since the stringers have little side support, blocking is nailed between them and the header.

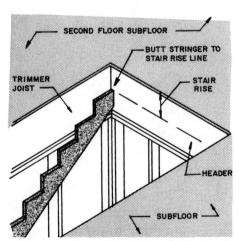

10-22   *Measure down from the subfloor to locate a line representing the stair rise.*

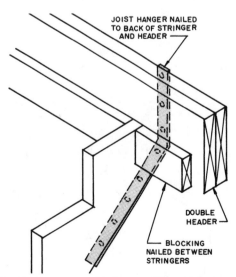

10-23   *Stringers can be hung with metal straps.*

173

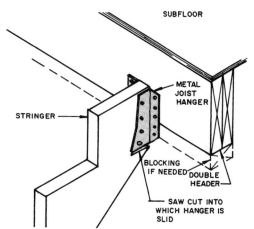

10-24 *Stringers can be hung with metal joist hangers.*

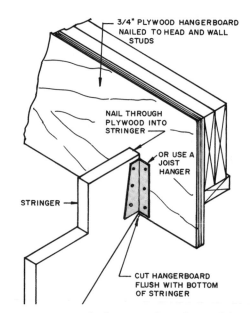

10-25 *Stringers can be hung with a plywood hangerboard.*

Another method uses metal joist hangers as shown in **10-24**. The stringer will need a relief cut to permit it to slip on the hanger. The hanger is nailed to the stringer and to the header.

A ¾in (19mm) thick plywood hangerboard can be used instead of metal joist hangers as shown in **10-25**. It is nailed to the header and to the wall studs if there is a wall below the header. The stringer can be secured by nailing through the plywood into the butting edge of the stringer. Some prefer to use the metal joist hangers. The hangerboard should run up to the top of the header and be cut flush with the bottom of the butting stringer.

Often there is a wall directly below the double header as shown in **10-26**. In such a case the top plate and additional blocking serve to back up the stringers. In this instance a wood ledger can be nailed to the wall and the stringer notched around it.

There are times when the top tread is designed to be flush with the second floor as shown in **10-13**. In

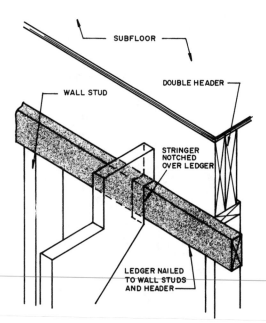

10-26 *Stringers can be hung on a ledger.*

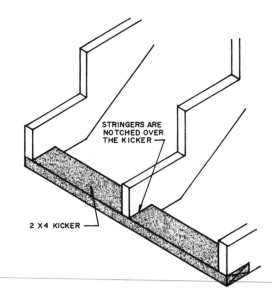

10-27 *Kickers are used to hold the bottom of the stringer.*

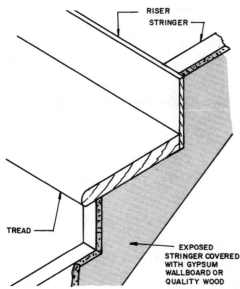

10-28 *The exposed stringer is covered with a finishing material.*

this situation the top end of the stringer fully butts the header and can be secured with metal hangers or a ledger.

The bottom end of the stringer is notched to sit on a kicker that is nailed to the subfloor. Toenail the stringer to the kicker (see **10-27**).

Treads and Risers for Carpeted Stairs

If stairs are to be carpeted, the treads and risers can be cut from ¾in (19mm) plywood. Some carpenters prefer to use 1⅛in (28mm) plywood for the treads. This decision must be made early on as the stair is planned, because it will influence the design of the stringer. Usually the drywall and skirt are in place before the tread and risers are installed. The treads and risers should be carefully cut square and fit close to, but not touch, the skirt. The small gap will be covered by the carpet and will eliminate a possible source of squeaks caused by the tread rubbing on the skirt board. If one side of the stair is to be exposed, the stringer will be covered by a finish skirt or drywall as shown in **10-28**.

Begin installation by gluing and nailing the risers first (see **10-29**). They can be nailed with 8d finishing nails that are set and covered. This is important as these are installed to take any bow out of the stringers. Some carpenters will install the bottom riser first, then the top riser, then move down a few to install several in the center to pull the stringers into line.

Finally install the tread boards with three 8d or 10d finishing nails into each carriage. Apply an adhesive to the top edge of the riser and the stringer before nailing. This will help reduce possible squeaks (see **10-30**).

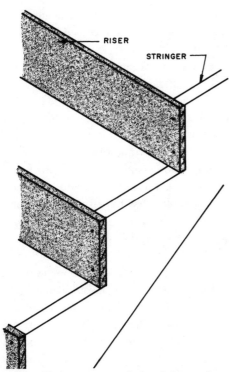

10-29 *Install the risers with finishing nails.*

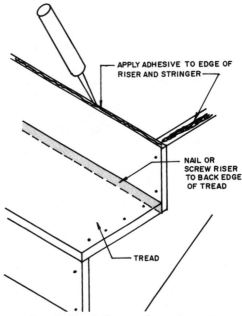

10-30 *Glue and nail the treads to the stringer. Plywood risers and treads are to be covered with carpet.*

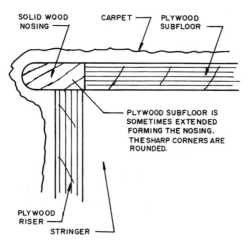

10-31 *Framing the top of the stair when the stair and landing will be covered with carpet.*

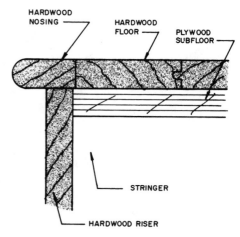

10-32 *Framing the top of the stair when hardwood treads and risers are used with a hardwood floor.*

Conditions at the top of the stair will vary. If the stair and second floor is to be carpeted, it will be framed as shown in **10-31**. The nosing will be the same as that used on the stair. However, sometimes the nosing is omitted on the stair.

If the second floor and stair are to be exposed hardwood, it can be framed as shown in **10-32**. The nosing is hardwood and overhangs the hardwood riser the same amount as the treads. The hardwood floor butts the stair nosing.

Another factor to consider at the top of the stair is that the nosing on the landing or second floor must be notched to receive the skirt as shown in **10-33**.

Treads and Risers for Hardwood Stairs

Hardwood treads and risers are available from stair parts manufacturers. Once received they will have to be cut to fit. Oak is the most commonly used wood. The risers are ¾in (19mm) thick and the treads are usually 1¹⁄₁₆in (27mm) thick.

There are several ways these can be installed. The riser may be nailed to the stringer with the end grain permitted to show or the finished skirt could be mitred and the riser mitred, forming a corner where no end grain is visible. Another approach is to mitre the riser and a bracket to hide the end grain (see **10-34**).

The mitred skirt has the riser cut on a 45-degree angle to meet the mitre on the end of the riser. The skirt is laid out much the same as the stringer except that the riser is extended beyond the edge of the riser cut on the stringer at a 45-degree angle (see **10-35**). Therefore, the mitred skirt layout would be like that shown in **10-36**. Cutting the riser mitre requires careful, accurate work. The exposed edge must be sharp and free from chips. Some cut the mitre slightly less than 45 degrees. The gap on top is covered by the tread (see **10-37**).

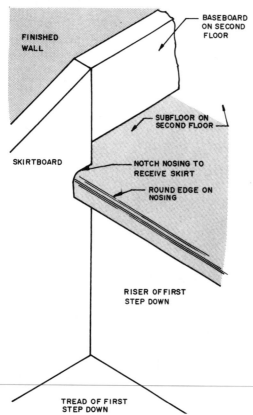

10-33 *The top nosing must be notched to receive the skirt board.*

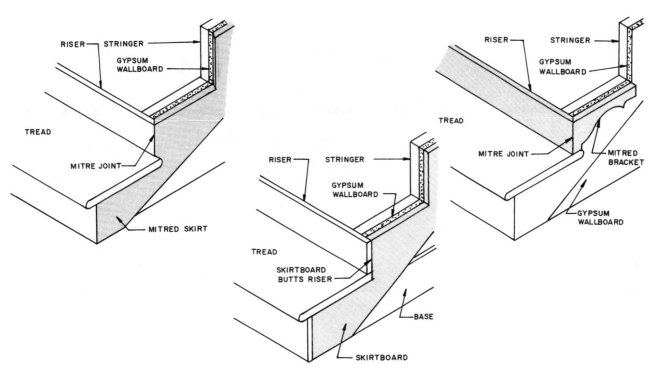

10-34 *Various ways to assemble hardwood risers on a stair.*

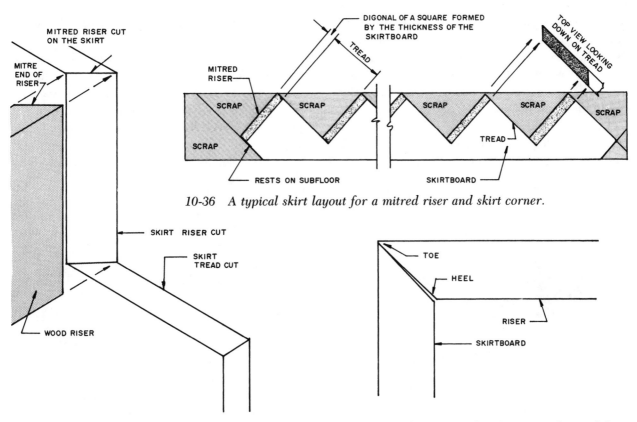

10-36 *A typical skirt layout for a mitred riser and skirt corner.*

10-35 *The skirt and riser can be mitred to conceal the end grain of the riser.*

10-37 *Cut the mitre so that the toe touches and there is a small gap at the heel.*

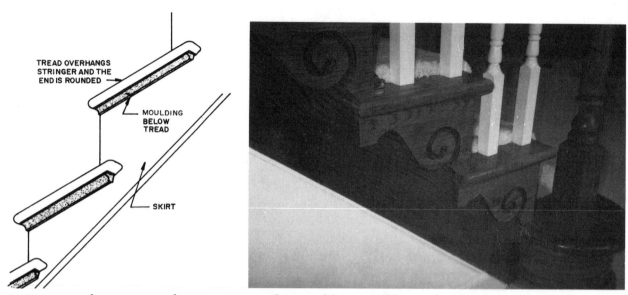

TREAD OVERHANGS
STRINGER AND THE
END IS ROUNDED

MOULDING
BELOW
TREAD

SKIRT

10-38   *A tread on an exposed stringer can overhang and have moulding or brackets below the tread.*

Installation details will vary but those shown in **10-34** are typical. In one case the stair is open below so that the mitred skirt is secured directly to the stringer. Some place ¼in (6mm) spacers between them to allow for adjusting the mitres. If there is a wall below the stair, gypsum drywall is nailed to the stringer, and the mitred skirt board is installed over this. The tread should bear on the stringer, not the skirt, so that the skirt is set a little below the tread. The gap is covered with a small moulding or bracket (see **10-38**).

The tread overhang can be return-mitred or shaped. The shaped return is cut with a router, and care must be taken to avoid splitting the end of the tread. Some prefer to shape from each end towards the center or clamp a backup block and shape towards it (see **10-39**).

The mitred return is more difficult to make. It should be made before the tread is cut to length. Begin by laying out the cuts on the treads (see **10-40**). Carefully cut to the lines. A fine-tooth blade is required so that a smooth, clip-free edge is left. Usually the returns are not installed on the treads until they are secured to the stringer and the newel posts are in place. The mitred returns are glued and nailed in place (see **10-41**). The back end is also mitred and a small return block finishes off the installation.

When installing the hardwood treads and risers, they are butted against the skirt. When notched stringers are used, the ends must be clearly cut and fit squarely against the skirt. Over time this may produce a small, visible gap. To avoid this, a housed stringer could be used. Glue and nail or screw the hardwood treads in place. The screw heads can be covered with wood plugs.

Building Landings

The actual framing of a landing will vary some with the specific installation. In all cases it must be very sound and well constructed. The following examples are typical.

A landing for an L-shaped stair should be as wide and deep as the finished width of the stair. Generally it is in the middle of the rise, but this is not neces-

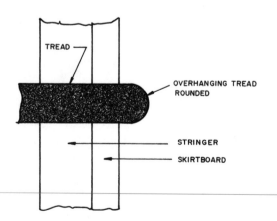

TREAD

OVERHANGING TREAD
ROUNDED

STRINGER

SKIRTBOARD

10-39   *The overhang of a stair tread can be shaped with a router.*

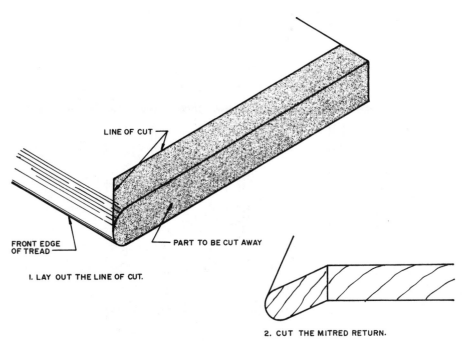

I. LAY OUT THE LINE OF CUT.

2. CUT THE MITRED RETURN.

10-40   Laying out and cutting the mitred return on the end of the tread.

sarily so. It can occur as needed, and this is determined by the floor space available.

The design of the landing and the two flights of stairs is the same as described for straight flights. Remember that the landing actually replaces a tread in the total distance. Therefore, figure the tread and riser sizes as described earlier for a straight stair. At one of the tread locations, position the landing. The treads and risers in both flights should be the same size.

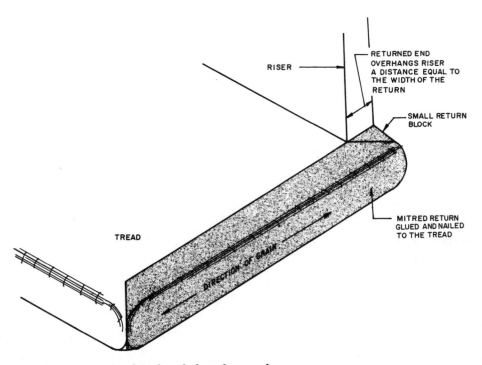

10-41   The mitred return is glued and nailed to the tread.

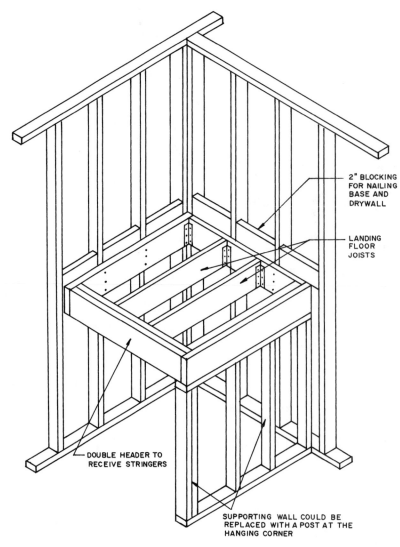

2" BLOCKING
FOR NAILING
BASE AND
DRYWALL

LANDING
FLOOR
JOISTS

DOUBLE HEADER TO
RECEIVE STRINGERS

SUPPORTING WALL COULD BE
REPLACED WITH A POST AT THE
HANGING CORNER

10-42   *Typical framing for the landing of an L-shaped stair.*

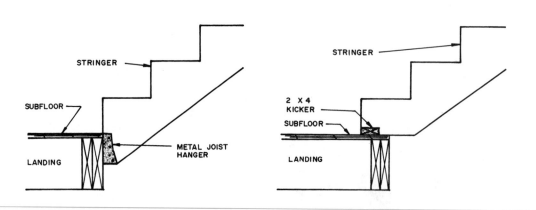

STRINGER

SUBFLOOR

LANDING

METAL JOIST
HANGER

STRINGER

2 X 4
KICKER

SUBFLOOR

LANDING

STRINGER MOUNTED WITH A METAL JOIST HANGER   STRINGER RESTS ON THE LANDING

10-44   *Two ways to mount a stringer on a landing.*

The landing is built much the same as framing the floor (see **10-42**). Usually 2×8 joists 16in (40.6cm) O.C. are used on small landings. They are nailed to the studs and hung with metal joist hangers. The header against which the stringers rest is often doubled. Posts or a wall are used to support corners without a wall to hold them (see **10-43**).

The tops of the stringers are secured to the landing as described earlier. The bottom of the second set of stringers can be fastened to the landing as shown in **10-44**.

Remember to allow space between the studs and stringer for the drywall and finish stringer, as described earlier.

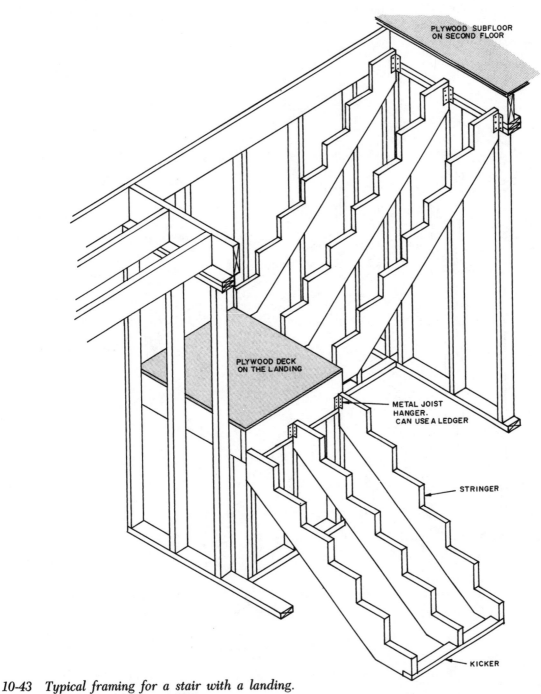

10-43 Typical framing for a stair with a landing.

Framing for a landing on a U-shaped stair is shown in **10-45**. It is framed as described for the smaller landing. A supporting wall or posts beneath the unsupported double joist add greatly to the stiffness of the landing.

Building Winders

Winders are used in the same way as landings, which is to enable a stair to make a 90-degree or 180-degree turn (see **10-46**). Before designing the winders be certain to check your local building code. Typical requirements are given earlier in this chapter.

Generally three triangular treads are used to turn a 90-degree corner as shown in **10-47**. This permits the stair to rise the required distance, turn a corner, and take considerably less floor space than if a landing were used.

To begin, calculate the number of treads and risers as discussed earlier. Since you know it takes three

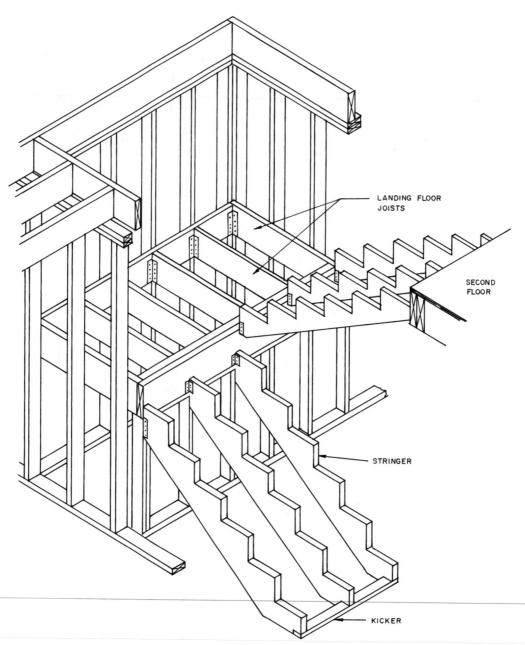

10-45 *Typical framing for a U-shaped stair.*

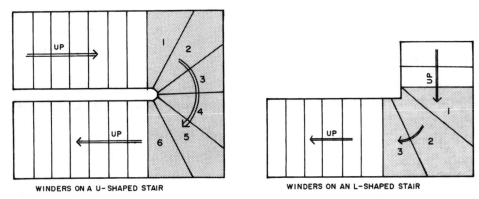

10-46   *Winders can be used to turn a stair around a corner.*

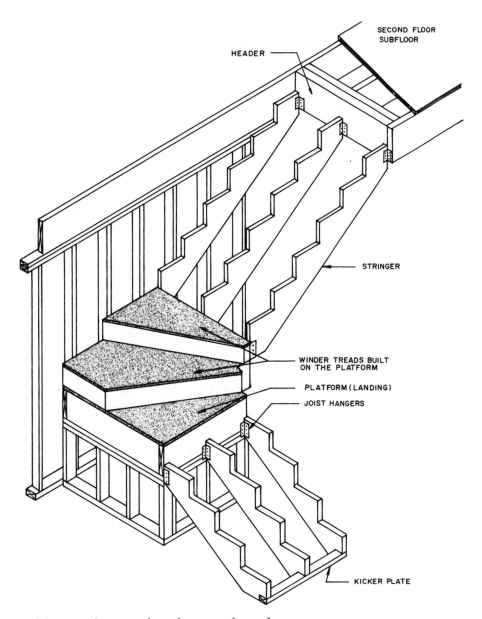

10-47   *Typical framing for an L-shaped stair with winders.*

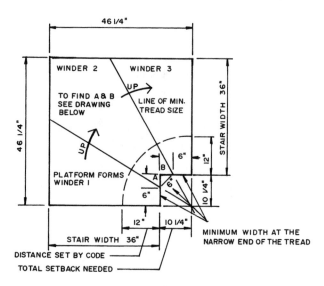

1. THE FINISHED WINDER DRAWING.

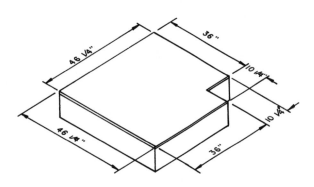

2. HOW TO FIND THE UNKOWN DISTANCES A AND B.

TO FIND THE LENGTH SIDES A AND B
USE THE PYTHAGOREAN THEOREM

$SIDE\ A^2 + SIDE\ B^2 = HYPOTENUSE^2\ (6^2)$

$A^2 + B^2 = 36$

$A^2 = 18 \quad B^2 = 18$

$\sqrt{18} = 4.25$

$A = 4.25 \quad B = 4.25$

MINIMUM WIDTH AT NARROW
END OF TREAD

3. THE FINISHED PLATFORM FOR
THE THREE TREAD WINDER.

10-48 How to lay out the winders for an L-shaped stair.

treads to turn the corner, the remaining number are divided between the two flights. Usually space requirements are such that the first flight is shorter than the second, but this is not mandatory. Notice in **10-47** that the installation begins by constructing a landing as described earlier. Then two triangular treads (the winders) are built on top of this, and the second flight joins the top or third winder. The basic construction is the same as described earlier in this chapter.

Laying Out the Winders

The layout of the winders is an important part of the job because, if not done properly, building codes may be violated.

After the platform is complete, it will have a ¾in (19mm) plywood subfloor. The winders can be laid out on this surface. The exact procedure will depend

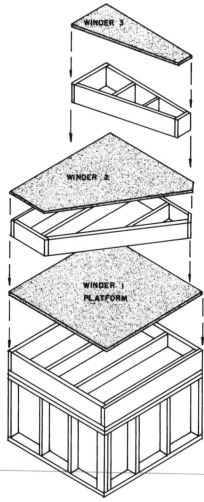

10-49 One way to frame a winder for an L-shaped stair.

on your local building code. It should be noted that most codes require a winder to be a minimum of 6in (152mm) wide at the narrow end and equal to the width of the tread, 12in (305mm), in the middle. This will require that for a 36in (915mm) wide stair the platform will have to be 46¼in (1174mm) as shown in **10-48**. The width of the stair (36in or 915mm) is laid out and the 6in (152mm) narrow end is drawn. To find the sides of the triangle forming the end of the second tread use the Pythagorean theorem as follows:

$$\sqrt{\text{side } \mathbf{A}^2 + \text{side } \mathbf{B}^2} = 6 \text{ (required small end)}$$
$$\sqrt{36} = 6$$
$$\mathbf{A}^2 = 18 \quad \mathbf{B}^2 = 18$$
$$\mathbf{A} \text{ and } \mathbf{B} = \sqrt{18} \text{ or } 4¼\text{in}$$

Building the Winders

While the winders can be built using carriages, as explained for straight stairs, it is easier to build each as separate units and mount one on top of the other. Typical construction details are shown in **10-49**. The stock used to form each winder unit is 2in (50mm) thick and must be ripped to width to get the correct riser height. For example, if you want a 7in (178mm) rise and use a ¾in (19mm) plywood tread, the 2in (50mm) stock must be cut 6¼in (158mm) wide. Assemble by gluing and nailing. Be certain the nails are flush or a little below the tread surface so that they do not penetrate the carpet.

Installing the Stringers

Install the stringers as explained earlier. Metal joist hangers or ledgers are commonly used (see **10-47**).

Housed Stringer Stairs

Housed stringers have dadoes cut in their sides into which the treads and risers are inserted. Usually these are bought machined to fit a particular job. However, a carpenter could lay out and route the dadoes on the job. The dadoes are typically routed ⅜in (9.5mm) into the stringer.

A housed stringer is shown in **10-50**. It is used when the stair is enclosed by walls on both sides.

Assembling Stairs with Housed Stringers

This discussion assumes the housed stringers are made by a stair manufacturer who also supplies the treads, risers, and wedges.

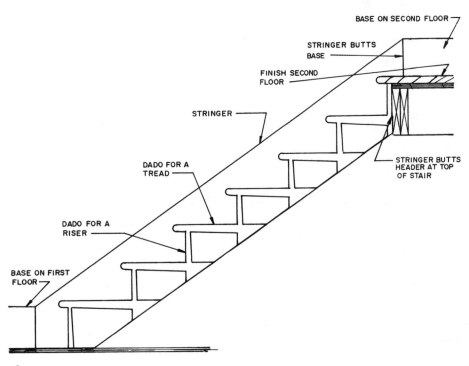

10-50 A housed stringer.

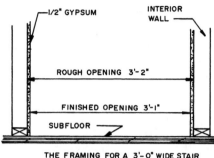

THE FRAMING FOR A 3'-0" WIDE STAIR
THAT WILL GIVE A 1/2" GAP ON EACH
SIDE AS SHOWN BELOW.

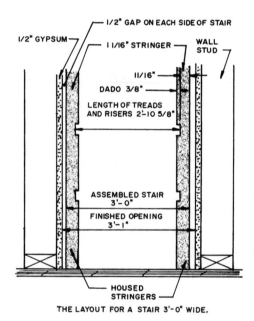

THE LAYOUT FOR A STAIR 3'-0" WIDE.

10-51   Determining the length of treads and risers for a stair with housed stringers.

1. Determine the length of the treads and risers. The factors involved are shown in **10-51**. Measure the distance between the studs forming the stairwell. For our example we will use a 3ft (91.5cm) wide stair. Then subtract twice the thickness of the finished wall covering material. Notice that the rough opening minus the gypsum drywall leaves a 1in (25mm) space for positioning the 3'-0" (91.4cm) assembled stair between the walls.

2. Examine the housed stringers. Typically they are 1 1/16in (27mm) thick and the dado is ⅜in (9.5mm) deep. The length of the treads and risers is equal to 3'-0" (91.4cm) minus 1⅜in (3.4cm) or 2'-10⅝" (88cm). The amount subtracted is found by sub-

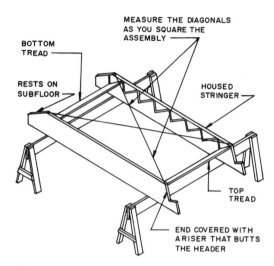

10-52   Begin assembly by installing top and bottom treads.

tracting the depth of the dado from the thickness of the stringer and doubling it (two stringers). Refer to **10-51**, step 2.

3. Check the treads and risers for width and length. Cut to size, as necessary. Notice that the top riser is 1⅜in (35mm) longer than the rest, because it is nailed to the face of the stringer at the top of the stair.

4. Place the stringers on sawhorses, as shown in **10-52**. Install the top tread first. Apply adhesive to the dado, and insert the tread so that the front nosing fits snugly into the rounded end of the dado (see **10-53**).

5. The treads are held in place with glued wedges (see **10-54**). Now apply glue to the wedge, and drive it in place between the bottom of the tread and the edge of the dado. Check the front side of the stair (which is facing the floor) to be certain the tread nosing is in place, before you set the wedge tightly in place. This may involve tapping the tread some and then tapping the wedge until the joint on the front is closed. Be certain the back edge of the tread is in line with the front of the dado to receive the riser. Drive several 8d box nails through the stringer into the edge of the tread. Be certain one is in the front nosing. These serve to pull the tread fully into the dado.

6. Now install the bottom tread in the same manner.

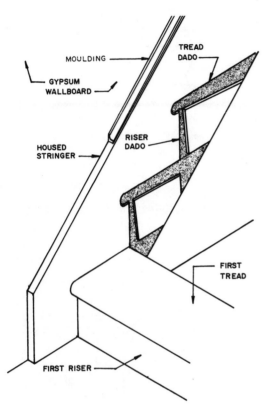

10-53   *Insert the tread in the dado.*

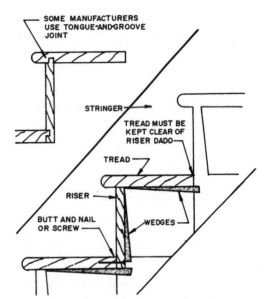

10-54   *Glue and wedge the treads and risers to the stringer.*

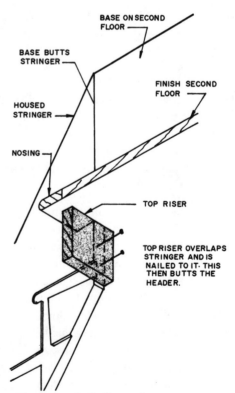

10-55   *The top end of a housed stringer is cut square to receive the riser and butt the header.*

7. Check to be certain that the stringers are straight and the rectangular unit formed is square. Squareness can be checked by measuring the diagonal from opposite corners (see **10-52**). If one diagonal is longer than the other, it is necessary to apply pressure on the long diagonal to move the unit square. It may be necessary to nail blocks to the sawhorses to hold the stringers in a square position.

8. Install the other treads as just described. Some carpenters prefer to install the next one in the center to help hold the unit square and keep the stringers straight.

9. Install the top riser. Remember that it is longer than the rest, because it is face-nailed to the back of the stringers (see **10-55**).

10. Install the bottom riser. It may be narrower than the rest because of conditions at the floor.

11. Install all the other risers. They are set in the dadoes, glued, and wedged the same as the treads. Nail through the bottom edge of the riser into the back edge of the tread and through the stringers into the end of the riser with 8d box nails. Space the nails about 8in (approx. 20cm) apart. Be certain that the joint between the back of the tread and riser is closed.

187

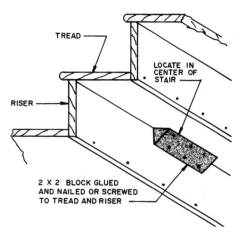

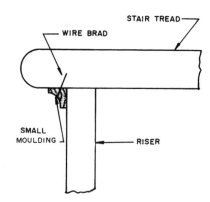

10-56 *Glue blocks can reduce possible squeaks.*

10-57 *A small moulding can be nailed below the tread.*

12. Nail or screw glue blocks about 6in (approx. 15cm) long joining the tread and riser in the center of the stair (see **10-56**). This helps stiffen the unit and reduces squeaking.

13. Turn the assembled stair over, and nail a small moulding under the nosing. Nail with 4d wire brads (see **10-57**).

Installing the Assembled Stair

The assembled stair is long and heavy. It will take several people to work it into position. If the gypsum drywall has not been applied to the walls yet, it enables workers to get underneath the stair to hold it or to provide temporary bracing. It would be very difficult to install these otherwise.

1. Slide the stair into the stair opening, and raise it up placing the top riser against the header on the second floor. Adjust it so that it is in the center of the rough opening, leaving room on each side for the gypsum drywall. The top edge of the top dado should be level with the top of the furnished floor on the second level (see **10-58**). Shim the stringer or trim it, as necessary, to get this level.

    If the first floor is to have a hardwood floor that has not been installed yet, set the stringers on wood blocks that are the same thickness as the wood floor.

2. Join the stringers to the header with metal joist hangers or a ledger, as explained for notched carriage stairs.

3. Some carpenters also nail the stringers to the wall studs; this will stiffen the stair and is done after the

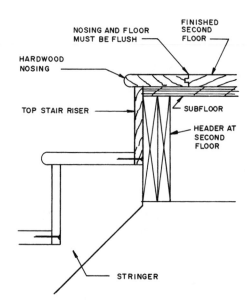

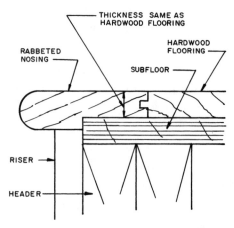

10-58 *Adjust the length of the stringer to get the nosing and finished floor to be flush.*

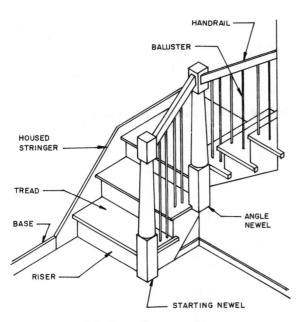

10-59 *Typical balustrade construction.*

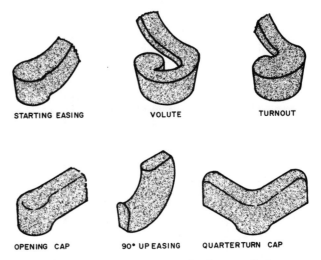

10-60 *Typical fittings designed to be installed on top of the newel post and change the direction of the rail.*

drywall is in place. Use finishing nails and set the heads so that they can be concealed.

4. Secure the bottom end of the stringers to the subfloor or finished hardwood floor. This can be 2×4 blocking nailed to the carriages and to the subfloor. This is located behind the riser.

5. Finally, install the top rabbeted nosing into the top dado. It should be joined securely to the top floor subfloor or the top of the header (depending on how the second floor will finally be finished).

6. After the drywall or other finished wall covering is installed, cut and nail a moulding on top of the stringer to cover the gap between the wall and the stringer.

Stock Stair Parts

Stock stair parts are available from lumber and millwork materials suppliers. They have available a wide range of sizes and designs from which to choose. This includes **dadoed stringers**, **treads**, **risers**, **rails**, **fittings**, **balusters**, and **newels**.

Stock Balustrades

A balustrade includes the rail, balusters, and newels (see **10-59**). The handrail is manufactured in straight lengths with a variety of fittings used to turn corners and change levels. Some of the fittings used to change direction are shown in **10-60**. These are designed to fit on top of the newel post. Examples are shown in **10-61** and **10-62**.

10-61 *This fitting permits the handrail to slope down the stair as it descends to a lower level.*

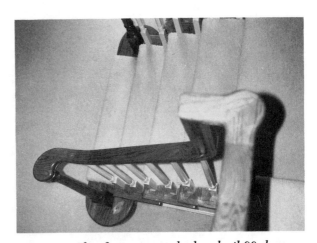

10-62 *This fitting turns the handrail 90 degrees.*

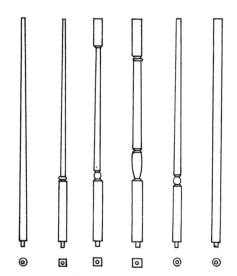

BALUSTERS – 1 1/4" DIAMETER TYPICAL
LENGTHS 31", 34", 36", 39", 41".

10-63   A few of the baluster designs available.

10-64   An angle newel is used in the balustrade when the stair changes angles.

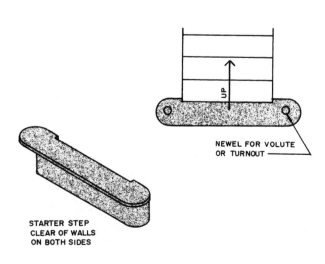

UP

NEWEL FOR VOLUTE OR TURNOUT

STARTER STEP CLEAR OF WALLS ON BOTH SIDES

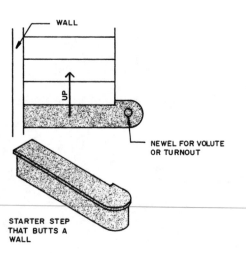

WALL

UP

NEWEL FOR VOLUTE OR TURNOUT

STARTER STEP THAT BUTTS A WALL

10-65   Typical starting steps.

10-66   A starting newel rests on a starting step.

The balusters are vertical rods running from the bottom of the rail to the treads. They are inserted into holes drilled in each tread. Typical designs are shown in **10-63**. The balustrade begins at the bottom of the stair with a large post called a newel. If the stair changes directions, an angle newel is used, as shown in **10-59** and **10-64**. These parts are very expensive, and only the most experienced finish carpenters install them. Often this is an area of specialization, and a stair builder is called to install the finished stair parts.

Other Stock Parts

Various types of starting steps are available, as shown in **10-65**. Applications of these are illustrated in **10-66** and **10-67**. Notice in **10-67** the use of brackets. These are made from ¼in (6mm) thick wood and are nailed to the stringer. They cover a possible gap between the tread and stringer and provide a decorative feature.

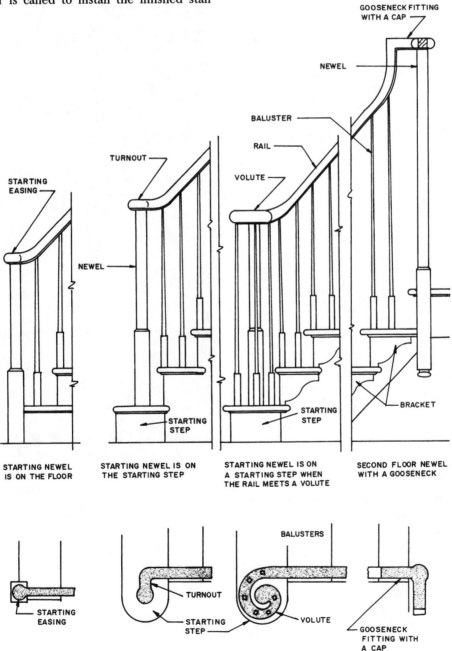

10-67 Typical over-the-post balustrade construction.

Two Balustrade Systems

Stock parts for balustrade construction are available for post-to-post and over-the-post construction. These are shown in **10-67** and **10-68**. Starting steps are required for over-the-post systems when the balustrade begins with a volute or turnout rail fitting. A finished over-the-post stair is shown in **10-69**.

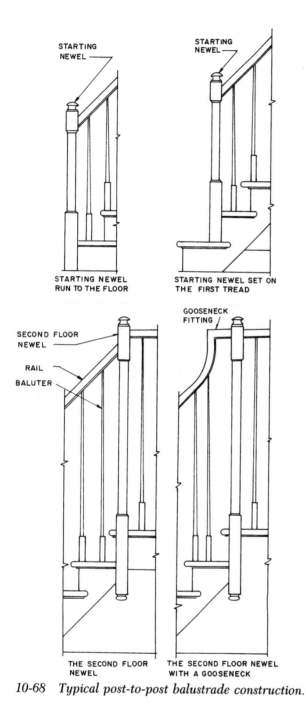

STARTING NEWEL

STARTING NEWEL

STARTING NEWEL RUN TO THE FLOOR

STARTING NEWEL SET ON THE FIRST TREAD

SECOND FLOOR NEWEL

RAIL

BALUTER

GOOSENECK FITTING

THE SECOND FLOOR NEWEL

THE SECOND FLOOR NEWEL WITH A GOOSENECK

10-68   Typical post-to-post balustrade construction.

10-69   A finished L-shaped stair with an over-the-post balustrade.

11

Installing Gypsum Drywall

Gypsum sheet products are used to finish interior ceilings and walls, essentially replacing the labor-intensive plaster lath of an earlier era. They consist of a gypsum core sandwiched between two sheets of special paper. The product is strong and highly fire resistant.

The most frequently used drywall is in sheets 4ft (122cm) wide and 8ft (244cm) long. However 9, 10, 12, and 14ft (274, 305, 366, and 427cm) lengths are available. The standard thicknesses are ⅜, ½, and ⅝in (10, 12, and 16mm). The thicker the sheet, the less likely it will sag after installation and the higher the fire-resistance rating. The long edges are tapered, forming a shallow valley when the sheets are butted (see **11-1**). This is filled with joint compound and tape to produce a smooth, concealed joint. The 4ft (122cm) ends of the sheets usually are cut square, which, when used to form an exposed joint, are harder to conceal with joint compound and tape.

Types of Gypsum Drywall

There are a variety of gypsum panels each with special properties. Those commonly used in finishing residential walls are regular panels which have **tapered, long side edges.** Type X panels have a specially formulated core that increases its ability to resist fire.

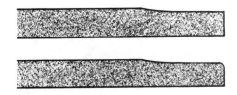

11-1 The long edges of some gypsum wallboard panels are tapered.

Another type has an aluminum-foil backing which forms a vapor retarder when applied with the foil backing next to the framing. A water-resistant panel is used as a base for the adhesive application of ceramic and plastic tile wall coverings. The paper covering of this type is chemically treated to resist the penetration of water; these are typically used on walls in bathrooms and kitchens. Predecorated standard panels are also available with a vinyl wall covering on the exposed face in a wide range of colors and designs. A variety of gypsum predecorated mouldings are available to cover the joints in predecorated-panel installations.

Joint Compounds

Drywall joint compound is used to conceal the butt joints between panels and the heads of the nails or screws used to secure the panels to the studs or joists. It is available in powdered or premixed form. The powdered type is mixed with water to the proper consistency. Premixed compounds are ready to use. They have the advantage of immediate use, correct consistency, and are free of lumps and air bubbles that often are found in site-mixed powdered compounds.

Powder type compounds are available in a number of setting times ranging from 20 to 360 minutes. They can be stored for long periods in dry storage and cold conditions. However, they should be brought to normal room temperature before mixing.

Premixed compounds are available in several types. The taping compound is used for embedding the tape. The topping compound is used for the second and third finish coats over the taping compound. An all-purpose compound can be used for taping, finishing, and texturing the surface.

193

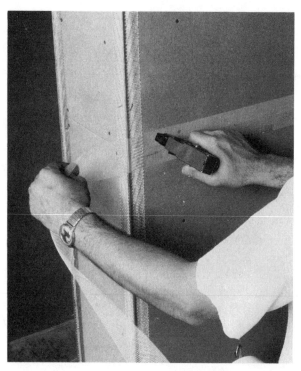

11-2 *Fibreglass mesh tape can be stapled to gypsum wallboard.* (Courtesy United States Gypsum Company)

Joint-Reinforcing Materials

The most commonly used joint reinforcement is a **reinforced, perforated paper tape** that can be seen in **11-30** under the section on taping the joints. It is 2in (51mm) wide and is available in rolls up to 500ft (139.5m) long. It has a crease in the center, making it easy to fold for reinforcing corners. It is bonded to the wall panels by the joint compound.

A **fibreglass, leno-weave mesh tape** is also available. There are several types of these. One type has a pressure-sensitive adhesive back and is pressed on the drywall. Another type is installed by stapling (see **11-2**). For general residential construction, paper tape is used and provides adequate joint control.

Corners are reinforced with galvanized steel or plastic **corner beads.** Several types are available. One has a bulb-like corner with mesh flanges and another has solid metal flanges with prepunched holes. They may be installed by nailing or stapling through the drywall into the stud (see **11-3** and **11-4**). A flexible

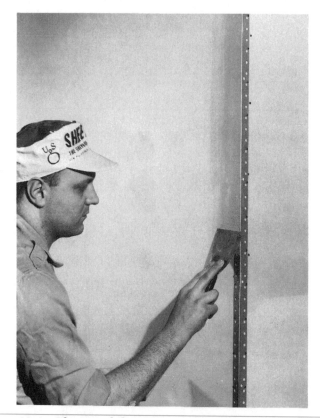

11-4 *This metal flange corner bead is nailed to the studs through prepunched holes. It is then covered with joint compound.* (Courtesy United States Gypsum Company)

11-3 *This mesh-type metal corner bead is being nailed through the wallboard into the stud.* (Courtesy United States Gypsum Company)

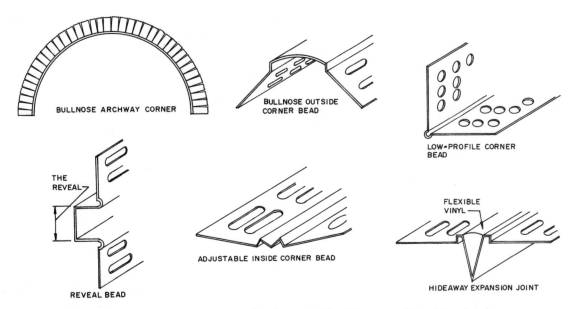

11-5 A *few of the many types of plastic corner beads available.* (Courtesy Trim-Tex, Inc.)

metal corner tape is available that is folded forming the bead. It can be used on curved corners. A few of the plastic corner beads that are available are shown in **11-5**. They are used for straight and curved corners and may be nailed or stapled. The reveal bead provides a ½in (13mm) deep reveal. The width of the reveal can be ½, ¾ or 1in (13, 19, 25mm). A hideaway expansion joint bead has a vinyl membrane over the V-shaped expansion area. Drywall compound is laid up to the edge but not over the vinyl membrane.

A bullnose corner bead gives the corner a round appearance. A bullnose archway corner bead has the nailing flange notched, permitting it to bend around the curved arch. The low-profile corner bead is most commonly used in residential construction. It provides a small but damage-resistant corner. The adjustable inside and outside corner beads will flex to cover corners on angles from 90 degrees to 135 degrees. Many other types of beads, mouldings, and trim are also available.

After the corner beads are in place they are covered with joint compound, which is feathered out on the drywall, as shown in **11-4**.

Exposed edges of gypsum drywall panels are reinforced and concealed with U-shaped metal trim, as shown in **11-6**. The trim is slid on the gypsum panel and nailed to the stud. It is concealed with joint compound. Several types of edges are available.

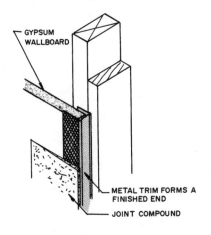

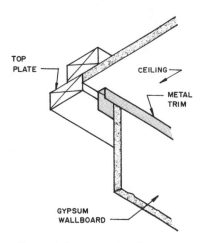

11-6 *Metal trim is used to give a finished edge to gypsum wallboard that is exposed to view.*

Drywall Finishes

Possibly the greatest number of square feet of installed drywall are finished by painting with an interior paint. Wallpaper is also widely used. Ceilings and some walls are given a textured finish. Compound manufacturers have available a variety of materials that can be brushed, rolled, or sprayed over the panels to produce such a textured surface (see **11-7**).

Temperature Control

The rooms in which gypsum panels are to be installed must be kept at 55° to 70°F (13° to 21°C), 24 hours a day, during periods when the outdoor temperature is below 55°F (13°C). Ventilation must be provided to remove excess moisture developed as the joint compound dries.

On-Site Storage

Gypsum drywall panels must be stored in a protected area. Typically this is inside the building where they are to be used. They should be stacked flat on a clean floor. Since the ceiling is installed first, the panels for this use must be on the top of the pile. Since gypsum panels are heavy, consideration must be given to the total weight that a pile will put on the floor joists.

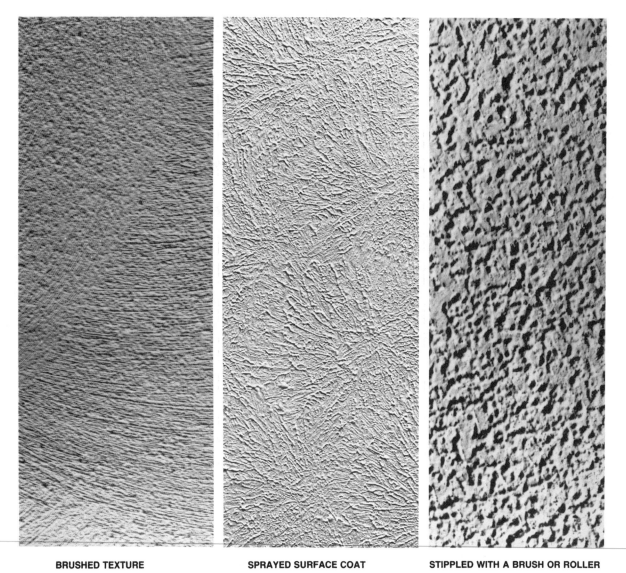

BRUSHED TEXTURE   SPRAYED SURFACE COAT   STIPPLED WITH A BRUSH OR ROLLER

11-7 A few of the surface textures that may be used on gypsum wallboard.
(Courtesy United States Gypsum Company)

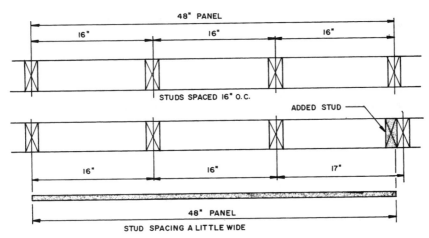

11-8 *Improperly spaced studs require that extra studs be installed to support the edge of the wallboard.*

Preliminary Preparation

Before beginning to install gypsum drywall, the framing should be checked for squareness and spacing. The standard 4ft (122cm) width panel will span four studs, and the 8ft (244cm) length will span seven studs spaced 16in (40.6cm) O.C. If they have not been carefully spaced, it will be necessary to nail scabs onto the misplaced studs so that the edges of the sheet rest firmly on a stud (see 11-8).

The studs and ceiling are checked for squareness by running a chalk line from one end of the wall to the other. Bowed studs can be straightened by sawing into the hollow sides at the middle of the stud, pulling the stud straight, and driving a thin wedge into the saw kerf until the stud remains straight. Then a 2ft

(61cm) long 1 × 4 scab is nailed across the cut on both sides of the stud to hold the stud straight (see **11-9**). Trim off the part of the wedge extending beyond the stud.

Ceiling joists can often be straightened by installing some form of strongback across them in the attic. One example is shown in **11-10**. When the joists are nailed to the strongback, they are pulled into line. The material used to make the strongback should be straight.

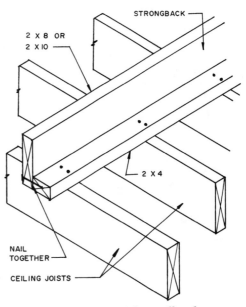

11-9 *Bowed studs must be straightened before installing gypsum wallboard.*

11-10 *Strongbacks are used to pull ceiling joists into a flat plane.*

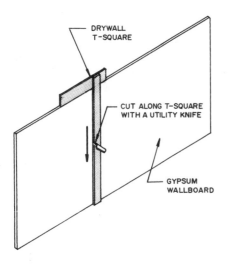

Cutting Gypsum Panels

Straight cuts across a panel are made by marking the location of the cut, placing a drywall T-square on the mark, and scoring the panel with a utility knife (see **11-11**). Then bend the board and it will snap along the scored line (see **11-12**). Cut through the paper on the back side of the panel (see **11-13**). The two pieces will separate (see **11-14**). Circular holes can be cut with a circular cutting tool or a keyhole saw. Drywall saws are also used to make various cuts in gypsum panels. Ragged edges can be smoothed with a knife, file, multiblade forming tool, or coarse sandpaper.

11-11   Straight cuts are made with a utility knife and a drywall T-square.

11-12   After scoring the panel with a knife, bend it to snap the gypsum core along the line that was cut. (Courtesy United States Gypsum Company)

11-13   After snapping the gypsum core, cut the paper on the other side. (Courtesy United States Gypsum Company)

11-14 *After the back paper has been cut, the wall-board parts will separate.* (Courtesy United States Gypsum Company)

Installing Drywall Panels

Panels may be installed using a **single-layer** or **double-layer application.** Single-layer application is used on interior ceilings and walls where economy is important. It provides for fast installation and fire protection. Most residential work uses single-layer installation. Double-layer application has one layer of gypsum drywall nailed or screwed directly to the studs and this is overlaid with a second layer. It offers greater strength, fire protection, and reduced sound transmission. The second layer is bonded to the first layer with an adhesive (see **11-15**). Some nails are used to hold the panels as the adhesive sets.

11-15 *Adhesive is applied to the back of a gypsum panel that will be bonded to another panel that has been nailed or screwed to the studs.* (Courtesy United States Gypsum Company)

Panels may be nailed or screwed to wood studs and screwed to metal studs. They may be single-nailed, double-nailed, attached with screws, or bonded with adhesives. Single-nailed panels must have the nails located ⅜in (9.5mm) from the edge of the panel. On wood frame construction they should be spaced 7in (178mm) apart on the ceiling and 8in (203mm) apart on the walls (see **11-16**). Screws are spaced 12in (305mm) apart on the ceiling and 16in (406mm) apart on the walls. The nails should be staggered by about 1in (25mm) on the butting joints (see **11-17**).

A double-nailed panel is shown in **11-18**. Double-nailing reduces the number of nail pops that occur as the wood framing shrinks and helps keep the panels tight to the studs. The nails are spaced 7in (178mm) around the perimeter of ceiling panels and 8in (203mm) on wall panels. Nails are doubled within the panel, spaced 2in (50mm) apart, and spaced 12in (305mm) on center.

Single-Layer Application over a Wood Frame

The panels can be applied with the long side **perpendicular** to or **parallel** with the studs. Check local codes to see if fire regulations specify the method to be used (see **11-19** and **11-20**). Generally perpendicular application is used, because it greatly reduces the lineal feet of joints, provides a stronger wall, and tends to bridge over irregularities in the line of the studs. For ceiling heights greater than 8'-1" (2.46m), parallel application is usually more practical.

All ends and edges of panels must occur over framing members, except when the joints are at right angles to the framing members.

Nails should be driven straight into the stud. If a nail misses the stud, remove it. The nail head should not break the paper cover. If it does, drive another nail about 2in (50mm) away (see **11-21**). These same recommendation apply to screws. Use a drywall hammer to drive nails, because it has a crowned face designed for setting the nails and producing the required dimple around the head. This hammer is shown in **11-20**.

NOTE: SCREWS 12" O.C. ON
CEILING 16" O.C. ON
WALLS

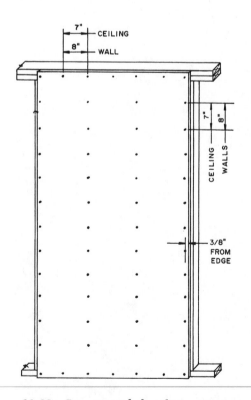

11-16 Recommended nailing pattern for single-layer wall and ceiling panels.

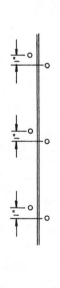

11-17 Stagger the nails from edge to edge on butting panels.

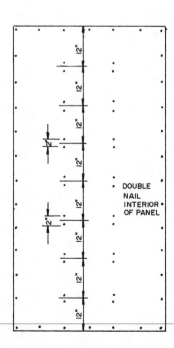

11-18 A double-nailed panel.

11-19 *Gypsum wallboard being applied with the long side in a horizontal position. Note that screws are being used to secure panels to the studs.* (Courtesy United States Gypsum Company)

11-20 *Gypsum wallboard being applied with the long side in a vertical position.* (Courtesy United States Gypsum Company)

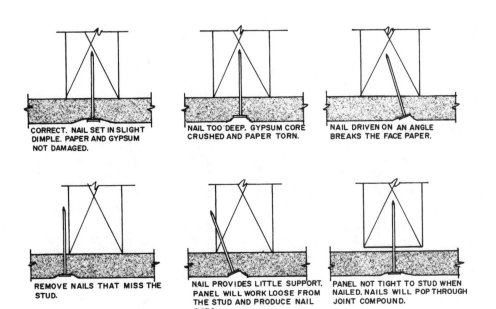

CORRECT. NAIL SET IN SLIGHT DIMPLE. PAPER AND GYPSUM NOT DAMAGED.

NAIL TOO DEEP. GYPSUM CORE CRUSHED AND PAPER TORN.

NAIL DRIVEN ON AN ANGLE BREAKS THE FACE PAPER.

REMOVE NAILS THAT MISS THE STUD.

NAIL PROVIDES LITTLE SUPPORT. PANEL WILL WORK LOOSE FROM THE STUD AND PRODUCE NAIL POPS.

PANEL NOT TIGHT TO STUD WHEN NAILED. NAILS WILL POP THROUGH JOINT COMPOUND.

11-21 *Nail installation influences the quality of the finished job.*

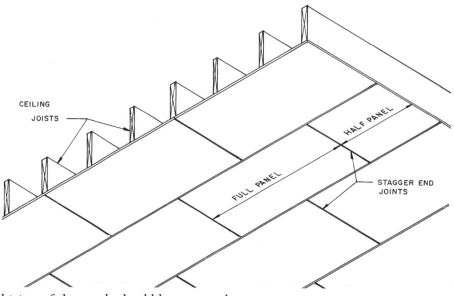

11-22 *The end joints of the panels should be staggered.*

11-23 *Gypsum panels on the ceiling can be held in place with an adjustable support such as this. (Courtesy Patterson Avenue Tool Co.)*

11-24 *A mechanical drywall lifter such as this can be used to place a panel on a high wall. (Courtesy Telpro, Inc.)*

11-25 *A mechanical drywall lifter such as this can be used to place a panel on a high ceiling. (Courtesy Telpro, Inc.)*

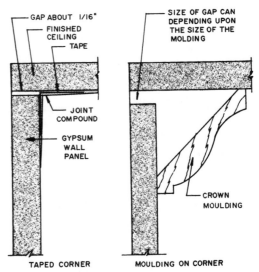

11-26 *Control the size of the gap between the gypsum wall panel and the finished ceiling.*

Begin by installing the ceiling panels. Start nailing in the middle of the panel, and work towards the edges and ends. If there are end joints, stagger them about 4ft (122cm) apart (see **11-22**). The panel can be held in place by two or more workers. The use of T-shaped supports or mechanical jacks greatly assists the process (see **11-23**, **11-24**, and **11-25**). If possible, get panel lengths long enough to cross the ceiling without requiring end butt joints. End butt joints are difficult to conceal. It is especially desirable to double-nail the ceiling, since it is the area most likely to sag or pop nails.

Next, nail the wall panels. Keep the edge and end joints about ¹⁄₁₆in (1.5mm) apart to allow for possible expansion. They should meet the ceiling neatly so that a sharp corner can be taped. If a moulding is to be used at the ceiling, the size of the gap is not critical (see **11-26**).

When installing wall panels horizontally, hang the top panels first (see **11-27**), and try to avoid end joints. Often a panel can butt a door or window frame, thus hiding the end with the wood casing to be installed around the door or window opening. Begin nailing the panel from the top edge in the middle of the panel. Work down and towards the ends. Next, install

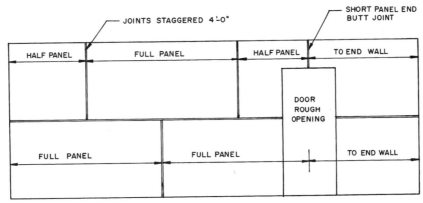

11-27 *Try to arrange panels to minimize the number of end butt joints.*

the bottom panel in the same way. If necessary, trim the bottom panel so that it clears the subfloor. This edge will be covered with a baseboard or carpeting. If a baseboard is used, it need not be a smooth cut. If the floor is to be carpeted it should be close to the subfloor and neatly trimmed.

Vertical panels are nailed by starting on the edge that butts another panel; nail towards the opposite ends and edges. Nail the interior of the panel and proceed towards the edges. The panels should be held tight to the framing as they are nailed.

A device that speeds up the installation of drywall panels is The Nailer, a plastic clip installed by the finish carpenters before the drywall crew arrives. The clips are nailed or stapled every 2ft (610mm) along the vertical corners and every 16in (406mm) around the tops

of the walls. These reduce the need to install the wood framing that is usually required for nailing the panels at the ceiling and in the corners. Once the panel is in place, it is nailed in the conventional manner (see **11-28**).

Installing Corner Beads

Corner beads are installed by nailing or stapling every 9in (228mm). Place the bead firmly against the panel and nail. The bead should stand out a little from the panel so that joint compound can penetrate through the holes in it to get behind the bead. Dimple the nail into the bead so that the head can be covered with joint compound. Try to avoid butting the ends of beads together to get a long piece; it is difficult to get a tight joint. The beads can be cut to length with tin snips (see **11-29**).

Taping the Joints

Be certain all nails and screws are properly set. Apply a continuous coat of taping compound to fill the space formed by the edges of the tapered panels. Center the tape over the joint, and lightly press it into the compound. Draw the finishing knife along the joint to remove excess compound, and cover the tape with a thin layer of compound (⅟₃₂in or 0.8mm), as shown in

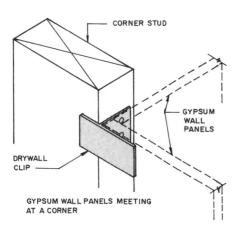

GYPSUM WALL PANELS MEETING AT A CORNER

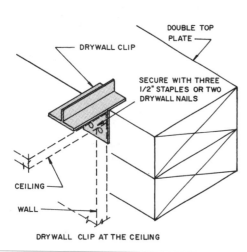

DRYWALL CLIP AT THE CEILING

11-28   Plastic drywall clips are used on the top plate and corner studs to position and hold the drywall panel while it is being nailed or screwed to the studs. (Courtesy Millennium Group)

11-29   Cutting the plastic corner bead to length with a snips. (Courtesy Trim-Tex, Inc.)

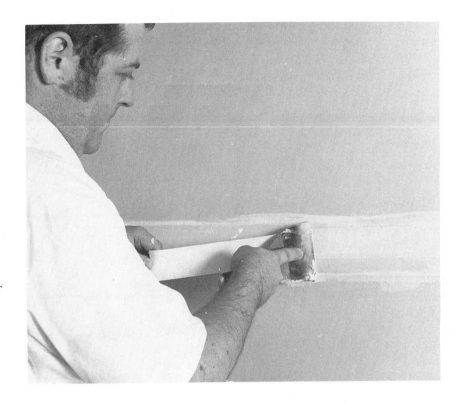

11-30 After applying a coat of taping compound over the joint, center the tape and lightly press it into the compound. (Used with permission of Georgia-Pacific Corporation)

11-30. Allow to dry before applying topping coats. Do not use topping compound for this first step.

Apply a taping compound over the nail heads. This should be enough to fill the depressions and bring them level with the surface of the panel.

After the tape coating has dried, apply a coating of topping compound. Using a wide finishing knife, feather a thin coat out to about 7 to 10in (2135 to 3050mm) wide. It should be at least 2in (50mm) beyond the edge of the tape coat (see **11-31**).

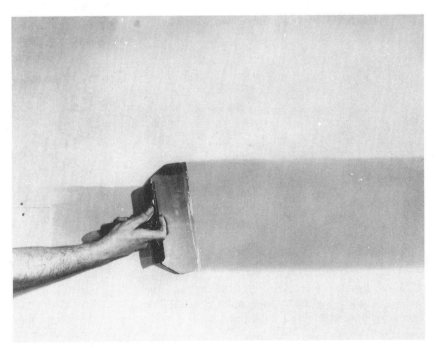

11-31 After the tape coating has dried apply a topping coat over it that is wider than the taping coat. (Used with permission of Georgia-Pacific Corporation)

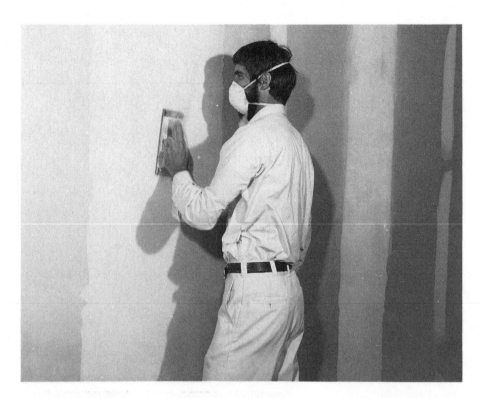

11-32 *The joint compound can be hand-sanded using a wide, flat sanding pad and fine sandpaper or abrasive cloth.* (Used with permission of Georgia-Pacific Corporation)

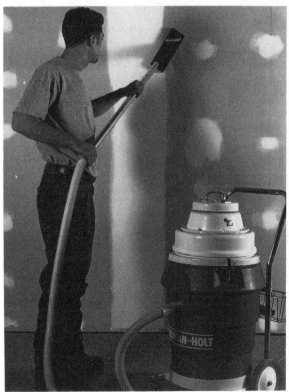

11-33 *A drywall joint sander, such as this San-duster, removes the dust at the point it is created.* (Courtesy Hyde & Meeks Industries, Inc., 26 Dudley St., Arlington, MA 02174)

11-34 *A drywall sander such as this one has filters that remove much of the dust created.* (Courtesy PermaGlas Mesh, Inc.)

11-35 A portable barrier such as this provides a flexible means for isolating dust to the area in which work is taking place. (Courtesy Curtain Wall Co., 246 Welfare Ave., Warwick, RI 02888)

After the second coat is dry, smooth out any tool marks or ridges with the finishing knife. Then apply the third coat using topping compound. Feather the edges until they are about 2in (50mm) or more beyond the edge of the second coat.

When the third coat is dry, the joint can be sanded. Use very-fine-grade sandpapers or abrasive cloths. Any depressions should be filled with topping compound, allowed to dry, and then be resanded. Dust is a severe problem; so respirators and safety glasses are required (see 11-32). Two types of sanding units that use a vacuum to remove much of the dust are shown in 11-33 and 11-34. These not only provide protection for the worker but help prevent the gypsum dust from spreading all over the house. Cleanup after a typical sanding operation is difficult and expensive; units are available with a special filter to increase the amount of dust collected.

Another technique for controlling dust during drywall sanding or other operations is to isolate the dust in the area of work with a curtain wall. One unit, shown in 11-35, has an adjustable metal framework that carries the dust-resisting curtain. Another product is a dust door; this unit fully seals off doors from dust-producing areas, as shown in 11-36.

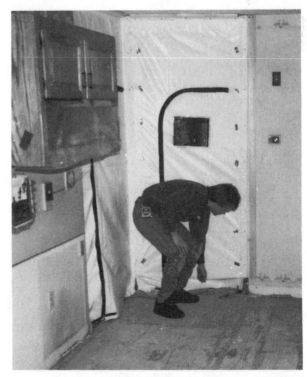

11-36 A system such as this seals off doors to areas in which dust will be produced. (Courtesy Brophy Design, Inc., manufacturers of the Dust Door & Wall System)

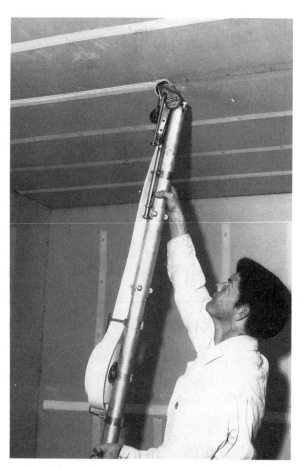

1. MECHANICALLY TAPE THE CEILING JOINT

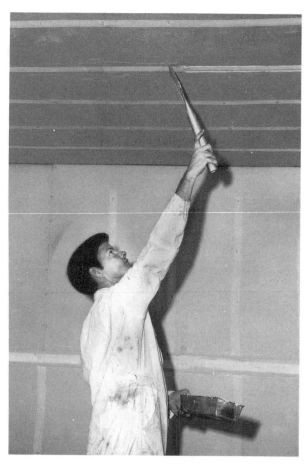

2. THEN WIPE DOWN THE JOINT WITH A BROAD KNIFE

3. APPLY THE FINISH COATS AFTER THE COMPOUND HAS HARDENED

11-37 Mechanical devices such as these make taping the ceiling easier. (Courtesy United States Gypsum Company)

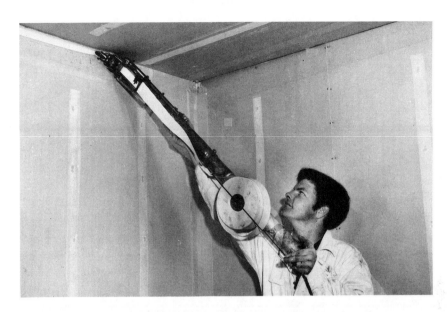

1. APPLY THE COMPOUND AND TAPE ON THE INSIDE CORNER

11-38 Devices such as these can be used to tape inside corners. (Courtesy United States Gypsum Company)

2. DRESS THE JOINT WITH A CORNER-FINISHER

There are a number of mechanical devices used to apply joint compound and tape. In **11-37** the device applies joint compound and tape. Then the joint is wiped down with a broad knife. Then finish coats can be mechanically applied. Interior corners can also have compound and tape applied as shown in **11-38**. Then dress the tape with a mechanical finisher.

A finished installation, using plastic corner beads, after sanding and painting is shown in **11-39**.

11-39 A finished gypsum wallboard installation. (Courtesy Trim-Tex, Inc.)

209

12

Installing Cabinets

A variety of cabinets are used in residential construction. Most common are kitchen and bath cabinets. Other rooms may have bookshelves, bars, and various built-in storage units (see **12-1**, **12-2**, and **12-3**).

Mass-Produced and Custom-Built Cabinets

Cabinets are produced in three basic ways. These include **mass-produced** assembled and unassembled units, cabinets **built on the site** by the carpenter, and **custom-built** units made in a local cabinet shop.

Mass-produced cabinets are manufactured in a factory by the same techniques used to make furniture. The use of production woodworking equipment permits the cabinet to be made using high-quality joinery and finishes applied in a controlled atmosphere. While most mass-produced cabinets used are completely assembled and finished in the factory, they can be purchased precut, but not assembled. The carpenter assembles these on the job. Most are designed so that they can be nailed or stapled together.

Manufactured cabinets, also referred to as architectural mill, are divided into three levels of quality. The **economy grade** is the lowest and least expensive. Joinery and construction is simple, and less costly wood products are used. **Custom-grade** cabinets have better-quality framing and joinery and possibly are the most commonly used grade. **Premium grade** cabinets use the best joinery, and expensive woods. They will use extensive mouldings and machined panels.

12-1 Kitchens typically contain a wide variety of cabinet sizes and styles. (Courtesy Wellborn Cabinet, Inc.)

12-2 Floor-to-ceiling cabinets are commonly used in rooms such as the den, family room, and living room for books, television, and general storage. (Courtesy Wellborn Cabinet, Inc.)

12-3 Cabinets are often used in the bedroom to provide drawers for storage, space for hanging clothes, and other special features such as a desk. (Courtesy Wellborn Cabinet, Inc.)

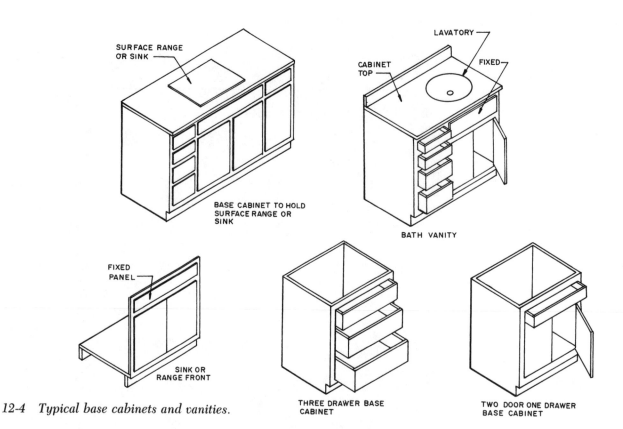

12-4 *Typical base cabinets and vanities.*

Site-built cabinets are constructed by the carpenter or a cabinetmaker on the job. Power tools, wood, and plywood are brought to the job. All the pieces are cut, assembled, and the units are then installed and finished. The joinery on these cabinets must be relatively simple and the finish applied under less than ideal conditions.

Custom-built cabinets are built by a cabinetmaker in a local woodworking shop. Their construction and finish is usually of higher quality than site-built units. Units not available from a mass-production supplier can be satisfactorily made this way. The quality depends on the skills of the cabinetmaker.

Kinds of Cabinet

Cabinets most commonly required in residential construction are in the kitchen, bath, utility room, and various built-in storage units such as bookcases and areas where articles are to be displayed.

In the kitchen the base cabinet rests on the floor and is designed for storage, to hold a sink, cooking top or range, and with a top that serves as a work surface (see **12-4**). It has both drawer and door sections.

Wall cabinets are mounted on the wall about 18in (approx. 46cm) above the top of the base cabinet. They usually have adjustable shelves and are used for

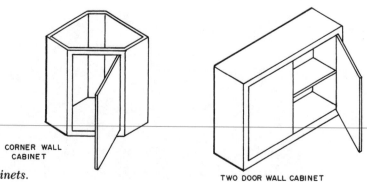

12-5 *Typical wall cabinets.*

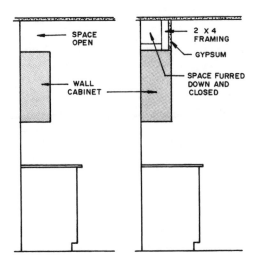

12-6 *The space above wall cabinets may be left open or furred down and enclosed.*

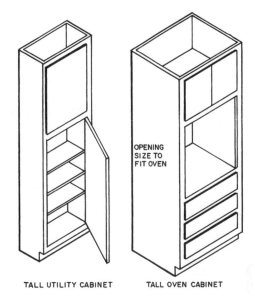

TALL UTILITY CABINET   TALL OVEN CABINET

12-7 *Typical tall cabinets.*

general storage (see **12-5**). Most wall cabinets are made 30in (approx. 76cm) high, which is about as high as the average person can reach. The space between the top of the wall cabinet and the ceiling can be left open or closed with a drop ceiling (see **12-6**). If left open, the area can be used to display interesting articles.

Tall cabinets are generally used to store nonperishable foods. They are built so that the top lines up with the top of the wall cabinets (see **12-7**).

Vanity cabinets of all types are used in the bathroom to hold the wash basin. They have drawers and doors below providing storage as shown in **12-8**.

12-8 *Cabinets in the bath provide storage for towels and clothing and form bases for sinks.* (Courtesy Wellborn Cabinet, Inc.)

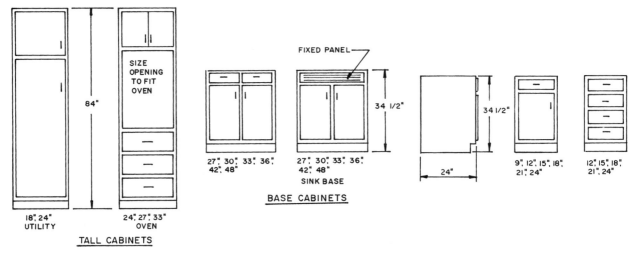

12-9   Standard sizes of base and tall cabinets.

Standard Kitchen and Bath Cabinet Sizes

The standard cabinet sizes in general use by many cabinet manufacturers are shown in **12-9**, **12-10**, and **12-11**. The designer uses these standard sizes to plan the cabinets in kitchens and baths. Manufacturers' catalogs also list the modular and other sizes of cabinets that they produce. There are design standards for cabinets that make them accessible to the physically handicapped. These are shown in **12-12**.

Cabinet Construction

The various parts of a cabinet are identified in **12-13**. These terms are commonly used in the industry. Cabinets can be divided into two major types based on their construction. These are units with a **face frame** and units **without a face frame** (often called **European style**).

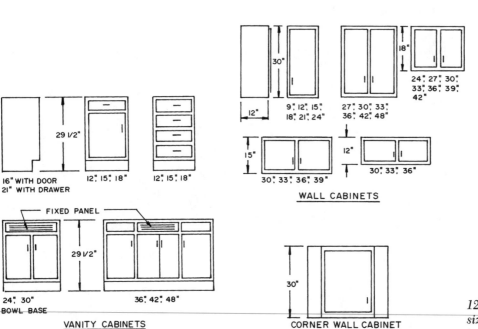

12-10   Typical standard vanity sizes.

12-11   Typical standard sizes of wall cabinets.

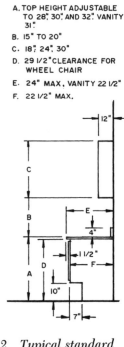

12-12   Typical standard sizes for cabinets designed to be used in households that include one or more persons with disabilities.

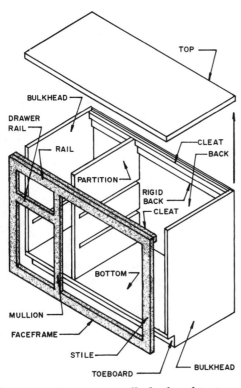

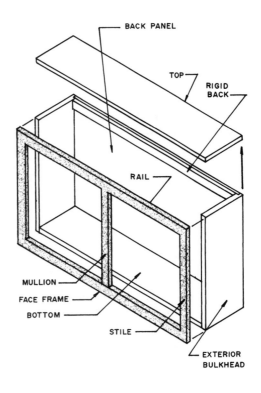

12-13 The parts of conventionally built cabinets.

Construction With a Face Frame

This type of construction can have doors and drawers flush with the face frame as shown in **12-14** or can overlap or overlay the face frame as shown in **12-15**. The flush construction is more expensive because of the necessity to fit the doors and drawers within the framed opening.

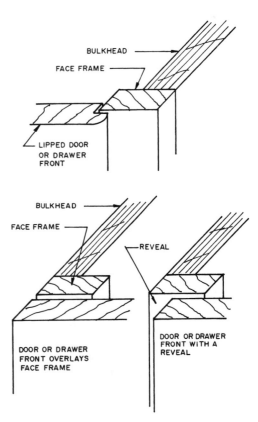

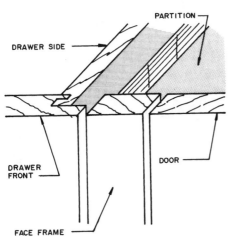

12-14 Conventional construction with doors and drawers flush with the face frame.

12-15 Conventional construction with doors and drawer fronts over the face frame.

215

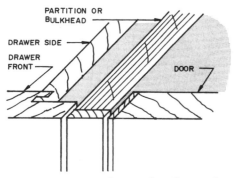

12-16 *Construction without a face frame; doors and drawer fronts are flush with the partition or bulkhead.*

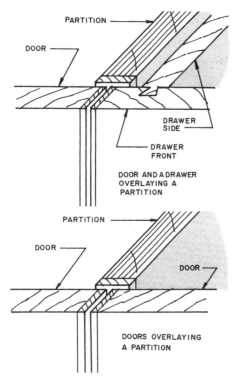

12-17 *Construction without a face frame with the doors and drawer fronts overlaying the partitions and bulkheads.*

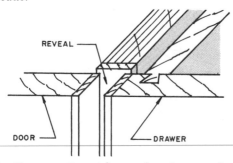

12-18 *Construction without a face frame with doors and drawer fronts overlaying the partitions but leaving a reveal.*

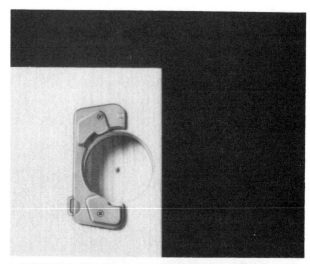

1. CUT RECESS INTO DOOR AND ATTACH ANCHOR PLATE

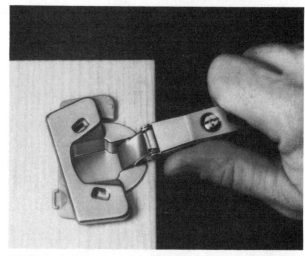

2. INSERT HINGE IN HOLE AND ROTATE TO LOCK IN POSITION

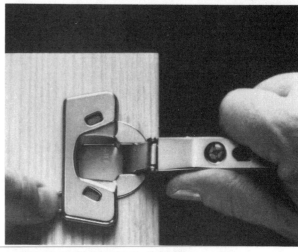

3. LEAF ON RIGHT OF INSTALLED HINGE IS READY TO BE SCREWED TO CABINET FRAME

12-19 *Steps to install one type of hinge for an overlaid door. (Courtesy Melpa Furniture Fittings)*

12-20 This hinge permits the door to be removed and reinstalled by pressing the lock on the end of the leaf. (Courtesy Melpa Furniture Fittings)

Construction Without a Face frame

This type of construction can have the doors set flush with the face of the bulkheads, top and bottom, as shown in **12-16**, or can overlay the bulkheads, top and bottom, as shown in **12-17**. The overlay can be adjusted to provide a reveal which accents the separation between the doors and drawer fronts (see **12-18**).

There are a variety of hinges designed to hang cabinet doors on Europe-style cabinets. The steps to install one type of hinge are shown in **12-19**. The hinge permits the door to be installed and removed when desired by pressing the lock pad on the end of the hinge (see **12-20**). The installation of doors with this hinge is shown in **12-21**.

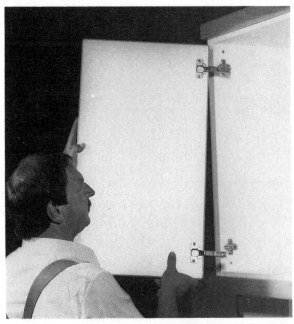

1. ONCE HINGE IS MOUNTED ON DOOR AND ANCHOR PLATE ON CABINET SIDE, INSERT HINGES ON ANCHORS

2. PRESS THE LOCK ON THE END OF HINGE DOOR IS LOCKED IN POSITION; IT CAN BE REMOVED BY RELEASING THE LOCK

12-21 This hinge is mounted on the door and inside the cabinet. The door can be removed by pressing the lock on the end. (Courtesy Melpa Furniture Fittings)

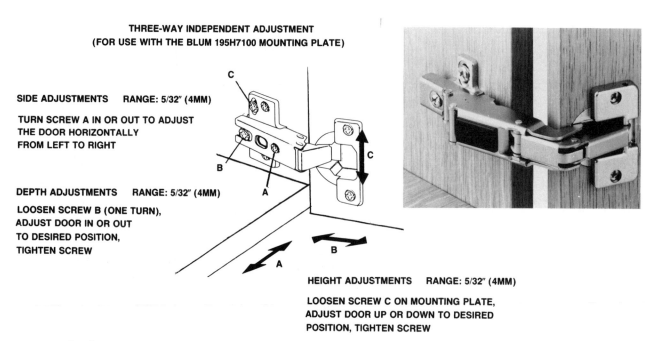

THREE-WAY INDEPENDENT ADJUSTMENT
(FOR USE WITH THE BLUM 195H7100 MOUNTING PLATE)

SIDE ADJUSTMENTS   RANGE: 5/32" (4MM)

TURN SCREW A IN OR OUT TO ADJUST
THE DOOR HORIZONTALLY
FROM LEFT TO RIGHT

DEPTH ADJUSTMENTS   RANGE: 5/32" (4MM)

LOOSEN SCREW B (ONE TURN),
ADJUST DOOR IN OR OUT
TO DESIRED POSITION,
TIGHTEN SCREW

HEIGHT ADJUSTMENTS   RANGE: 5/32" (4MM)

LOOSEN SCREW C ON MOUNTING PLATE,
ADJUST DOOR UP OR DOWN TO DESIRED
POSITION, TIGHTEN SCREW

12-22   *This hinge permits the door position to be adjusted in three directions.*
(Courtesy Julius Blum, Inc.)

Another hinge has adjustments that permit the door to be repositioned slightly after the hinges have been installed. This enables the cabinetmaker to get the best position possible (see **12-22**).

Working Design Drawings

The designer conceives and executes **working design drawings** for the kitchen, baths, and other areas in which cabinets are wanted. The **specifications** for the job detail technical information about the cabinets. The **floor plan** shows the plan view of the required cabinets, and **elevations** of each wall are drawn showing the location of doors, drawers, shelves, and other features. An example of a typical floor plan of a kitchen is shown in **12-23**, and the cabinet elevations are shown in **12-24**. Before the cabinets are ordered or custom-built, the cabinetmaker or building materials supplier must visit the house and take measurements

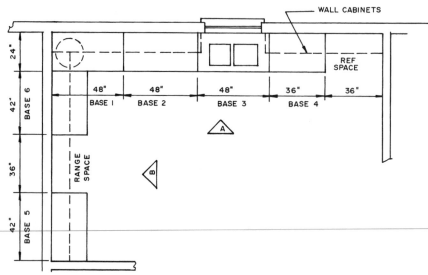

12-23   *A floor plan for a kitchen.*

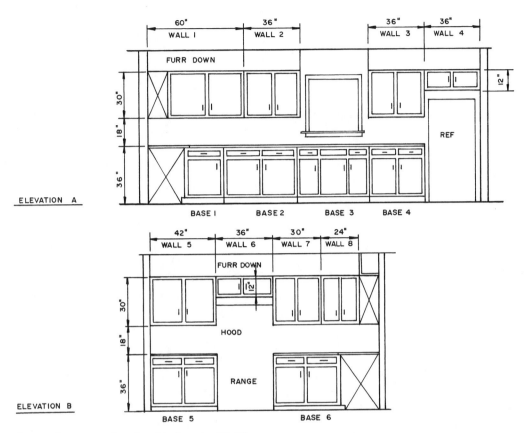

12-24 *Cabinet elevations for the kitchen in 12-23.*

of the finished room to verify the exact sizes required. The dimensions given on the architectural drawings while close to existing conditions are not accurate enough to use for ordering the cabinets. Also, things not on the plan may be found to exist such as a heating duct, plumbing, or an electrical outlet. As you measure the room make a layout similar to that shown in **12-25**.

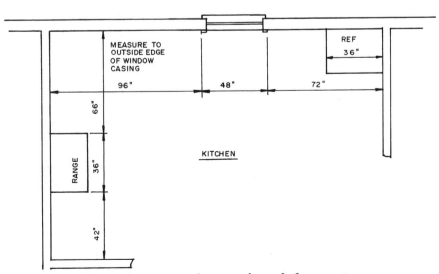

12-25 *Measure the room and locate features, such as windows, before starting to prepare the actual cabinet specifications.*

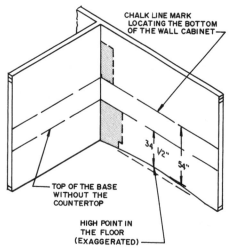

12-26 *Locate the top of the base unit and the bottom of the wall cabinets on the wall.*

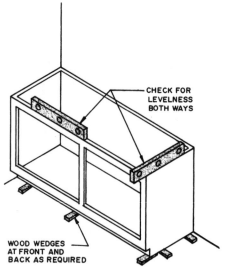

12-27 *Set the first base cabinet in a corner and check for levelness.*

Installing Cabinets

Factory-produced cabinets are delivered to the site finished and ready to install. Often they are in protective cardboard cartons. They must be stored on a site where they are clear of dust and possible damage. All drywall or plasterwork must be completed, and the moisture content of the air should be normal before cabinets are moved into the building.

Preliminary Preparation
Before attempting installation, be certain the room is clean and the walls free of any obstructions. If it is a remodelling job, remove the base. Next locate and

mark the studs. Check the floor with a level on a long straightedge to see if there are any high spots. If there are, mark them on the floor. Then at this point measure up the wall 34½in (87.7cm)—the height of the base unit—and 54in (137.2cm)—the height of the bot-

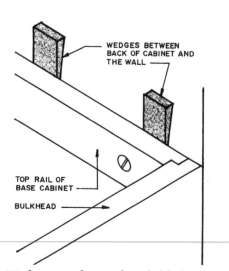

12-28 *Wedges can be used to hold the base level when the wall inclines.*

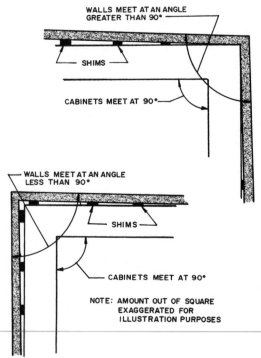

12-29 *Check to see whether the walls meet at a 90-degree angle.*

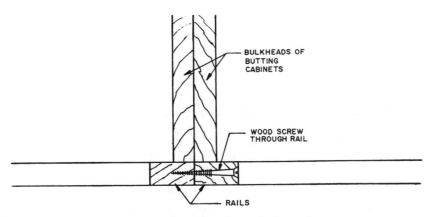

12-30   Butting cabinets should be joined with wood screws through the rails.

tom wall unit. Snap a level chalk line through these points to locate the top of the base and wall cabinets (see **12-26**).

Many carpenters prefer to install the base cabinets first and use them to support the wall cabinets. Others feel the base cabinets get in the way; so they hang the wall cabinets first.

Installing the Base Cabinets

The following is a commonly used procedure for installing base cabinets.

1. Begin with a corner unit. If the floor is not level, shim it with wood wedges, keeping the top on the line on the wall, and checking to be certain it is level as well as parallel and perpendicular to the wall (see **12-27**).

2. Next, check the back of the cabinet as it butts the wall. If the wall has a bow, shim the back of the cabinets so that they line up straight (see **12-28**).

3. If a cabinet turns a corner, check to see whether the walls are perpendicular. If they are not, shim as shown in **12-29**.

4. The base is joined to each stud by wood screws through the rigid back. Drill holes through the rigid back and secure the base to the wall with No. 8 or 10 flathead wood screws that go into the stud at least ¾in (**19mm**).

5. Butt the second base unit to this first one. Clamp the butting ends together with C-clamps. Join the units with flathead wood screws through the frame of one unit into the next unit (see **12-30**). Then level as needed, and fasten to the wall studs.

In many cases the stock base and wall cabinets will not provide the exact length required. When this happens, filler strips are added to the face frame to fill the gap. These strips are available prefinished to match the grain and color of manufactured cabinets. They must be cut to width and joined to the base or wall cabinet, as shown in **12-31**.

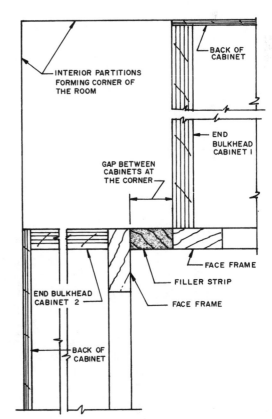

12-31   A filler strip is used to fill the gap between cabinets forming a corner.

221

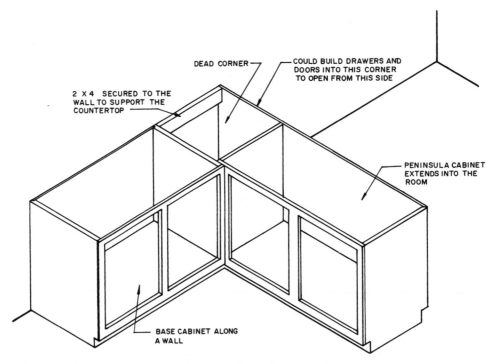

12-32   *Peninsula-base cabinets project into the room from the units along the wall.*

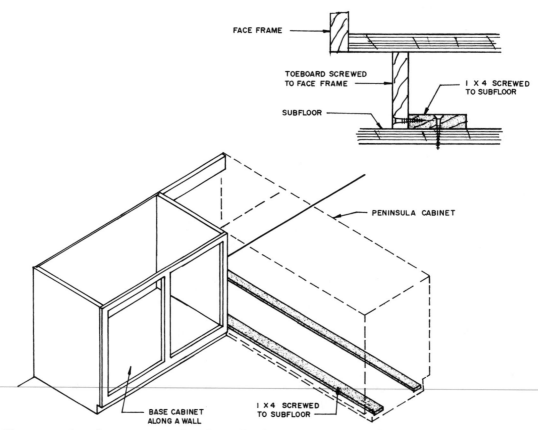

12-33   *The peninsula cabinet is screwed to the wall cabinet and to the subfloor.*

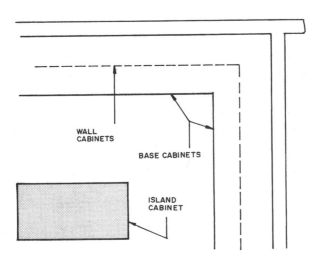

12-34 An island cabinet is freestanding.

Installing Peninsula and Island Base Units

Peninsular units connect to a wall base cabinet and project into the room, as shown in **12-32**. They are available in a variety of designs, but installation is much the same as with wall base cabinets. They are joined to the wall base unit by screws through the face frame. The toe board is secured to the floor by screwing or nailing it to a wood blocking screwed to the subfloor (see **12-33**). The island base unit is freestanding. It is secured to the subfloor in the same manner as the peninsula base unit (see **12-34** and **12-35**).

12-35 This island counter holds the cooking unit and provides storage space. (Courtesy Wellborn Cabinet, Inc.)

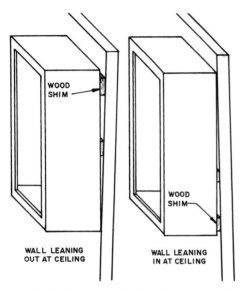

12-36 *If the wall is not plumb, shim the cabinets so that they are plumb.*

WOOD SHIM

WOOD SHIM

WALL LEANING OUT AT CEILING

WALL LEANING IN AT CEILING

Installing the Wall Cabinets

1. As with base cabinets, check the wall to see if it has any bows. Make note of these, because they will require that the wall cabinets be shimmed to keep them straight. The wall may also be out of plumb and require shimming as shown in **12-36**.

2. Check the corners of the room to see whether the walls are square. If not, this may require shimming as shown in **12-29**.

3. Start the installation of wall cabinets in a corner. Some carpenters use wood support units that rest on top of a temporary plywood or particleboard top on the base cabinets. The wall cabinets can rest on these as they are levelled and plumbed (see **12-37**). A commercial support used for this purpose is shown in **12-38**.

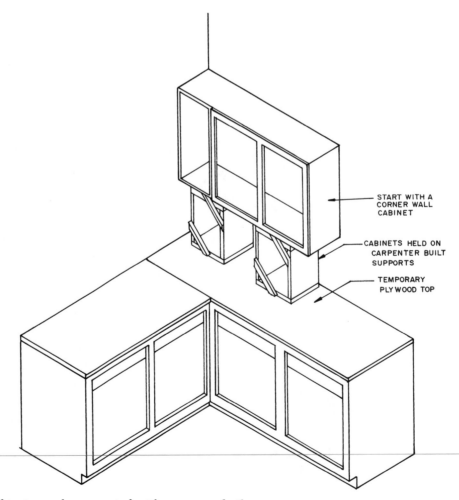

START WITH A CORNER WALL CABINET

CABINETS HELD ON CARPENTER BUILT SUPPORTS

TEMPORARY PLYWOOD TOP

12-37 *Wall cabinets can be supported with carpenter-built supports.*

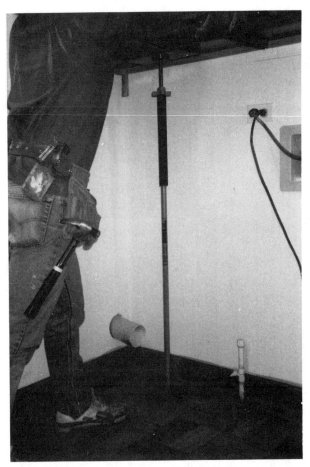

12-38 *Stands such as these are available for temporarily supporting cabinets over the base cabinet or from the floor.* (Courtesy Patterson Avenue Tool Co.)

4. When the wall cabinet is level and plumb, it can be fastened to the studs through the rigid back. Many prefer to hang the wall cabinets on wood or metal cleats, fastened to the wall where the top back of the cabinet will be positioned. Butting cabinets are joined by screws through the rails.

Installing the Countertops

It is common practice for the building materials supplier who furnishes the cabinets to supply finished, properly sized countertops. When this occurs, the carpenter must position them on the base cabinet and secure them to the base through corner braces located at each corner of the base cabinet. When necessary, screws can be installed through the rail into the top (see **12-39**). Openings must be cut for sinks once their exact size is established.

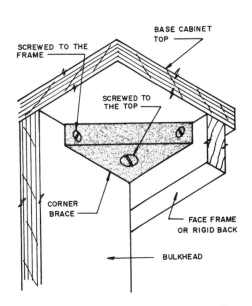

12-39 *Countertops can be joined to the base with corner braces.*

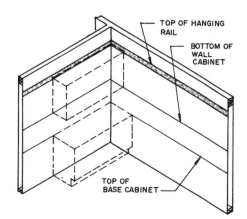

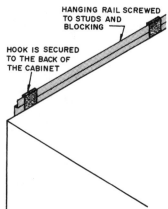

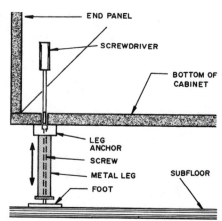

12-40   How to lay out the cabinet level lines for European-style cabinets.

12-41   The wall cabinet is hung on metal hanging rails.

12-42   The base cabinet is set on adjustable metal legs.

Installing European-Style Cabinets

European-style cabinets have no face frame, as shown in **12-16** and **12-17**. Some American cabinet manufacturers make European-style cabinets, but most prepare them to be installed as explained earlier in this chapter. The European-style cabinet installation system is fast and efficient. The upper cabinets are hung from a steel rail cleat or suspension fitting that is screwed to the wall studs. The base cabinets stand on metal legs secured to the bottom of the cabinet. The legs may be adjusted to level the base.

To install the cabinets snap a chalk line on the wall locating the top of the base cabinet, the bottom of the wall cabinet, and the top of the wall cabinet hanging rail. This is generally a little above the top of the cabinet when it is hung (see **12-40**).

The hanging rail that is screwed to the studs is usually about 1¼in (32mm) wide. It has an offset bend in the top into which hanging hooks screwed to the back of the cabinet will fit. The hanging rail is hung with 2½in (64mm) wood screws. A stronger installation is made by installing 2in (25mm) blocking between the studs where the hanging rail will be located. Then run screws through the rail and drywall into the blocking every 2 or 3in (25 to 76mm).

The upper cabinet has hanging hooks secured to the back rail. The hook has two adjusting screws. One is used to move the cabinet in and out from the wall. The other adjusts the cabinet up and down so that it can be levelled (see **12-41**). If the hanging rail is exposed to view, a crown moulding may be used to conceal it.

After the wall cabinets are hung and levelled, they are bolted together with bolts supplied with the cabinets. Clamp the cabinets together and finish drilling the holes located for the bolts inside the cabinets. If bolts are not available, the cabinets can be joined with wood screws.

The base cabinet has metal levelling legs fitting into plastic sockets secured to the bottom of the cabinet. A hole in the cabinet floor above each leg permits the length to be adjusted with a screwdriver, or the legs can be turned by hand (see **12-42**). A cap is supplied to cover the hole.

European-style cabinets are usually narrower than the standard 24in (610mm) American cabinet. This means that the countertop must be made narrower or the base cabinet held out from the wall with a wood strip nailed or screwed to the studs. Europeans do not secure their base cabinets to the wall. However, it is a good practice to screw them to the studs or the spacer strip.

The toe kick is covered with a plywood or particleboard strip covered with a plastic laminate. It can be cut to the required width. This depends on the finish floor and whether it has been installed. On the back of the toe kick board, mark the location of each leg. The manufacturer supplies clips that fit into a groove in the back of the toe kick board. The clips fit around the leg, holding the board in place.

It should be noted that this is only a general description; there may be differences in cabinets made by various manufacturers.

13

Cornice Construction

The **exterior cornice** is the trim on the projection of the roof where it meets the exterior wall. On gable roofs it occurs on the sides where the roof meets the wall. Hipped roofs have a cornice on all sides. Flat roofs have the cornice constructed by extending the rafters/ceiling joists beyond the exterior wall. This will occur on all sides of the building.

The three basic types of cornice are **box** or **soffit**, **close**, and **open**. The box cornice is the most frequently used type because it provides an attractive appearance and protects the exterior walls and windows from rain and, in some cases, exposure from the sun. The close cornice finishes off the ends of the rafters but has no overhang; it therefore provides no protection. The open cornice is much like the box because it provides overhang, but it gives quite a different appearance. It is used where a rustic appearance is desired and is also less costly to build.

Box or Soffit Cornices

The width of the box cornice will be specified on the working design drawings. The width can vary considerably and depends in part on the slope of the roof. The soffit **return** must meet the exterior wall above the head of the windows. Several roof slopes are drawn in **13-1** showing how they influence the amount of overhang. Low-sloped roofs can have wider soffits than more steeply sloped roofs.

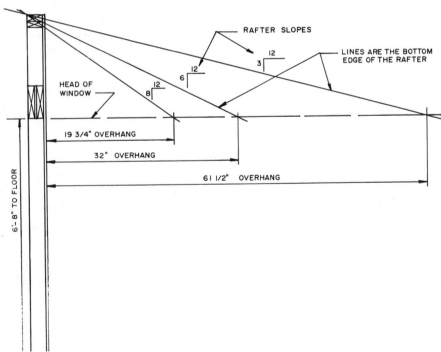

13-1 The slope of the roof limits the amount of cornice projection.

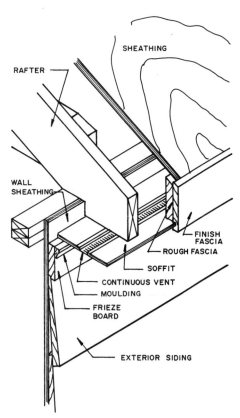

13-2 A narrow box cornice as installed on a building with wood siding.

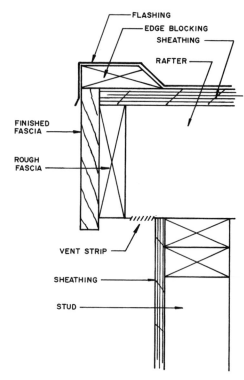

13-3 A narrow box cornice as used on a flat roof.

A narrow box cornice has the rafter projection cut so that it serves to hold the **fascia** and soffit (see **13-2**). A **frieze board** is used to cover the gap between the soffit and the siding. Often a moulding is added to complete the joint. A narrow box cornice for a flat roof is shown in **13-3**. Notice the inclusion of vents to clear the air above the insulation.

A wide box cornice is used when more overhang is wanted. It uses lookouts nailed to the end of the rafter and to a ledger that is nailed to the wall studs (see **13-4**). The soffit can be plywood, oriented strand board, hardboard, gypsum, vinyl, or metal. There are a number of new sheet products on the market that can also be used as soffit material. The thickness required depends on the spacing of the lookouts. Typical spacing is 16in (406mm) and 24in (610mm) O.C. Vents are located in the soffit.

The rough fascia is 2in (50mm) thick material and the finish fascia is 1in (25mm) thick. The rough fascia is nailed to the ends of the rafters, and the finish fascia is nailed to it.

A frieze board is commonly used with wide box cornices. It is usually a 1in (25mm) thick board rabbeted to receive the wood siding.

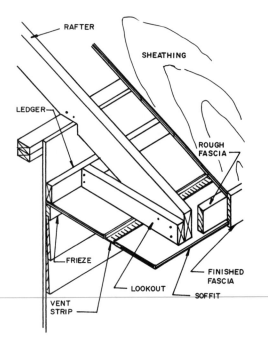

13-4 Framing for a wide box cornice.

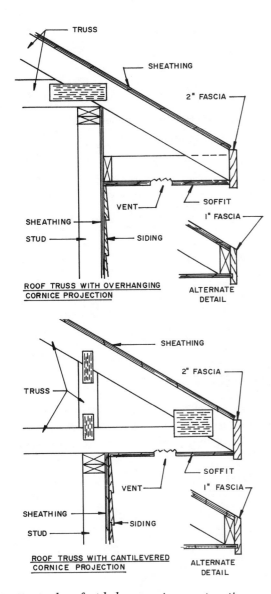

13-5 *Examples of wide box cornice construction on a roof framed with wood trusses.*

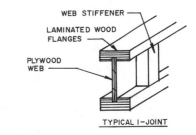

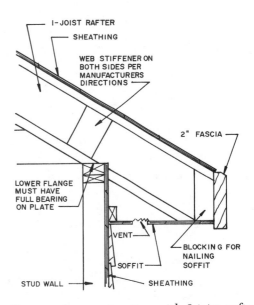

13-6 *Box cornice construction with I-joist rafters.*

Details for constructing other box cornices are shown in **13-5**, **13-6**, **13-7**, and **13-8**. These include truss-framed roofs, I-joist rafters, flat roofs, and brick veneer construction.

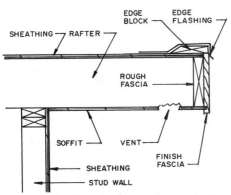

13-7 *Construction for a wide cornice projection on a flat roof.*

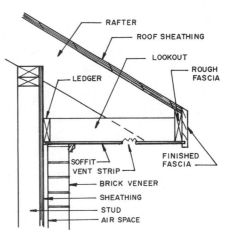

13-8 *Construction details for a box cornice when brick siding is used.*

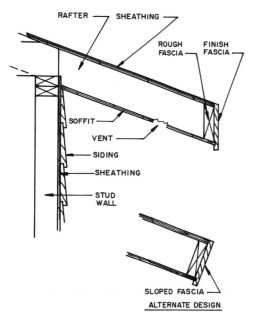

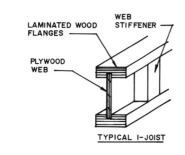

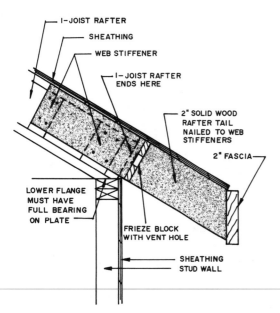

13-9 *A box cornice with a sloping soffit.*

13-11 *Typical open-joist cornice construction when framing the roof with I-joist rafters.*

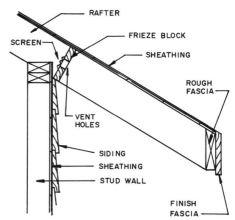

13-10 *Construction details for an open cornice with a wide projection.*

A box cornice without lookouts has a sloped soffit that is nailed to the bottom of the rafters as shown in **13-9**. The construction is the same as described for other box cornices.

Open Cornices

Open cornices are built in the same manner as wide box cornices without lookouts, except that the soffit is omitted. Instead a frieze block is installed between the rafters, and vents are placed in it (see **13-10**). Open cornice construction with I-joist rafters is shown in **13-11**. Open cornice construction when trusses are used is shown in **13-12**.

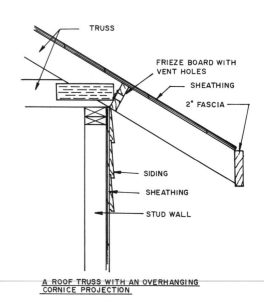

13-12 *Open cornice construction when framing the roof with wood trusses.*

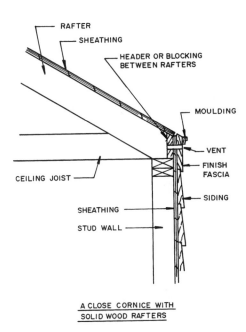

13-13 *Construction details for a close, or snub, cornice with wood exterior siding.*

Close Cornices

A close cornice has the rafter cut off flush with the outside of the **top plate**. The sheathing extends up over the ends of the rafters. A frieze board butts the bottom of the shingles and is rabbeted to receive the wood siding. Usually a moulding is installed to close the joint and provide support for the shingles as they

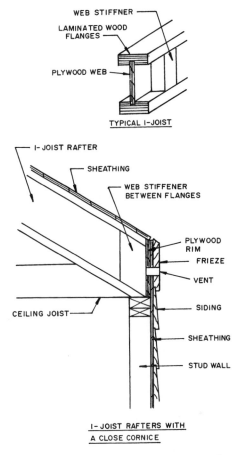

13-14 *Typical close cornice construction when using I-joist rafters.*

extend over the exterior wall (see **13-13**). Close cornices for roofs using I-joists, trusses, and flat roof construction are shown in **13-14**, **13-15**, and **13-16**.

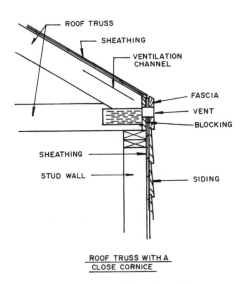

13-15 *A close cornice with wood roof-truss construction.*

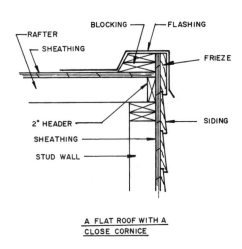

13-16 *Close cornice construction with a flat roof.*

231

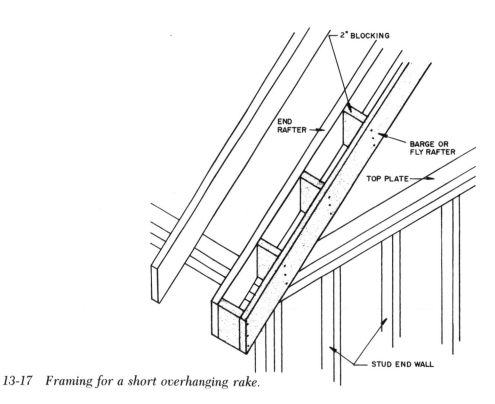

13-17 *Framing for a short overhanging rake.*

Finishing the Rake or Gable End

The **rake** is the finished edge of the roof on the gable end. It may be a boxed rake, open rake, or close rake. The boxed and open rake project beyond the gable

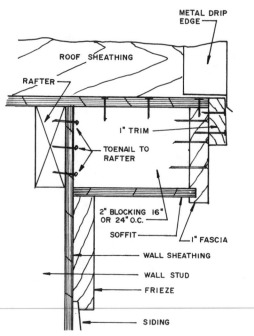

13-18 *A section through a rake with a small overhang.*

end. When the rake projection is small, such as 4 to 8in (100 to 203mm), the fascia and soffit are nailed to short **lookout** blocks spaced 16in (406mm) O.C. The lookouts are toenailed to the end rafter. The fascia is nailed to the lookouts and through the roof sheathing (see **13-17**). A frieze board is placed butting the soffit and a moulding can be added, if desired (see **13-18**).

If the extension is in the range of 8 to 18in (203–457mm), it is necessary to build a **"ladder" extension** that is nailed through the sheathing into the end rafter. A 2in (50mm) **fly** or **barge rafter** is nailed to the other end of the lookouts (see **13-19**). The lookouts are spaced 16 to 24in (406 to 610mm) O.C. The ladder is built on the ground, hoisted in place, and nailed to the end rafter. After the assembly is nailed to the end rafter, the finished fascia is nailed over the fly rafter, and a soffit is nailed to the bottom of the lookouts. A frieze board and moulding can be used below the soffit.

Moderate cornice projections are sometimes framed as shown in **13-20**. The fly rafter is nailed to the end of the ridge board and is mitred and nailed to a 2in (51mm) thick fascia board. Blocking can be added to support the soffit. The sheathing is nailed to the fly rafter and adds stiffness to the assembly.

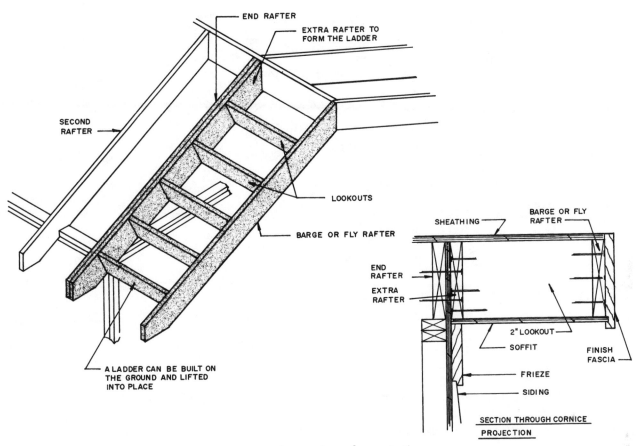

13-19 *A "ladder" can be used to frame a moderate-size rake projection.*

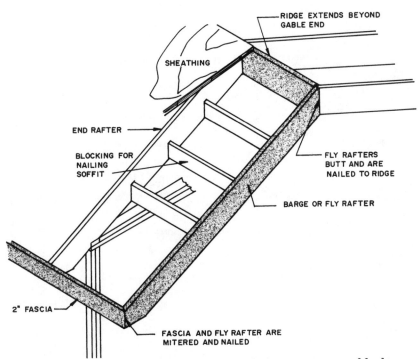

13-20 *The fly rafter may be supported by the ridge board, fascia extension, blocking, and sheathing.*

233

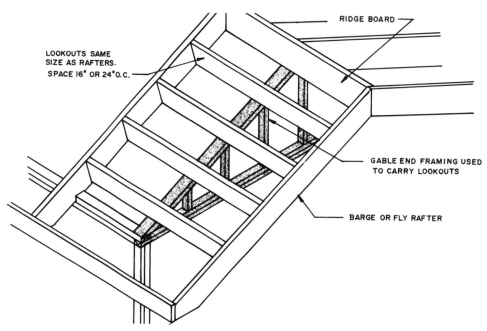

13-21 Wide rake projections can be framed using lookouts supported by the top plate of the gable end framing.

A rake with a wide projection, usually considered 18in (457mm) or more, requires a rigid frame to resist snow and wind loads. A series of lookouts is used. In one case the lookouts rest on the top plate of the gable-end framing and extend to the next rafter, which is doubled. The lookouts are secured to the rafter with metal joist hangers (see 13-21). Another procedure uses 2×4 lookouts laid flat and notched

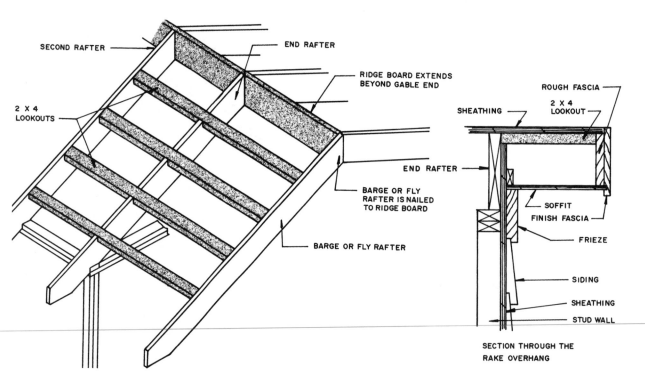

13-22 A wide rake projection built using lookouts set into notched rafters.

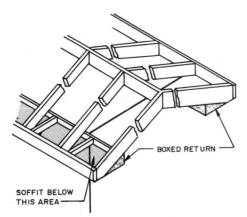

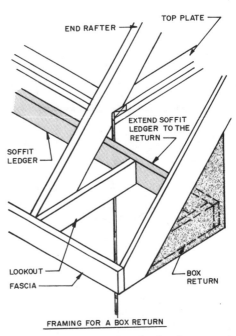

13-23 *Boxed returns can be used on projecting cornices on gable roofs.*

into the two end rafters and face-nailed to the third rafter (see **13-22**). Notice in the illustrations that the ridge board extends beyond the end rafter or gable end and provides support for the fly rafter and fascia. These ladder-type frames plus the roof sheathing provide adequate support for the fly rafter and the finished fascia.

Cornice Returns

The **cornice return** provides a finished end on the cornice as it runs from the fascia to the wall of the building. Hip and flat roof buildings have the cornice running continuously around the building. Gable roof buildings require that a finished return be con-

13-24 *Typical framing details for box cornice returns.*

structed. The type required will be shown on the working design drawings. Two frequently used returns are the **soffit return** and the **Greek return**. A narrow cornice can be finished using a boxed return as shown in **13-23**. This is framed as shown in **13-24**. When the cornice is a box type without horizontal lookouts, the soffit continues up the projected overhang, as shown in **13-25**.

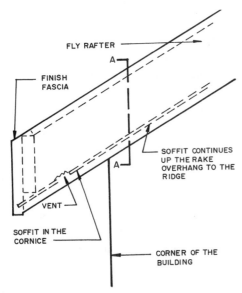

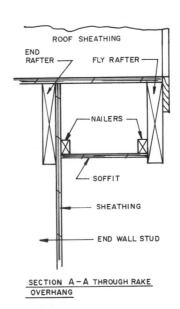

13-25 *The soffit on a sloped box cornice extends up the rake projection to the ridge.*

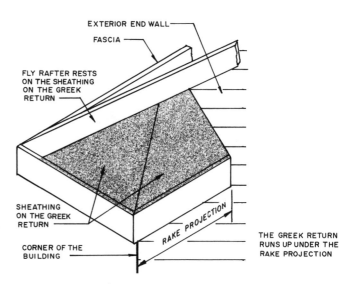

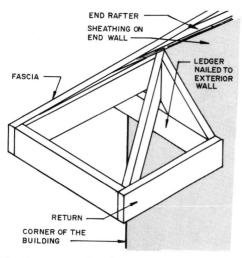

13-26 *Framing a Greek cornice return.*

The Greek return provides the most attractive cornice return. This is actually a little hip-type frame. Typical details are shown in **13-26**.

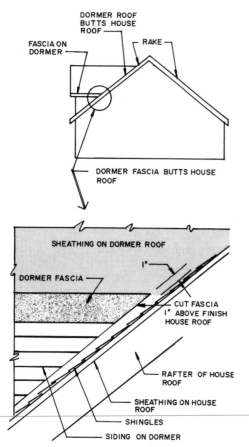

13-27 *Fascias that butt other roofs must be cut so that they clear the roof by at least one inch.*

There are situations where a fascia butts another roof. In this case the butting end of the fascia is cut at the slope of the abutting roof. Keep the sloped end of the fascia at least 1in (25mm) above the surface of the shingles on the abutting roof (see **13-27**).

Aluminum and Vinyl Soffit and Fascia Systems

A typical detail for installing aluminum and vinyl soffits and fascias is shown in **13-28**. Exact details will vary depending on the manufacturer of the product. Installation directions are available from the manufacturer. The cornice has the rough fascia installed. It supports the fascia and soffit. The soffit panel is perforated so that it also serves as the attic vent.

Attic Ventilation

The two major problems occurring in an attic are the collection of **moisture** and the development of **high temperatures.** Even though the ceiling has a vapor barrier, moisture does tend to gravitate to the attic space. In the winter this warm moisture hits the cold roof of sheathing, condenses, and drips onto the insulation, reducing its effectiveness. In very cold climates the moisture freezes on the sheathing and eventually melts as the weather gets warmer. Attics need adequate ventilation to remove this moisture.

In the summer the air in the attic gets very hot. Even though the ceiling is well insulated, air-conditioning costs are increased by the transfer of some of this heat into the living area below. Ventilation in the summer is vital to reducing the air temperature in the attic.

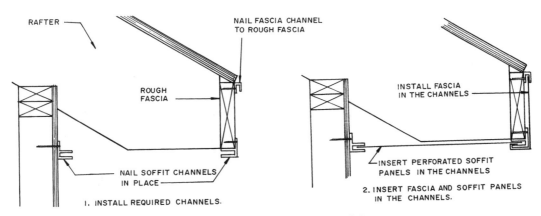

13-28 *Typical installation details for aluminum and vinyl soffits and fascias.*

The amount of **ventilator area** needed is established by the local building code. Typically the **net free area** of the vents should not be less than $\frac{1}{150}$ of the area (square feet) of the space ventilated. If the area is ventilated by vents in the upper portion of the attic space, the required net area of the vents can be $\frac{1}{300}$ of the area (square feet) to be ventilated. All vents should be covered with some form of mesh. The **net area** of a vent is the amount of open unrestricted air space. Since vents are covered with wire mesh the actual size of the vent unit should be double the required net area.

The air movement in the attic begins with vents in the soffit, and it exits the attic with some type of vent mounted high on the roof. Commonly used roof vents include gable end vents, ridge vents, metal ventilators near the ridge, dormer-ventilators, cupolas, and power fans (see **13-29**, **13-30**, and **13-31**).

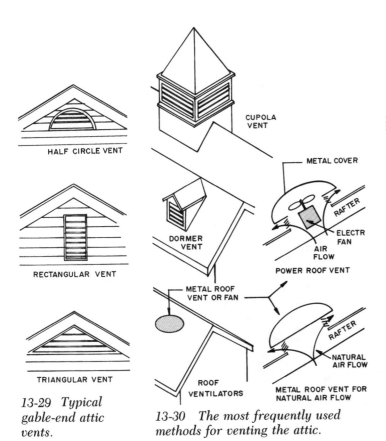

13-29 *Typical gable-end attic vents.*

13-30 *The most frequently used methods for venting the attic.*

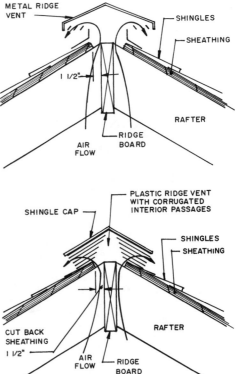

13-31 *Ridge vents are an effective way to ventilate an attic.*

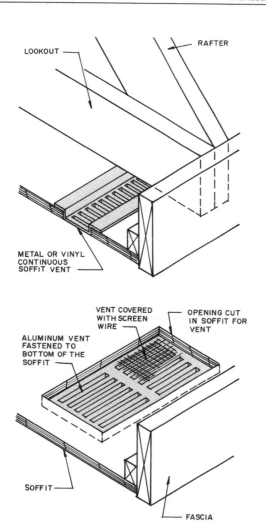

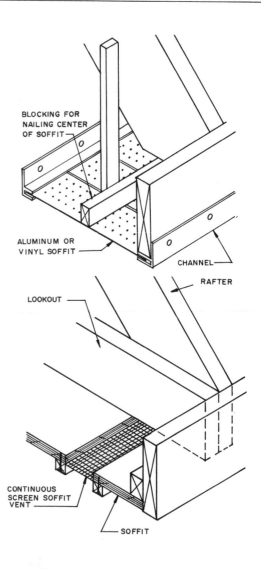

13-32   *Types of soffit vents for boxed cornices.*

13-33   *A vinyl soffit and fascia.* (Courtesy Alcan Building Products)

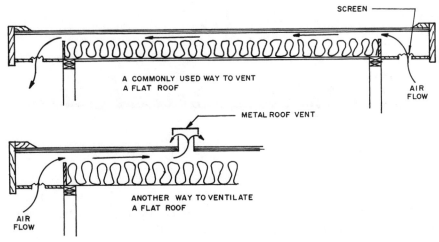

13-34 *Ways to ventilate a flat roof.*

The vents in the soffit may be individual vents spaced evenly along the soffit, continuous vents, or aluminum or vinyl soffits that are perforated so that the entire soffit becomes a vent (see **13-32**). A vinyl soffit and fascia are shown in **13-33**.

Flat roofs require each rafter space to be vented. The insulation must allow an air space between the top of the insulation and the roof sheathing. The most common way to ventilate a flat roof is with continuous vents in the projecting soffit (see **13-34**). Flat roof ventilators and parapet wall ventilators also help vent flat roofs.

Open soffit construction requires that the vents be placed in the frieze block that closes the opening above the exterior wall. Variations for venting an open soffit are shown in **13-35**.

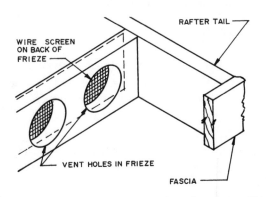

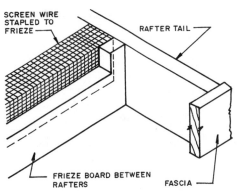

13-35 *Several ways to vent roofs with open-soffit construction.*

14

Finishing the Roof

Roofing materials shield the interior of the building from the elements, provide fire protection, and enhance the exterior appearance. The finished roof is often the dominant feature seen when viewing a house.

The type of finished roofing material to be used is shown on the working design drawings and detailed in the specifications. The local building code also has a bearing on the type of material that can be used.

Roofing Material Choices

On steep-sloped roofs (a slope of 3 in 12—written 3:12—or greater) these materials are used:

1. Fibreglass asphalt and organic asphalt shingles.

2. Wood shakes and shingles.

3. Natural slate.

4. Clay tile and concrete tile.

5. Metal sheet and tile roofing.

Flat and low-sloped roofs (usually a slope of 3:12 or less) the following materials are used:

1. A built-up membrane.

2. A single-ply plastic or rubber membrane.

3. Certain types of metal sheet roofing.

Building Codes

Building codes will specify the physical requirements that a roofing material must meet and the method of installation. For example, in areas that have occasional high winds, the local code may specify the approved type of nail to use and ban the use of staples for installing asphalt or fibreglass shingles. Codes will also specify the level of fire resistance. The American So-

ciety for Testing and Materials standards are used to classify fire resistance into four groups.

Class A materials have the highest resistance to fire. These include materials such as slate, concrete, tile, and clay tile.

Class B materials are used where moderate resistance to fire is required. These include some types of composition shingles and metal roofing.

Class C materials are effective against light exposure to fire and include some asphalt shingles and fire-retardant-treated wood shingles.

Nonclassified materials include untreated wood shingles. The manufacturers indicate the verified rating for each of these materials.

Roofing Materials

A wide choice of roofing materials is available to the architectural designer and home owner. Things considered include the appearance, architectural style, cost, weight, availability, and fire rating. Following are those materials in general use.

Asphalt shingles are made using a felt layer that is constructed of organic materials such as cellulose fibres, and that is saturated with asphalt and has a finished, exposed surface of granular material, such as marble chips, slate, or granite.

Fibreglass asphalt shingles are made similar to the asphalt shingle, except that they are made on a fibreglass base (see **14-1**).

Wood shingles are sawed from Western red cedar, Eastern white cedar, Tidewater cypress, California redwood, and Southern pine logs. The grading differs for the various species. For example, Western red cedar shingles are graded as No. 1 (the best), No. 2, No. 3, and No. 4 (used for undercourses). They are available in 16, 18, and 24in (406, 457, and 609mm) lengths.

14-1 *Asphalt shingles are available in a range of styles and thicknesses.*

14-2 *Wood shakes are hand-split, producing a rough surface.*

Wood shakes are much like wood shingles, except that they are *split* from the logs rather than sawed. Some are split and resawed, producing a shake with a rather smooth side and a rough split side, whereas others have the rough split surface on both sides. They are available in various thicknesses ranging from ½ to ⅝in (12 to 16mm) and lengths of 18 and 24in (457 and 609mm) as shown in **14-2**.

Slate is a natural rock that is mined, cleaved along natural planes of weakness, and then cut to standard

sizes. It has holes drilled in it for nailing to the sheathing. Roofing slate is available in a variety of colors including red, green, purple, blue-grey, grey, black, and blue-black. It is very heavy, and the roof framing must be designed to carry this extra load (see **14-3**).

Clay tile roofing is made from mined clays much the same as those used for brick. It is available in a variety of stock sizes and colors. The finished tile may be glazed or unglazed. Like slate, it is heavy, and the roof structure must be designed to carry it (see **14-4**).

14-3 *Slate shingles are available in a range of colors and hues.* (Courtesy Evergreen Slate Co., Inc.)

14-4 *Clay tile roofing is heavy, durable, and fire-resistant.* (Courtesy Gladding McBean Co.)

14-5 *Concrete tile is made in several styles and a wide range of colors.* (Courtesy Monier)

14-6 *Metal roofing is available in sheets and individual tiles.* (Courtesy Berridge Manufacturing Co.)

Concrete tiles are extruded and steam-cured, producing a strong, dense, stain-resistant roofing material. They are sealed so that they are waterproof and have a semigloss finish. Concrete tiles are available in standard sizes similar to those used for clay roofing tiles. They are also very heavy (see **14-5**).

Metal roofing that is most commonly used is made from steel or aluminum sheet. Steel is usually galvanized and has a colored finish coat. Aluminum roofing also is made with a wide range of colors as a finish coating. Such roofing is manufactured in stock sizes and has a variety of systems for securing it to the sheathing and for locking the panels together to get a waterproof joint. **Metal roof tiles** that look like clay tiles are also available (see **14-6**).

14-7 *This roof has been covered with roofing felt, and the roofer is working the asphalt shingles up to the ridge.* (Courtesy CertainTeed Corp.)

Installing Asphalt and Fibreglass Asphalt Shingles

While the finish carpenter may on occasion be required to install the shingles, they are usually installed by the crew of a roofing contractor. Before starting the installation of the shingles, be certain the sheathing is covered with 15- or 30-pound roofing felt. Make certain there are no nails or other projections that might pierce the shingles. Finally sweep the surface clear of any loose objects such as nails or wood blocks (see **14-7**).

Check to see that all flashing has been completed and that anything that must pierce the roof, such as a sewer vent stack, has been installed and the flashing for it is available (refer to **14-14** and **14-15**).

If a metal drip edge is specified, be certain that it is in place. It is installed on the rake and cornice as shown in **14-8**. This helps prevent water from running back under the end shingle and getting behind the fascia. This material is available preformed from your building materials supplier.

While there are a variety of these types of shingles, this discussion will center on the one most commonly used, the 12 by 36in (approx. 30 by 91cm) square butt, three-tab shingle (see **14-9**).

Begin by installing the starter strip at the eave. It can be cut from a roll of roofing that matches the shingles or it can be a row of actual shingles turned upside down so that the space between the tabs is up (see **14-10**). This should overhang the fascia by about ½in (13mm). This gives coverage below the slots in the first row of shingles.

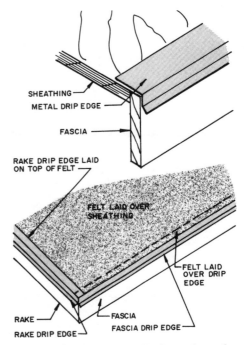

14-8 *Metal drip edge is installed on the rake and cornice.*

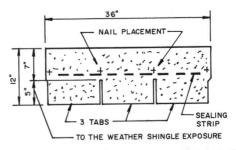

14-9 *A typical three-tab organic asphalt of fibreglass asphalt shingle.*

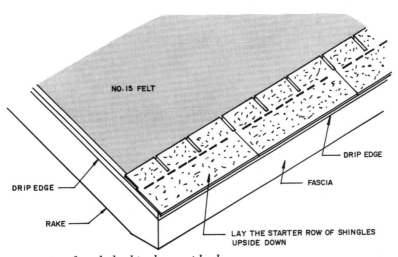

14-10 *Lay the starter strip of asphalt shingles upside down.*

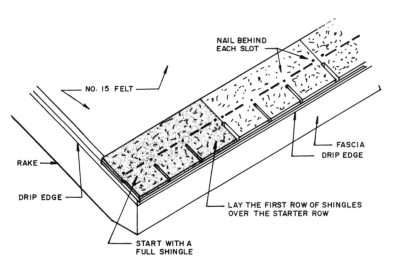

14-11   *Start the first row of shingles with a full shingle.*

Lay the first course on top of the starter strip. Start it with a full shingle as shown in **14-11**. The second row is begun one-half of a tab off the first. This allows the space between the tabs to line up vertically (see **14-12**). The third course is started with a full shingle, and then the procedure repeats itself (see **14-13**).

Before actually nailing the first row, check it out across the roof to the other side. You do not want to end up with a very narrow tab on the other edge; these usually break off over time. If this configuration occurs, move the first row over to allow a wider end tab on the other side.

Place one nail behind the slot between each tab, as shown in **14-11**. As additional courses are laid, the lower edge of the shingle should line up with the top of the slot on the course below it. This gives the ex-

posure required by the shingles being used. The dark asphalt strips above the exposure area are used to seal the shingles together; as the sun heats the shingles, this strip softens, bonding the shingles together. This process is essential if the shingles are to resist high winds.

When the shingles reach something projecting through the roof, the shingle is cut to fit over it. Then the flashing is placed over the shingle, and the roofing continues (see **14-14**).

When the shingles reach flashing, such as on a chimney, lay the shingles up to the chimney. Then install the flashing so that it is over the shingles on the front of the chimney. If the flashing is already in place, slip the shingles under it. Then proceed to install the shingles around the chimney, letting them overlap

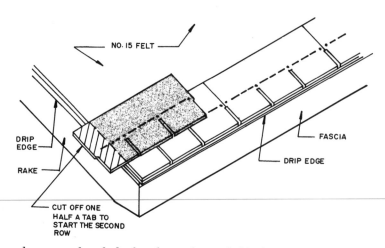

14-12   *Start the second course of asphalt shingles with one half of one of the tabs removed.*

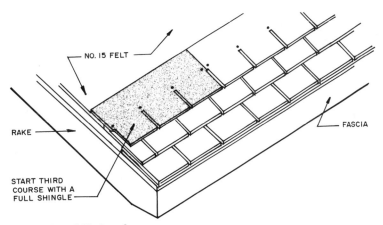

14-13   *Start the third course with a full shingle.*

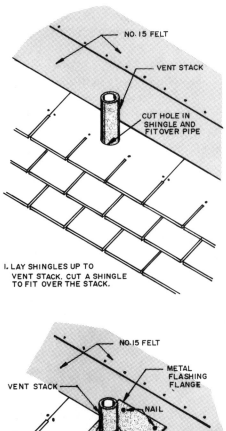

1. LAY SHINGLES UP TO
VENT STACK. CUT A SHINGLE
TO FIT OVER THE STACK.

the flashing as shown in **14-15**. Notice that the flashing is in two parts. The base flashing rests on the roof sheathing, laps up the chimney, and is bonded to it with mastic. The counter-flashing is set in a mortar joint and overlaps the base flashing.

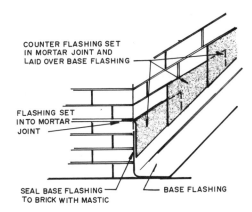

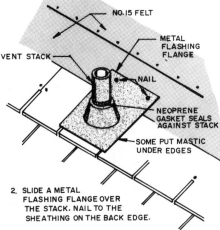

2. SLIDE A METAL
FLASHING FLANGE OVER
THE STACK. NAIL TO THE
SHEATHING ON THE BACK EDGE.

14-14   *Cut the shingle to fit over the pipe and place flashing on top of the shingle.*

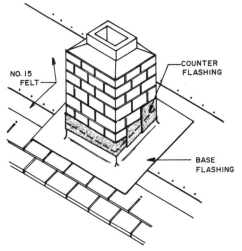

14-15   *Flashing used around a chimney.*

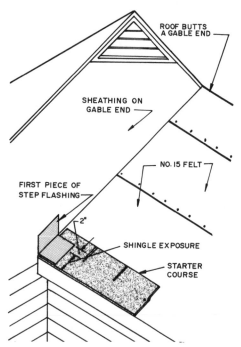

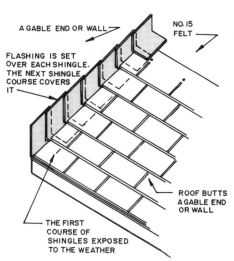

14-16 *When shingles meet a wall, the flashing is placed against the sheathing and over the shingle. The starter course is shown.*

14-17 *The flashing is placed over each course of shingles and is covered by the next course.*

When the shingles butt against a vertical wall, such as a dormer wall, the joint is flashed using metal flashing shingles that are applied over each course of shingles (see **14-16**). The flashing is usually 10in (254mm) longer and 2in (51mm) wider than the shingle expo-sure. It is bent to extend 5in (127mm) over the roof and 5in (127mm) up the wall. It is not nailed to the wall or roof sheathing. This permits movement to oc-cur without breaking the seal formed by the flashing. As the flashing shingles are installed with each course, they are covered by the course above them (see **14-17**). The flashing on the wall is covered with the finish siding. Keep the siding about 1in (25mm) above the roof surface, and paint the sawed end. This helps pre-vent decay on the end of the siding (see **14-18**).

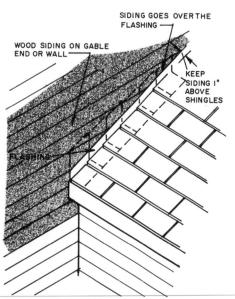

14-18 *The flashing on the sheathing is covered by the siding.*

14-19 *The hip is covered by the hip shingles.* (Cour-tesy CertainTeed Corp.)

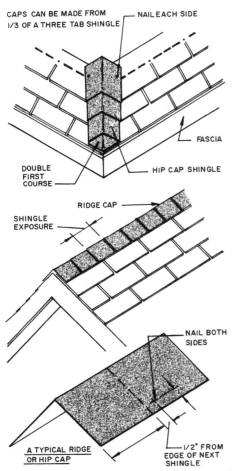

14-20 *Install the ridge cap and hip cap shingles to complete the job.*

The ridge and hips on a hipped roof are covered with ridge shingles that are available from the manufacturer or can be made by cutting the butt shingles into 9 × 12in (approx. 23 × 30cm) pieces (see 14-19). They are laid over the ridge or hip and nailed to the sheathing. The same exposure is used for the roof (see 14-20). The nails are placed behind the exposure, and one nail is placed on each side.

A common way to handle valleys is to interlace the shingles to form a woven valley. The valley must have a 36in (91.4cm) wide flashing of 50-pound roll roofing nailed to the sheathing. The shingles are interlaced as shown in 14-21.

Asphalt shingles can be nailed or stapled. In some areas, as mentioned, building codes regulate what is used because of a need to resist high winds. In 14-22 asphalt shingles are shown being installed with a roofing coil nailer. The nails are coiled in the cylinder below the handle and are driven by compressed air.

14-22 *Asphalt shingles can be rapidly laid with a roofing coil-nailer operated by compressed air. (Courtesy Senco Products, Inc.)*

14-21 *Shingles can be interlaced to form a woven valley.*

247

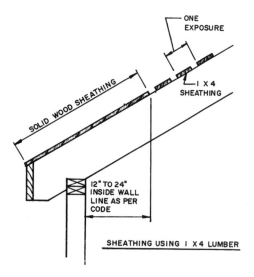

SHEATHING USING 1 X 4 LUMBER

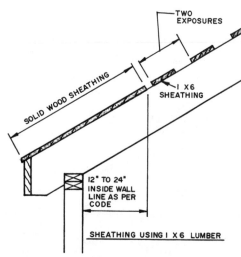

SHEATHING USING 1 X 6 LUMBER

14-23 Spacing wood sheathing for the installation of wood shingles.

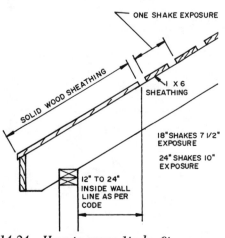

14-24 How to space 1in by 6in sheathing when wood shakes are to be used.

Installing Wood Shingles and Shakes

The minimum roof slope for which wood shingles are recommended is 3:12 and for wood shakes it is 4:12. Lower sloped roofs can use these materials if special methods of application are used.

The sheathing may be plywood, oriented strand board, or solid wood. If solid wood is used, it is spaced so that air can circulate between it and the wood shingles. There are two ways to install spaced, wood sheathing for use with wood shingles. If 1 × 4in lumber is used, it is spaced from the front edge of one board to the front edge of the next by a distance equal to the exposure to be used. If 1 × 6in lumber is used, the distance is equal to two exposures (see 14-23). There are exceptions to this for some exposures.

When using wood shakes, the sheathing should be 1 × 6in stock with the spacing equal to the exposure, but never more than 7½in (19.1cm) for 18in (45.7cm) shakes and 10in (25.4cm) for 24in (61cm) shakes (see 14-24).

14-25 Recommended exposure for Western cedar shingles and shakes.

	Shingles	
Length	Slope 3/12 to 4/12	4/12 and steeper
16"	3¾"	5"
18"	4¼"	5½"
24"	5¾"	7½"
	Shakes	
Length	Slope 3/12	4/12 and steeper
18"	Cannot use on this slope	7½"
24"	"	10"

(Courtesy Cedar Shake and Shingle Bureau)

14-26 Recommended nail type and length for use on cedar shakes and shingles.

Shingles—New Roof	Nail Type	Nail Length
16" and 18"	Box	3d (1¼")
24"	Box	4d (1½")
Shakes—New Roof	**Nail Type**	**Nail Length**
18" Straight Split	Box	5d (1¾")
18" and 24" Split and Resawn	Box	6d (2")
24" Tapersplit	Box	5d (1¾")
18" and 24" Tapersawn	Box	6d (2")

(Courtesy Cedar Shake and Shingle Bureau)

Solid sheathing should be installed from the edge of the rafters to a point 12 to 24in (30.5 to 61cm) inside the exterior wall. Solid sheathing is recommended on the entire roof in areas where wind-driven snow is expected. A 36in (91.4cm) wide layer of No. 15 felt is installed at the eave and extends up the roof over the exterior wall.

The allowable exposure depends on the grade of wood shingle or shake and the slope of the roof. Recommended data for No. 1 Western cedar shingles and shakes are given in **14-25**.

The nails used should be corrosion-resistant aluminum, zinc-coated, or stainless steel. Recommended sizes are shown in **14-26**. They should penetrate at least ½in (13mm) into the sheathing; deeper penetrations are required by some codes. They must be flush with the surface of the shingle or shake. Two nails must be used with very shingle or shake. Units over 8in (203mm) wide should be split to form two shingles or shakes.

If codes permit the use of power-driven staples, they should be aluminum or stainless steel, 16 gauge, with 7/16in (11mm) minimum crowns. They should penetrate at least ½in (13mm) into the sheathing and be driven flush with the surface of the shingle. Two staples must be driven in each shingle or shake in the same location as specified for nails. Nails or staples should be placed ¾ to 1in (19 to 25mm) from the side edges of the shingles or shakes and 1½ to 2in (38 to 51mm) above the butt line of the following course.

Installing Wood Shingles

Begin the installation of wood shingles by laying a course of starter shingles with the butt edges overhanging the finished fascia 1½in (38mm). Then go over this with a course of standard-size shingles, making certain the joints between shingles are no closer than 1½in (38mm) as shown in **14-27**. Space the edges of the shingles at least ¼in (6mm) apart, but no more than ⅜in (10mm).

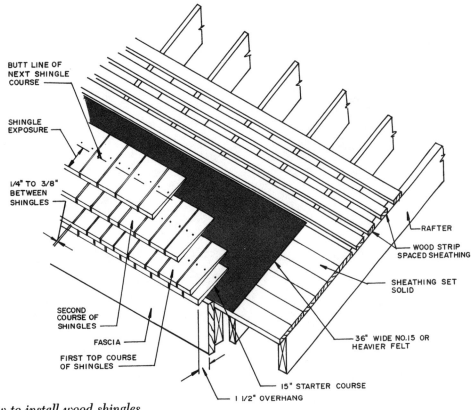

TWO NAILS PER SHINGLE SPACED 3/4" TO I" IN FROM EACH SIDE OF SHINGLE AND I 1/2" TO 2" BEHIND BUTT LINE OF NEXT COURSE.

BUTT LINE OF NEXT SHINGLE COURSE

SHINGLE EXPOSURE

1/4" TO 3/8" BETWEEN SHINGLES

SECOND COURSE OF SHINGLES

FASCIA

FIRST TOP COURSE OF SHINGLES

RAFTER

WOOD STRIP SPACED SHEATHING

SHEATHING SET SOLID

36" WIDE NO.15 OR HEAVIER FELT

15" STARTER COURSE

I 1/2" OVERHANG

14-27 How to install wood shingles.

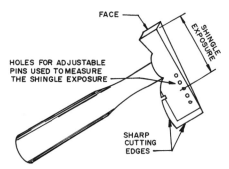

14-28   *A typical shingler's hatchet*

Start the second course with the butt above the butt of the first course a distance equal to the required exposure, to maintain the desire exposure. Set the pin on the head of the shingling hatchet so that the exposure is the distance from the pin to the face of the hatchet. Another way is to run a chalk line or wood straightedge across the roof (see **14-28**). Continue each course, observing the required 1½in (38mm) spacing between edge joints.

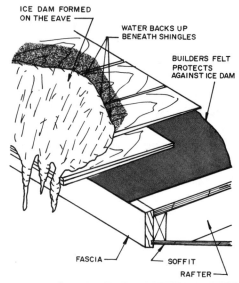

14-29   *An ice dam forms on the eave when heat lost to the attic melts some of the snow on the roof.*

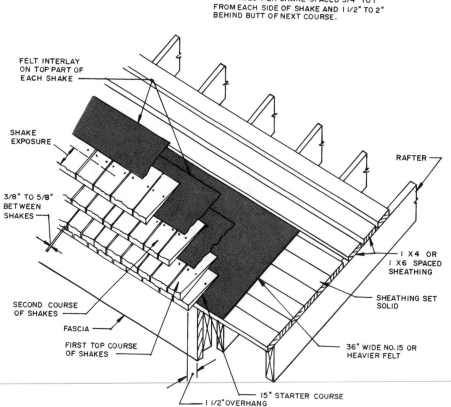

14-30   *A roofing felt interlay is used when installing wood shakes.*
(Courtesy Cedar Shake and Shingle Bureau)

14-31 *The installation of wood shakes.* (Courtesy Cedar Shake and Shingle Bureau)

Usually a felt interlay is not required when using wood shingles. It is usually required, however, with wood shakes; consult the local codes on this requirement. In both cases, a felt layer is installed over the solid wood sheathing at the eave. This provides protection from possible water damage to the inside of the house by ice dams that may form on the cornice. These occur when snow on the roof is melted by heat lost to the attic; the water drains to the cornice and freezes there, forming an ice dam. The water then begins to back up under the shingles and leaks into the attic. In areas where this is a likely problem, additional felt may be required over the cornice and on the roof sheathing over the interior of the building (see **14-29**).

Installing Wood Shakes

A 36in (91.4cm) wide, No. 15 felt is installed at the eave. The first course uses a 15in (38.1cm) starter shake which is covered with a second course of standard-length shakes. The butts of the first course overhang the fascia by 1½in (38mm). The joints between shakes should be spaced at least ⅜in (10mm), but no wider than ⅝in (16mm).

An 18in (45.7cm) wide, No. 30 felt interlay is placed between each course of shakes (see **14-30**). The bottom edge of the felt is located above the butt a distance equal to twice the exposure (see **14-31**). There are some cases where this felt can be omitted; consult local codes, as always, for specific requirements.

251

Other Installation Details

Hips and ridges are capped with preassembled hip and ridge units. These can be factory-made or site-made caps. When installed, the overlap joint must alternate sides of the ridge or hip (see **14-32**). The exposure to the weather is the same as that used for the roof. It requires longer nails because they penetrate both the cap and the roof shingle. Most codes require that the nails penetrate the sheathing ½in (13mm) or go completely through it. The end cap is always doubled (see **14-33**).

Valleys are flashed by first installing a layer of No. 15 or heavier felt up the valley. Metal flashing is installed over this. It should be painted galvanized steel (paint both sides) or aluminum. The metal flashing should extend over the fascia to the butt of the first course of shingles (see **14-34**). The grain of the shingles should not be parallel with the centerline of the valley. Joints between the shingles should not break into the valley.

With valleys for wood-shingle roofs over a slope of 12:12, the flashing should extend not less than 7in (17.8cm) on each side of the centerline. For roof slopes less than 12:12 this distance should be increased to 10in (25.4cm) as shown in **14-35**.

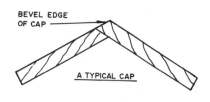

A TYPICAL CAP

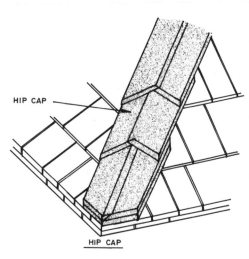

HIP CAP

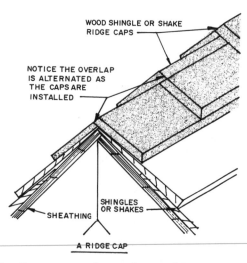

A RIDGE CAP

14-32 *Caps are used on ridges and hips.*

14-33 *Wood shake caps close the roof at the hip.* (Courtesy Cedar Shake and Shingle Bureau)

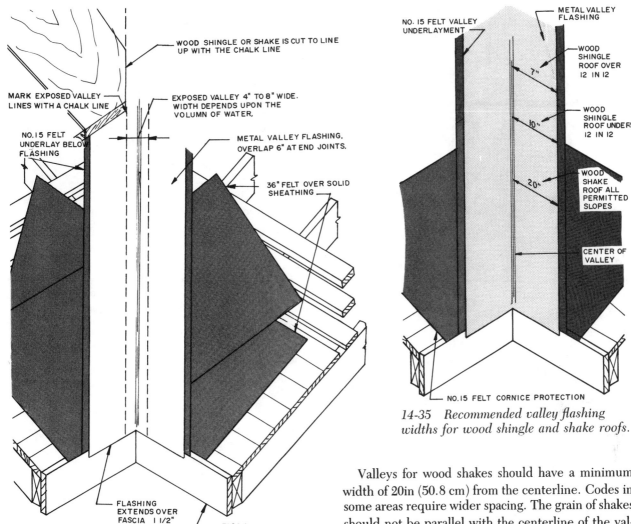

14-34 *How to flash a valley when installing wood shingles or shakes.*

14-35 *Recommended valley flashing widths for wood shingle and shake roofs.*

Valleys for wood shakes should have a minimum width of 20in (50.8 cm) from the centerline. Codes in some areas require wider spacing. The grain of shakes should not be parallel with the centerline of the valley. Joints between shakes should not break into the valley (see **14-35** and **14-36**).

14-36 *A metal valley is used with wood shingles and shakes.* (Courtesy Cedar Shake and Shingle Bureau)

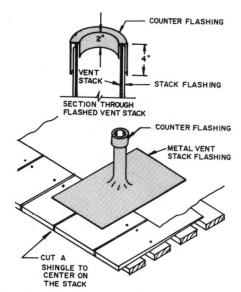

14-37 *Typical vent stack flashing.*

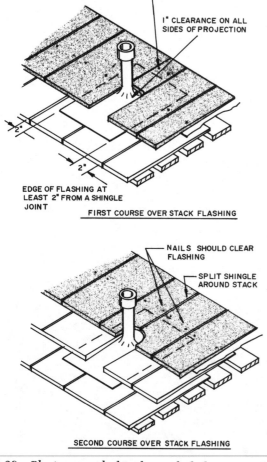

14-38 *Placing wood shingles and shakes around a flashed vent pipe.*

Projections through the roof, such as a vent stack, should be flashed and counter-flashed (see **14-37**). The flashing should extend 3in (76mm) under the sheathing paper. It should be long enough to cover the shingle or shake course just below the pipe and extend up under the straight course above the pipe. The positioning of shingles and shakes around the projection is shown in **14-38**.

Details for flashing and installing shingles or shakes when the roof butts a wall or chimney are shown in **14-39** and **14-40**. Nails should not penetrate the flashing.

Additional technical information is available from the Cedar Shake and Shingle Bureau, 515 116th Ave., NE, Suite 275, Bellevue, WA 98004-5294.

Clay and Concrete Tile

Roofing tile is available as a clay or concrete product. The shapes and sizes are about the same. The manufacturers of these products can supply information on the sizes they produce and their recommended installation details (see **14-41**).

Clay roofing tile may be glazed or unglazed. Interlocking-type tiles are used on roofs with slopes of 3:12 or higher. Flat shingle-type tiles are used on roofs with slopes of 5:12 or more. The roofing is heavy, durable, and fire-resistant.

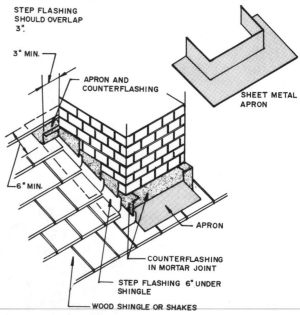

14-39 *Flashing a chimney when installing wood shingles or shakes.*

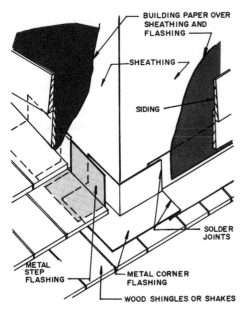

14-41   *These concrete circular roofing tiles are nailed to the sheathing.* (Courtesy Monier)

14-40   *Flashing a roof that butts a wall when using wood shingles or shakes.*

Concrete tiles are manufactured in a wide range of colors and tend to be less heavy than clay tile. Following are examples of typical installation recommendations.

Flat interlocking shingle tiles are installed over solid sheathing that is covered with roofing felt. The installation at the eave begins with a flat under-eave tile or metal drip edging. The gable rakes are covered with right- and left-side rake tiles or metal drip edging. Special V-shaped tiles are used on the ridge and hips. A typical installation is shown in **14-42**.

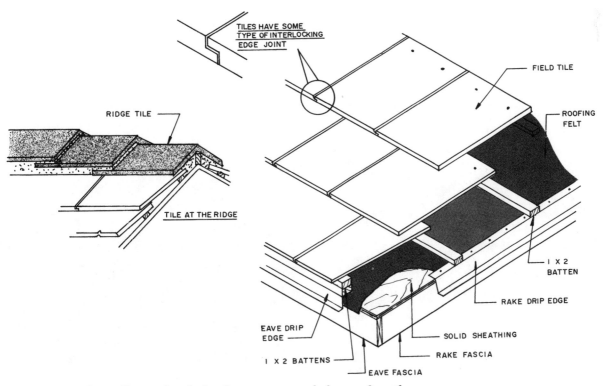

14-42   *Typical installation details for flat concrete and clay roofing tile.*

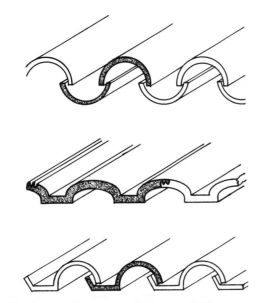

14-43   Some of the curved tiles available.

Curved clay and concrete tiles are made in several ways. Two types are shown in **14-43**. Installation details for one type are shown in **14-44**. The hips and ridges are covered with curved tiles that are set in a cement mortar and nailed in place (see **14-45**).

Both types are flashed in the same manner as other roofing materials.

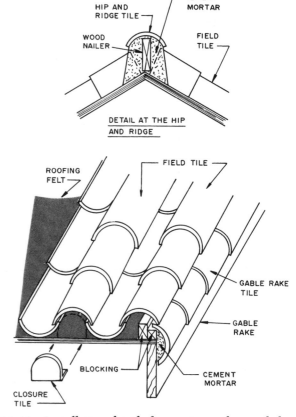

14-44   Installation details for one type of curved clay and concrete roofing tile.

14-45   The concrete ridge caps finish the roof. (Courtesy Monier)

14-46   The metal standing-seam roof panels run from the ridge to the eave as a single panel. (Courtesy ATAS Aluminum Corporation)

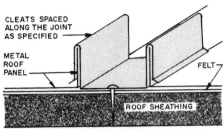

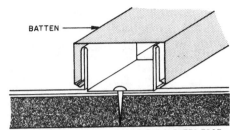

1. INSTALL THE ROOF PANELS OVER THE ROOFING FELT AND JOIN THEM WITH THE METAL CLEAT.

2. SNAP THE BATTEN CAP OVER THE CLEATED EDGE.

14-47 *Construction details for a metal panel steep-sloped roof with batten seams.*

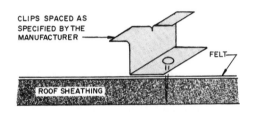

1. FASTEN THE CLEATS TO THE ROOF SHEATHING.

Metal Roofing

Two types of metal roofing in common use are panels and tiles. The panels can cover a long section of roof (see **14-46**). They are joined at the edges with watertight joints. The design of the joints depends on the manufacturer of the roofing. On steep-sloped roofs, batten, capped, and standing seams are used (see **14-47**, **14-48**, and **14-49**). Some panels must be installed over solid sheathing, whereas others have sufficient strength to span unsupported distances between purlins.

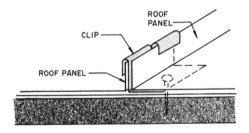

2. BUTT METAL ROOF PANELS TO THE SERIES OF CLIPS AND BEND CLIPS OVER THE FLANGES.

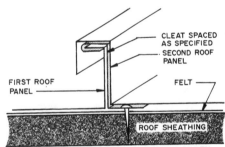

1. FASTEN FIRST ROOF PANEL TO SHEATHING WITH A SERIES OF CLEATS. BUTT SECOND ROOF PANEL TO THE CLEATS.

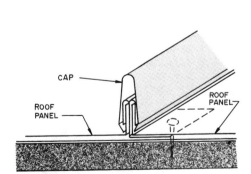

3. SNAP THE CAP OVER THE SEAM.

14-48 *Construction details showing the use of a capped seam on a steep-slope metal panel roof system.*

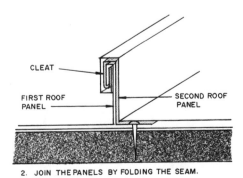

2. JOIN THE PANELS BY FOLDING THE SEAM.

14-49 *A typical detail for a standing-seam assembly for a steep-slope metal panel installation.*

14-50   These metal tiles look like clay tiles but are much lighter. (Courtesy ATAS Aluminum Corporation)

Metal shakes and shingles are lightweight, yet have the appearance of heavier roofing materials such as tile and slate. The surface is embossed in a range of textures, patterns, and colors (see **14-50**). They are fastened to the roof sheathing with metal clips. One system is shown in **14-51**. The actual system used depends on the design provided by the tile manufacturer.

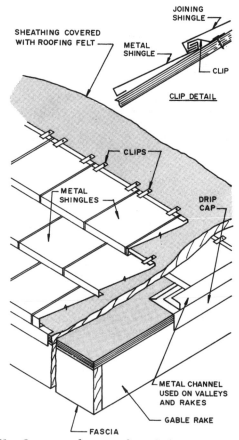

14-51   One way that metal roof tiles are fastened to the roof sheathing.

15

Finishing the Exterior

The carpenter must examine working design drawings of the elevations and wall sections of the building to ascertain the specified exterior finish material. Among these are solid wood, hardboard, plywood, wood shingles, aluminum, steel, vinyl, and masonry products.

Wood Siding

Quality wood siding is easy to work, relatively free from warp, and holds paint well. Best-quality wood siding should be free from knots and pitch pockets, because they will tend to bleed through the paint. It should have a moisture content of 10 to 12 percent, except in dry areas, where the moisture content could be as low as 8 percent. Wood siding should be stored flat and protected from the weather. It should be primed as soon as it has been installed.

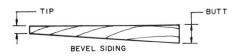

15-1   Bevel siding (see 15-2 for sizes).

The architectural drawings should specify the specie of wood. Some species hold up better, and others are more expensive. The best species include cypress, redwood, cedar, Eastern white pine, sugar pine, and Western white pine. Yellow poplar, spruce, Ponderosa pine, and Western hemlock are also good. Southern pine, Western larch, and Douglas fir are rated as fair.

Horizontal Wood Siding

Horizontal wood siding is available in three types: **bevel**, **drop**, and **boards**. They are manufactured in a variety of patterns, from solid wood, hardboard, and plywood.

Wood Bevel Siding

Typical sizes for **bevel siding** are given in **15-1** and **15-2**. These will vary some with the different lumber manufacturing associations in various parts of the United States or Canada. Usually one side has a rough-sawn surface and the other a smooth planed surface. The rough surface is often exposed when a stain is to be used.

15-2   Bevel siding sizes.

Nominal (inches)		Dressed Dry (inches)	
Thickness	**Width**	**Thickness**	**Width**
½″	4	all	3½″
	5	15/32″ butt	4½″
	6	3/16″ tip	5½″
¾″	8	all	7¼″
	10	¾″ butt	9¼″
	12	3/16″ tip	11¼″

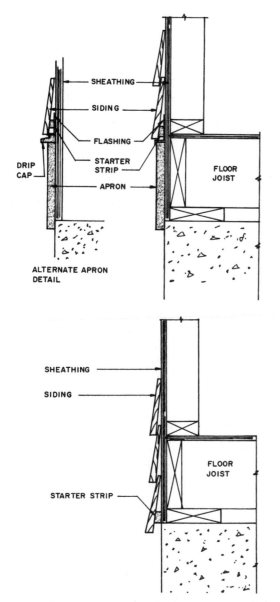

15-3 *Two ways to start the installation of bevel siding.*

15-4 *Wood siding nailing recommendations.*

Siding Thickness	With Plywood Sheathing	With Nonnail-bearing Sheathing
½″	7d	2″ plus thickness of sheathing
¾″	8d	2¼″ plus thickness of sheathing

Installing Solid-Wood Bevel Siding

Bevel siding begins with the bottom course at the sill. There are several ways to start the bottom course (see **15-3**). One uses a wood **starting strip** that holds the bottom of the first course out from the foundation. Another uses an **apron board,** sometimes called **fascia**, around the sill and has a **drip cap** of some kind on top. The choice depends on the decision of the architect and will appear on the elevations and wall section.

Bevel siding should overlap at least one inch. The exact overlap and exposed surface depend on the width of siding required and the need to space around windows. If possible the top edge of the siding should butt up against the bottom of the windowsill. To see if this is possible, measure the distance from the windowsill to the top of the foundation, allowing some overlap of the foundation. If this distance can be divided to give one inch overlap or more and have a course end at the bottom of the window, then this is the measurement used. If not, then the course at the window will have to be notched around the window. This should be carefully done so that a minimum of space is left.

The size of nail to use depends on the type of sheathing and the thickness of the siding. The nail must penetrate the stud 1½in (38mm) (see **15-4**).

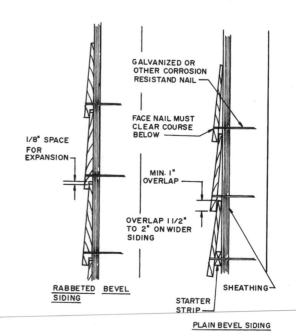

15-5 *Nailing wood bevel siding.*

When nailing the siding, the nail should be placed so that it misses the bottom edge of the course below (see 15-5). This is necessary to allow for expansion and contraction of the siding.

There are several ways to frame external corners when installing bevel siding (see 15-6). One mitres the siding and the other butts it against corner boards. A one-inch nominal square strip is used to form an internal corner. Metal corner strips are also used for inside and outside corners.

Whenever you are able to, try to avoid having to butt wood siding to complete a course. If this turns out to be unavoidable be certain that the butt joint is made with clean, square cuts. Some dip the cut end in a water-repellent preservative to protect it from rot.

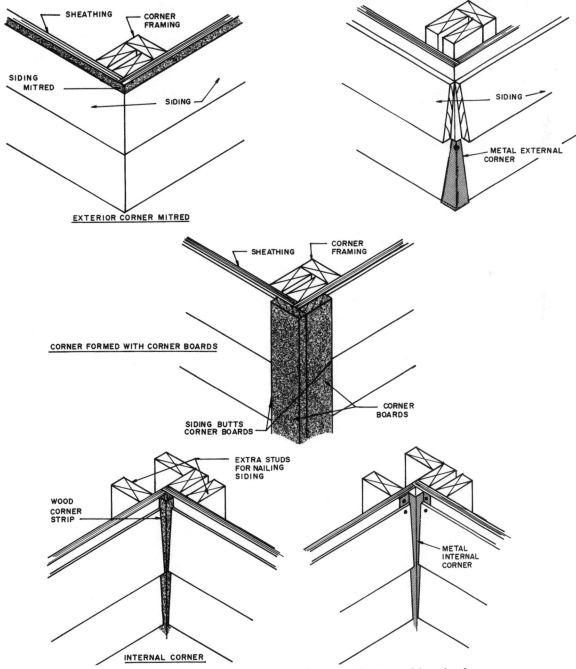

15-6 Ways to construct internal and external corners when installing wood bevel siding.

Other Solid-Wood Siding Profiles

There are many patterns of **drop siding** manufactured. Some of these are shown in **15-7**. While the sizes of drop siding available vary, those given in **15-8** are typical.

Installing Other Wood Siding Profiles

These siding materials are installed in the same manner as bevel siding, except that they are placed flat against the sheathing. The tongue on each piece is inserted in a groove or rabbet in the adjoining piece. A space is left between each to allow for expansion and contraction (see **15-9**) The siding is face-nailed with galvanized nails. Six-inch-wide siding is nailed through the siding into a stud with only one nail. Wider stock requires two nails. Details for starting the first course are shown in **15-9**. Internal and external corners are formed in the same way as described for bevel siding.

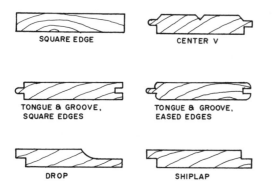

15-7   *Several types of rabbeted wood siding.*

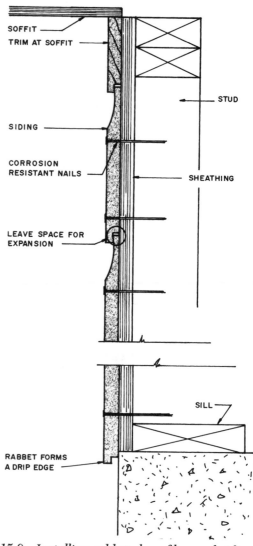

15-9   *Installing rabbeted profile wood siding.*

15-8   *Wood siding sizes.*

Nominal (inches)		Actual (inches)		
		Shiplap	**Tongue-and-Groove**	**Drop Siding**
1 × 4	Overall	—	3⅜	—
	Face	—	3⅛	—
1 × 6	Overall	5½	5⅜	5⅜
	Face	5⅛	5⅛	5
1 × 8	Overall	7¼	7⅛	7⅛
	Face	6⅞	6⅞	6¾
1 × 10	Overall	9¼	9⅛	9⅛
	Face	8⅞	8⅞	8¾
1 × 12	Overall	11¼	11¼	11⅛
	Face	10⅞	10⅞	10¾

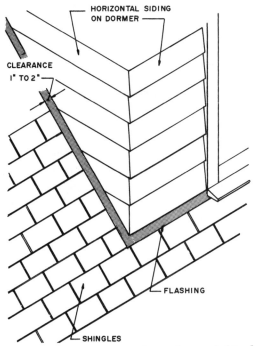

-10 *Keep the siding away from the roof shingles.*

Other Applications

Dormers usually have wood siding in a horizontal application. The siding is applied as just described, except that it is cut 1 to 2in (25 to 51mm) short of meeting the roof. This cut end must be coated with water-repellent material and carefully painted to keep moisture out of the wood (see **15-10**).

Another frequently occurring situation is when the siding changes to another pattern. A typical example is the use of horizontal siding on the end wall and then vertical siding or panel siding on the gable end. One way to handle this is to install a drip cap and flashing on top of the horizontal siding (see **15-11**). This provides a means of drainage for water coming down the gable end. Another technique is to set out the gable end framing, and cut the ends of the vertical siding on an angle, providing a drip edge (see **15-12**).

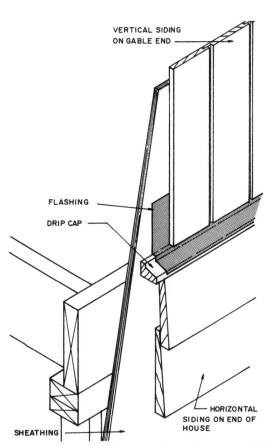

!5-11 *A transition of materials can be accomplished with a flashed drip cap.*

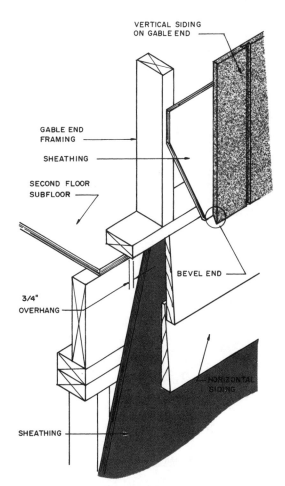

15-12 *A transition of materials on the gable end can be made by setting out the gable-end framing.*

Vertical Solid-Wood Siding

Vertical solid wood siding includes **tongue-and-groove** and **rabbeted siding** and some form of **board-and-batten.** The tongue-and-groove and rabbeted siding fits flat against the sheathing, and is one board thick (see **15-13**). The board-and-batten uses square-edged boards flat against the sheathing and to cover the space between the boards (see **15-14**).

Recommended nailing patterns are shown in **15-13** and **15-14**. The nails are placed to allow for expansion and contraction.

Whereas horizontal siding can be nailed to the studs, vertical siding requires other preparation. Solid 2×4 blocking 24in (61cm) O.C. between the studs provides good nailing. If nonnailable sheathing is used, 1×4 furring strips can be nailed 24in (61cm) O.C. across the wall and the siding nailed to them. If ⅝in (16mm) or thicker plywood sheathing is used, the siding can be nailed into the sheathing. Place a layer of permeable building paper that allows water vapor trapped in the wall to escape over the sheathing.

Installation at the sill and soffit and forming inside and exterior corners are shown in **15-15**.

Nails Used with Wood Siding

Nails commonly used to install wood siding are shown in **15-16**. They should be galvanized steel or a corrosion-resistant material. Ring-threaded or spiral-threaded nails have the greatest holding power. Smooth-shank nails may loosen over a period of years.

There are three types of points available. The blunt point reduces splitting. The diamond point is possibly the most commonly used point. The needle point has good holding power but is more likely to split the siding than the other two.

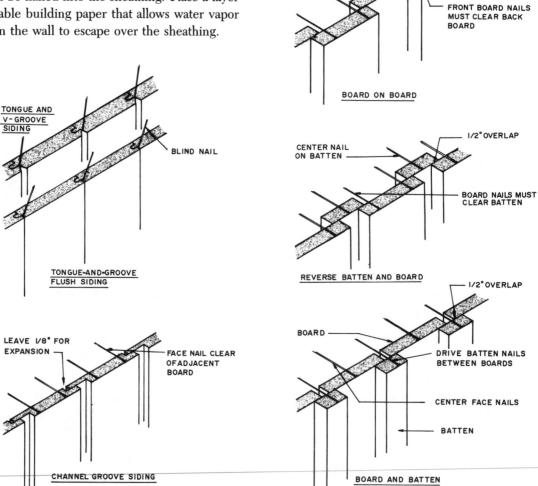

15-13 *Typical vertical installations of wood siding.*

15-14 *Types of wood board-and-batten siding.*

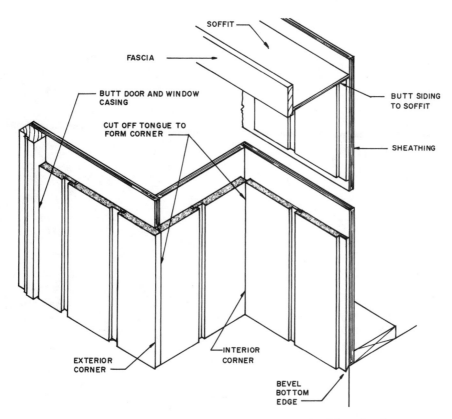

15-15   *Installation details for vertical wood tongue-and-groove and rabbeted siding.*

Wood Shingles and Shakes

Wood shingles and shakes are made from cedar, redwood, and cypress, and they are available in a variety of sizes and patterns. **Shingles** are sawed flat on both sides and are available in *random widths* as well as uniform widths of 4, 5, and 6in (10.2, 12.7, and 15.2cm)—also called **dimension shingles.** They are available in four grades and at lengths of 16, 18, and

24in (40.6, 45.7, and 61cm). Examples of some of the patterned dimension shingles are shown in **15-17**. **Shakes** are available as **straight split, tapersplit,** and **handsplit-and-resawn.** They are available in 18, 24, and 32in (45.7, 61, and 81.3cm) lengths and random widths. The surface is very rough because it is formed by splitting the log (see **15-18**).

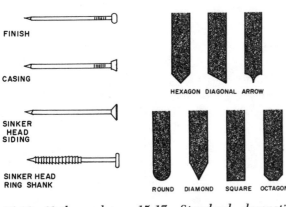

15-16   *Nails used to install wood siding.*

15-17   *Standard decorative sawn-wood shingles.*

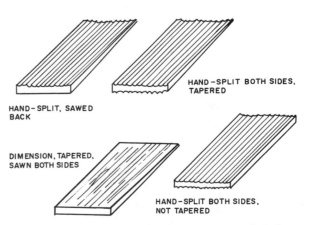

15-18   *Common types of wood shingles and shakes.*

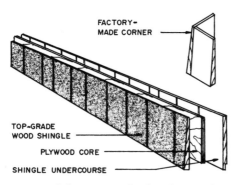

FACTORY-MADE CORNER

TOP-GRADE WOOD SHINGLE

PLYWOOD CORE

SHINGLE UNDERCOURSE

15-19   *A typical factory-made shingle panel used as exterior siding.*

Grading of shingles had shakes varies with the species of wood. Western red cedar grades are No. 1, No. 2, and No. 3; redwood grades are No. 1 and No. 2; and bald cypress grades are No. 1, Bests, Primas, Economy, and Clippers. The No. 1 grade in each case is the best.

Random-width shingles are packed by the **square** (100 square feet) while dimension widths are packed 1000 shingles per **bundle.**

Another wood shingle product is a **panel** product having wood shingles bonded to a plywood backer board. Panels are usually one shingle wide and 8 feet long (see **15-19**). Prefabricated corner boards are available.

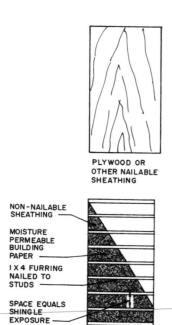

PLYWOOD OR OTHER NAILABLE SHEATHING

NON-NAILABLE SHEATHING

MOISTURE PERMEABLE BUILDING PAPER

I X 4 FURRING NAILED TO STUDS

SPACE EQUALS SHINGLE EXPOSURE

NON-NAILABLE SHEATHING

15-21   *Preparing the wall to receive wood shingles.*

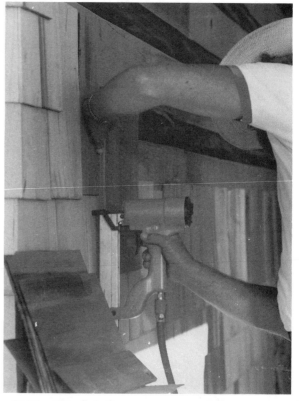

15-20   *Wood shakes are power-nailed to 1 × 4 wood furring when applied over non-nail-holding sheathing.* (Courtesy Senco Products, Inc.)

Installing Wood Shingles and Shakes as Siding

The wall to receive the shingles must have a sheathing, such as plywood, that will hold nails. If soft sheathing, such as foam plastic, is used, 1 × 4 furring strips must be nailed over the sheathing and into the studs (see **15-20**). The spacing between the furring strips equals the shingle exposure (see **15-21**). The sheathing must be covered with a building paper that permits the passage of vapor from inside the building.

The shingles are laid in uniform courses, similar to bevel siding. The amount exposed to the weather can be varied to help meet the heads and sills of windows in a proper manner. Recommended shingle exposures are given in **15-22**.

Wood shingles are applied as a single or double course. Single-course application is shown in **15-23**. The first course is doubled, providing a drip edge on the outside shingle. It should overlap the foundation by one inch. Each course is nailed over the one below, leaving the calculated exposure. It is nailed so

15-22   *Wood shingle and shake siding exposure length recommendations.*

(inches)	Shingles			Shakes		
Length	16	18	24	18	24	32
Single Course	6–7½	6–8½	8–11½	8½	11½	15
Double Course	8–12	9–14	12–16	14	20	—

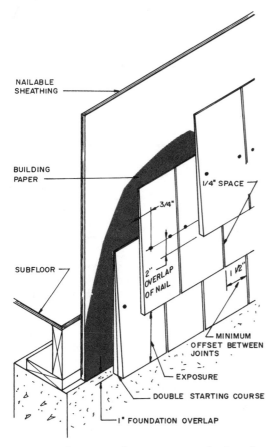

15-23   *Applying single-course wood shingles and shakes.*

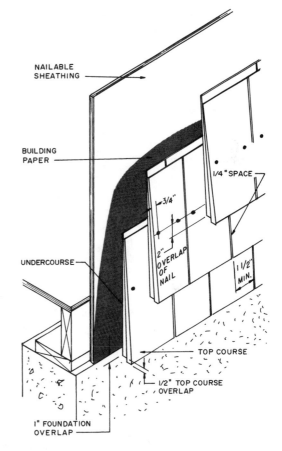

15-24   *Double-course application of wood shingles and shakes.*

that the shingle above overlaps the line of nails by 2in (51mm). A ¼in (6mm) space is left between shingles and the space should be offset at least 1½in (38mm) from a joint above or below it.

The double-course application is shown in **15-24**. Each course is doubled. The top shingle in each course overhangs the undershingle by ½in (13mm). In both cases the lower-grade shingles are used on the under layers.

When the shingles are laid, they can have the bottom edge staggered to form a "random" pattern (see **15-25**).

15-25   *The butt end of wood shingles and shakes can be staggered to produce a rougher, textured appearance.*

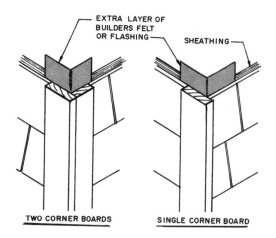

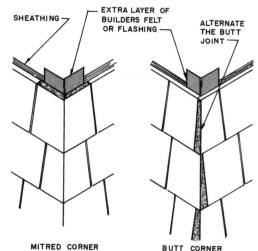

15-26 Ways to frame corners when installing wood shingles and shakes.

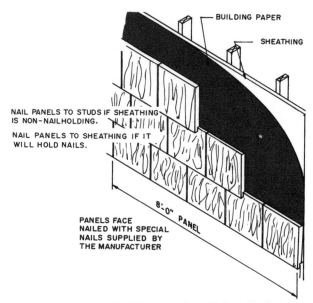

15-27 Wood shingle panels cover large areas rapidly.

Interior and exterior corners can be formed using corner boards or by cutting and fitting the shingles (see **15-26**).

The long shingle panels available are installed by applying building felt over the sheathing and nailing the panel directly into the studs. If nail-holding sheathing is used, they can be nailed to it (see **15-27**). Factory-assembled corner units are available for interior and exterior corners (see **15-28**).

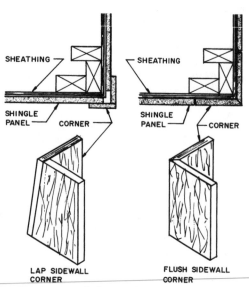

15-28 Factory-made lap and flush wood shingle corners are available.

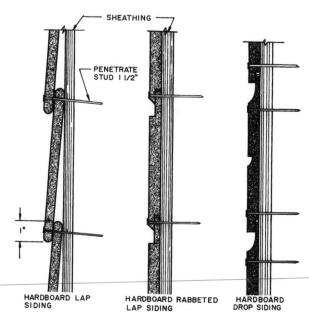

15-29 Nailing hardboard siding.

Nails Used with Wood Shingles

Rust-resistant nails are required. The screw type are recommended. Normally, 3d nails are used on the undercourse and 5d on the overcourse. Longer nails can be used, if needed. The nails are placed about three-quarters of an inch from each edge of the shingle. Shingles narrower than eight inches require two nails. Those wider require three nails. The nails should be driven flush with the surface of the shingle but should not crush the wood below the head.

15-30   *Typical sizes of hardboard lap siding.*

Siding Width (inches)	Maximum Exposure (inches)
12	11
8	7
6	5

15-31   *Typical sizes of hardboard panels.*

Panel Sizes (feet)	Thickness (inches)
4×8	7/16
4×9	7/16

Hardboard Siding

Hardboard siding is manufactured in a variety of patterns and is available as **lap siding** and **panel siding**. The lap siding is applied as described for wood lap siding, except that the nail penetrates both pieces, whereas rabbeted siding is face-nailed (see **15-29**). Typical siding widths and recommended minimum exposures are given in **15-30**. Panel sizes and thicknesses are given in **15-31**.

The spacing of studs required for various hardboard products is specified by the manufacturer.

Nails should penetrate the studs 1½in (38mm). For most hardboard lap siding, 8d galvanized box nails are used, spaced a maximum of 16in (40.6cm) O.C. Hardboard panel siding uses 8d galvanized box nails, spaced 6in (15.2cm) O.C. around the perimeter and 12in (30.5cm) O.C. at stud locations inside the panel (see **15-32**). The nail must be snug or flush with the surface of the siding. If it breaks the surface and is recessed, it must be painted or caulked. Nailing recommendations of the American Hardboard Association are shown in **15-33**. Hardboard siding joints are handled the same as plywood siding (refer to **15-38** following under *Installing Plywood Panel Siding*).

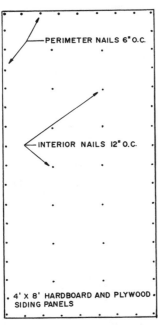

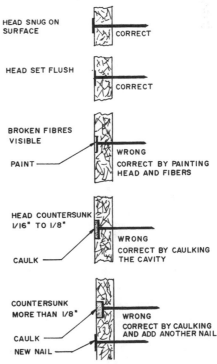

15-32 *Nailing pattern for hardboard and plywood siding panels.*

15-33 *Recommended nailing head placement for hardboard siding.*

15-34 *Plywood siding panels are used for soffits and exterior wall finish.* (Courtesy APA—The Engineered Wood Association)

Plywood Siding

Plywood siding is also available as lap siding and panel siding. Plywood siding is made by bonding wood veneers with a waterproof adhesive. It is available in a variety of wood species and textures (see **15-34**). The most common texture is a rough-sawn top veneer. Another type, Medium Density Overlaid (MDO), has a resin-treated fibre overlay sheet bonded to it. This provides a smooth, tough, check-free surface that holds paint well.

Siding manufactured to the standards of the American Plywood Association is identified by a grade mark on each panel. Several such grade marks are shown in **15-35**.

Plywood siding panels are available in a variety of surface patterns. Some are shown in **15-36**. Panels most frequently used are 4 × 8ft, but, panels 9 and 10 feet long are available.

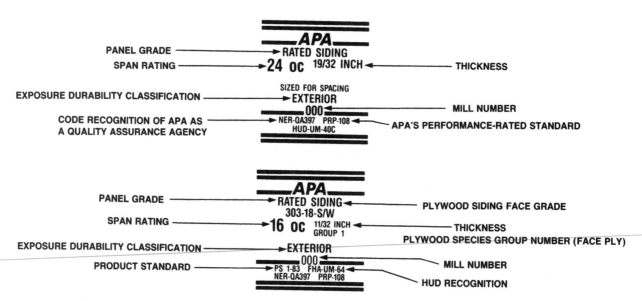

15-35 *Grade marks used on APA-Rated Siding.* (Courtesy APA—The Engineered Wood Association)

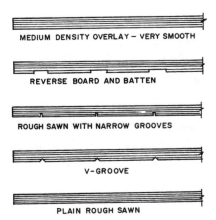

15-36 *Typical plywood siding panel patterns.*

Installing Plywood Lap Siding

Plywood lap siding is available in a range of widths up to 12in (30.5cm). It requires a minimum overlap of 1in (25mm) and ⅛in (3mm) clearance between butted siding ends and unions with casings on doors and windows and other trim. This clearance must be caulked.

Plywood lap siding can be nailed directly to studs or to nailable sheathing if it has a Span Rating on its

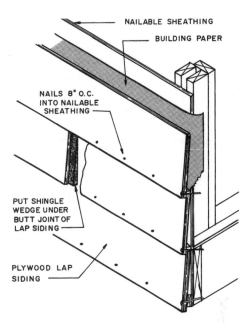

15-37 *Installing plywood lap siding over nailable sheathing.*

grade mark. The Span Rating is the allowable maximum spacing of the studs. The studs must be braced with diagonal bracing or a structural sheathing. Building paper is stapled to the studs before installing the siding.

Plywood lap siding when applied over nailable sheathing is nailed to 8in (20.3cm) O.C. along the bottom edge of the siding with nails driven to penetrate the top edge of the lower course (see **15-37**). Use 6d nonstaining box, casing, or siding nails for siding ¾in (19mm) or thicker. If nailed directly to the studs or over nonnail-holding sheathing, nail the lap siding at the bottom edge at each stud.

Installing Plywood Panel Siding

American Plywood Association Rated Siding has four basic classes identified by the series number 303. Each of the series 303 classes is subdivided into categories depending on appearance standards.

APA-Rated Siding panels can be applied directly to the studs, and no diagonal bracing is needed, if the stud spacing does not exceed that shown on the grade mark (see **15-38**). Building paper can be omitted, if the panel joints are battened or shiplapped. Square-edge joints require backing with building paper. Plywood siding panels can also be applied over any type of sheathing.

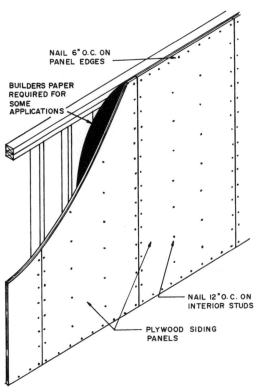

15-38 *Plywood siding can be applied directly to the studs. This is a vertical panel application.*

271

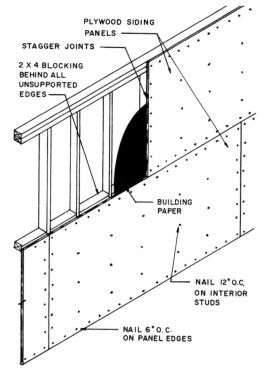

15-39 *Horizontally applied plywood panel siding requires blocking at all unsupported edges.*

APA-Rated Siding panels can be applied horizontally, if the horizontal joints are backed with 2×4 blocking (see **15-39**).

A ⅛in (3mm) clearance between panels and the door and window casings is required. The panel should be nailed at 6in (15.2cm) O.C. on the edges and 12in (30.5cm) O.C. at interior studs. Some typical installation details are shown in **15-40**.

Oriented Strand Board Siding

Oriented strand board siding is a nonveneer sheet material made by bonding wood strands with a special binder, arranging them into layers, and bonding them with extreme heat and pressure. The product is strong, of consistent quality, and free of open knotholes and hidden voids. The panels are finished with an exterior primer overlay. The surface can be finished with exterior paint. The overlay surface is embossed with a cedar grain texture and the edges are sealed to provide protection (see **15-41**). The siding is available in 4×8, 4×9, 4×10ft panels and as lap siding 6, 8, 9½ and 12in (15.2, 20.3, 24.2, and 30.5cm) wide. The product is 7/16in (11mm) thick.

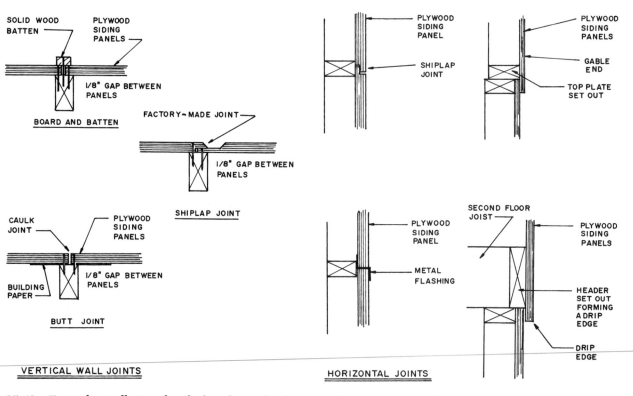

15-40 *Typical installation details for plywood siding panels. Hardboard siding joints are handled in the same manner. (Continued next page.)*

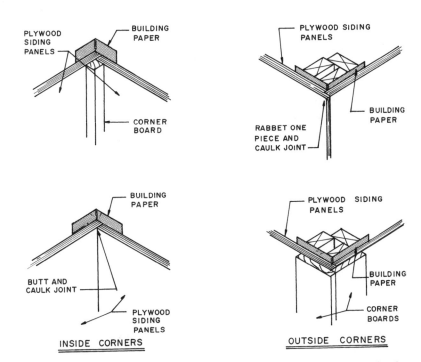

INSIDE CORNERS   OUTSIDE CORNERS

15-40 (Continued) Typical installation details for plywood siding panels. Hardboard siding joints are handled in the same manner.

The materials are installed much the same as other wood siding products. They can be applied over sheathing or directly to the studs spaced 16 and 24in (40.6 and 61cm) O.C. It is also available for use as exterior trim and fascia (see 15-42).

15-41 Oriented strand board siding has a cedar grain finish and a factory-applied prime coating. (Courtesy Louisiana-Pacific)

15-42 Oriented strand board siding can be applied over sheathing or directly to the unsheathed studs. (Courtesy Louisiana-Pacific)

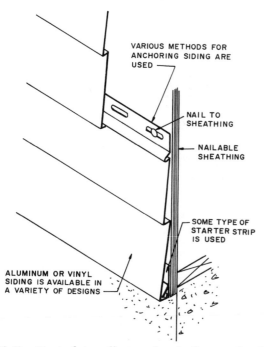

15-43 *Typical installation details for vinyl siding.*

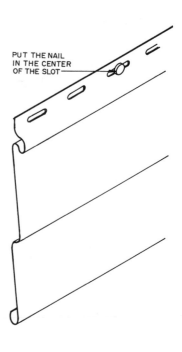

15-45 *Place the nail in the center of the nail slot.*

Vinyl and Aluminum Siding

Vinyl and **aluminum siding** are available in a variety of patterns, surface textures, and colors. The factory-applied finish requires no additional coatings after installation. These materials are generally not installed by the framing crew but by contractors specializing in their installation. Typical installation details are shown in **15-43** and **15-44**.

Proper nailing is important to a satisfactory installation. The nails should be placed in the center of the slots at the top of the panels. This allows for expansion and contraction (see **15-45**). The nails should be driven straight in and left about $\frac{1}{16}$ (1.5mm) clear of the siding to permit the panel to expand and contract and not bind on the nail (see **15-46**). When vertical

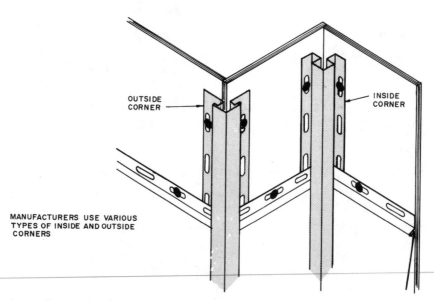

15-44 *Typical installation details for aluminum siding.*

274

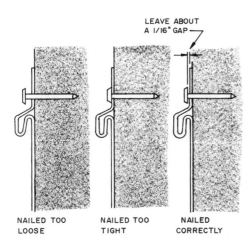

15-46 *Properly driven nails are left with a very slight gap with the siding.*

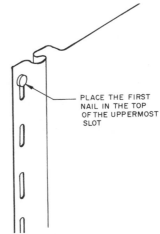

15-47 *When nailing vertical siding, place the first nail in the top of the first slot at the top of the panel.*

panels are installed, the first nail is placed in the upper edge of the topmost nailing slot as shown in **15-47**. Nails should be spaced about 16in (40.6 cm) apart into the nailable sheathing, otherwise they should go into the studs. Allow for expansion and contraction where the panel meets any trim, as shown in **15-48**. Follow the spacing recommended by the manufacturer.

The exterior wall must be straight. If it is wavy, the siding will follow the surface. To correct uneven walls, nail 1 × 3 furring strips that have been shimmed out to produce a straight nailing surface.

Vinyl siding has no structural strength and must be nailed to nailable sheathing or 1 × 4 furring. Corrosion-resistant nails are supplied by the siding manufacturer. Aluminum siding is installed much the same as vinyl siding. Some types use a fibre backing panel behind each piece. Manufacturers of these products supply detailed instruction manuals (see **15-49**).

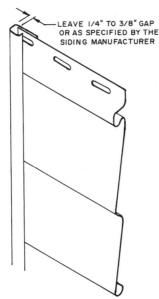

15-48 *Leave room for expansion where the siding meets the trim.*

15-49 *Aluminum and vinyl siding provide attractive, low-maintance exterior walls, fascias, and soffits. (Courtesy Alcan Building Products)*

275

Stucco Wall Systems

Another exterior wall finish material is **stucco.** It is usually not installed by the finish carpenter or, for that matter, by the framing crew, but rather, by craftsmen who specialize in this work. Typical installation details are shown in **15-50**. Traditional stucco is made of cement, sand, and lime. Generally, it is applied in three coats, producing a thickness of three-quarters of an inch or more.

The sheathing is covered with 15-pound builder's felt to protect it from the moisture in the stucco. A layer of **stucco wire** or **metal lath** is nailed over the builder's felt. It is nailed directly to nailable sheathing or to the studs when nonnailable sheathing is used. A good sheathing to use is ⅝in (16mm) plywood or oriented strand board.

The first coat, called the **scratch coat,** has a rough raked finish. The second coat, called the **brown coat,** has a smoother floated finish. The final coat, called the **color coat,** is tinted the desired color and can have any of a number of finished textures.

A new and increasingly popular form of stucco is sometimes referred to as **synthetic stucco** or **synthetic plaster.** One type uses an expanded polystyrene insulation board bonded to an approved substrate. A glass-fibre reinforcing mesh is bonded to this with a special adhesive mixed with Portland cement. A typical installation is shown in **15-51**. The finish coat is an acrylic coating mixed as directed by the manufacturer. It is trowled over the glass-fibre mesh (see **15-52**). A finished building is shown in **15-53**.

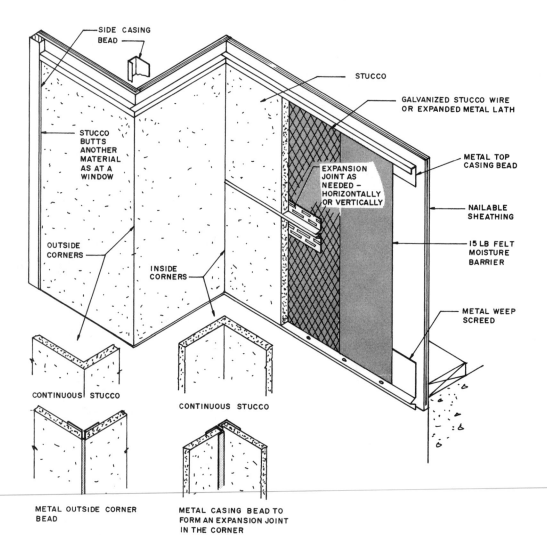

15-50   *Typical installation details for stucco.*

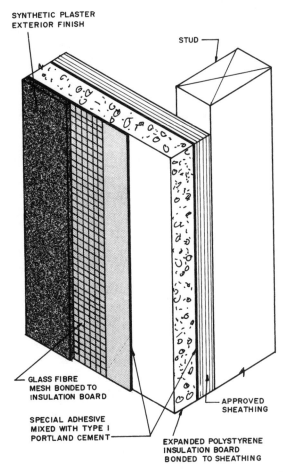

SYNTHETIC PLASTER
EXTERIOR FINISH

STUD

GLASS FIBRE
MESH BONDED TO
INSULATION BOARD

SPECIAL ADHESIVE
MIXED WITH TYPE I
PORTLAND CEMENT

APPROVED
SHEATHING

EXPANDED POLYSTYRENE
INSULATION BOARD
BONDED TO SHEATHING

15-51   *The components making up a system of synthetic stucco.*

15-52   *The base coat is being trowled over the insulation board.* (Courtesy Dryvit Systems, Inc.)

15-53   *A finished Dryvit exterior.* (Courtesy Dryvit Systems, Inc.)

Nail Types and Sizes

Nail Lengths and Diameters

Size	Length (inches)	American Steel Wire Gauge Numbers*		
		Common	Box and Casing	Finishing
2d	1	15	15½	16½
3d	1¼	14	14½	15½
4d	1½	12½	14	15
5d	1¾	12½	14	15
6d	2	11½	12½	13
7d	2¼	11½	12½	12½
8d	2½	10¼	11½	12½
9d	2¾	10¼	11½	12½
10d	3	9	10½	11½
12d	3¼	9	10/12	11½
16d	3½	8	10	11
20d	4	6	9	10
30d	4½	5	9	
40d	5	4	8	

* The smaller the gauge number, the larger the diameter of the nail

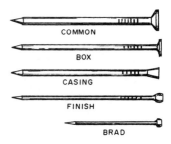

Wire Brads	
Length (inches)	Gauge Number
½	20
¾	20
1	18
1¼	16
1½	14

Metric Conversion

Inches to Millimetres and Centimetres						
mm—millimetres			cm—centimetres			
inches	mm	cm	inches	cm	inches	cm
⅛	3	0.3	9	22.9	30	76.2
¼	6	0.6	10	25.4	31	78.7
⅜	10	1.0	11	27.9	32	81.3
½	13	1.3	12	30.5	33	83.8
⅝	16	1.6	13	33.0	34	86.4
¾	19	1.9	14	35.6	35	88.9
⅞	22	2.2	15	38.1	36	91.4
1	25	2.5	16	40.6	37	94.0
1¼	32	3.2	17	43.2	38	96.6
1½	38	3.8	18	45.7	39	99.1
1¾	44	4.4	19	48.3	40	101.6
2	51	5.1	20	50.8	41	104.1
2½	64	6.4	21	53.3	42	106.7
3	76	7.6	22	55.9	43	109.2
3½	89	8.9	23	58.4	44	111.8
4	102	10.2	24	61.0	45	114.3
4½	114	11.4	25	63.5	46	116.8
5	127	12.7	26	66.0	47	119.4
6	152	15.2	27	68.6	48	121.9
7	178	17.8	28	71.1	49	124.5
8	203	20.3	29	73.7	50	127.0

Feet and Inch Conversions

1 inch = 25.4mm
1 foot = 304.8mm
1 psi = 6.89kPa
1 psf = 0.048kPa

Metric Conversions

1 mm = 0.039 inch
1 m = 3.28 feet
1 kPa = 20.88 psf

mm = millimetre
m = metre
kPa = kilopascal
psi = pounds per square inch
psf = pounds per square foot

Index

(Illustrations are referenced with italic page numbers.)